In Russian Political, Economic and Security Issues

RUSSIAN POLITICAL, ECONOMIC AND SECURITY ISSUES

Russian Political, Economic and Security Issues

Russian Political, Economic and Security Issues
Harold J. Kowen
2009 ISBN: 978-1-60692-407-5

In Russian Political, Economic and Security Issues

Russian Political, Economic and Security Issues

Harold J. Kowen
Editor

Nova Science Publishers, Inc.
New York

LIBRARY OF CONGRESS CATALOGING-IN-PUBLICATION DATA
Available Upon Request

ISBN: 978-1-60692-407-5

Published by Nova Science Publishers, Inc. ✢ New York

CONTENTS

Preface		**vii**
Chapter 1	Russian Political, Economic, and Security Issues and U.S. Interests *Stuart D. Goldman*	**1**
Chapter 2	Towards a New Russia Policy *Stephen J. Blank*	**25**
Chapter 3	Russia's Economic Performance and Policies and their Implications for the United States *William H. Cooper*	**97**
Chapter 4	Russia's Accession to the WTO *William H. Cooper*	**121**
Chapter 5	Nuclear Cooperation Agreement with Russia: Statutory Procedures for Congressional Consideration *Richard S. Beth*	**147**
Index		**167**

PREFACE

East-West relations have noticeably deteriorated during the Bush administration, and Russia's behavior has become commensurately more self-assertive. Key arms control achievements are in jeopardy, and Russia claims to be facing an array of growing threats, most prominently from America. In fact, Russia demands more respect from and equality with Washington and a free hand in world politics. In key respects, Moscow's new foreign policy grows out of the logic of its ever more autocratic and neo-imperial political structure. As analyzed in the book, this structure reinforces the long-standing Russian tendency to view other states as being inherently adversarial, i.e., it has a disposition to see world politics in terms of a presupposition of a priori enemies. Thus it views arms control issues from the standpoint of deterring enemies not working with strategic partners. The danger of a foreign policy that relies on truculent rhetoric, inflated and aggressive threat assessments, and an autocratic and neo-imperial political structure based on the ideology of Russia's desire for a free hand in world politics and ingrained belief that others are inherently the same is that it will stimulate precisely the adversarial behavior in Washington that it claims to see. There are already growing signs that certain sectors of the policymaking community are increasingly inclined to view Russia as a question mark, if not a rival of American policy.

Chapter 1- Dmitry Medvedev, Putin' s chosen successor and long-time protege, was elected President of the Russian Federation on March 2, 2008 with about 70% of the vote. Medvedev, formerly First Deputy Prime Minister, announced during the campaign that if elected, he would propose Putin as Prime Minister. Medvedev was inaugurated as President on May 7; Putin was confirmed as Prime Minister the next day. The Kremlin's Unified Russia party had previously swept the parliamentary election (December 2, 2007), winning more than two-thirds of the seats in the Duma. U.S. and EU observers criticized both elections as unfairly controlled by the governing authorities. Nevertheless, Putin's widespread popularity in Russia led many to conclude that the election results corresponded to Russian public opinion.

The economic upturn that began in 1999 is continuing. The GDP, domestic investment, and the general living standard have been growing impressively after a decade-long decline, fueled in large part by profits from oil and gas exports. There is a budget surplus, and the ruble is stable. Some major problems remain: 15% of the population live below the poverty line; foreign investment is relatively low; inflation is rising; and crime, corruption, capital flight, and unemployment remain high.

Russian foreign policy has grown more self-confident, assertive and anti- western, fueled by its perceived status as an "energy superpower." Russia's drive to reassert dominance in and integration of the former Soviet states is most successful with Belarus and Armenia but arouses opposition in Georgia, Ukraine, Azerbaijan, and Moldova. The Commonwealth of Independent States as an institution is failing. Washington and Moscow have found some common ground on the Iranian and North Korean nuclear concerns, but tension is rising on other issues such as NATO enlargement, Kosovo, and proposed U.S. missile defenses in Eastern Europe.

The military has been in turmoil after years of severe force reductions and budget cuts. The armed forces now number about 1.2 million, down from 4.3 million Soviet troops in 1986. Readiness, training, morale, and discipline have suffered. Russia's economic revival has allowed Putin to increase defense spending. Major weapons procurement, which virtually stopped in the 1990s, has begun to pick up. Some high-profile activities such as multinational military exercises, Mediterranean and Atlantic naval deployments, and strategic bomber patrols, have resumed.

After the Soviet Union's collapse, the United States sought a cooperative relationship with Moscow and supplied over $14 billion to encourage democracy and market reform, for humanitarian aid, and for WMD threat reduction in Russia. Direct U.S. foreign aid to Russia under the Freedom Support Act fell in the past decade, due in part to congressional pressure. U.S. aid in the form of WMD threat reduction programs, and indirect U.S. aid through institutions such as the IMF, however, was substantial. The United States has imposed economic sanctions on the Russian government and on Russian organizations for exporting nuclear and military technology and equipment to Iran and Syria. There are restrictions on aid to Russia in the FY2008 foreign aid bill. This CRS report will be updated regularly.

Chapter 2- East-West relations have noticeably deteriorated, and Russia's behavior has become commensurately more self-assertive. Key arms control achievements are in jeopardy, and Russia claims to be facing an array of growing threats, most prominently from America. In fact, Russia demands more respect from and equality with Washington and a free hand in world politics. In key respects, Moscow's new foreign policy grows out of the logic of its ever more autocratic and neo-imperial political structure. As analyzed in the monograph, this structure reinforces the long-standing Russian tendency to view other states as being inherently adversarial, i.e., it has a disposition to see world politics in terms of a presupposition of a priori enemies. Thus it views arms control issues from the standpoint of deterring enemies not working with strategic partners.

The danger of a foreign policy that relies on truculent rhetoric, inflated and aggressive threat assessments, and an autocratic and neo-imperial political structure based on the ideology of Russia's desire for a free hand in world politics and ingrained belief that others are inherently the same is that it will stimulate precisely the adversarial behavior in Washington that it claims to see. There are already growing signs that certain sectors of the policymaking community are increasingly inclined to view Russia as a question mark, if not a rival of American policy. This is particularly the case regarding issues of arms control and nuclear policy. Thus the current rhetorical belligerence seen in Russian policy and the increasing amount of interest in higher defense spending and inflated threat assessments could bring about exactly what Russian elites already claim to observe.

Accordingly, it is necessary for the United States to understand the scope of the challenge posed by Russia and to take steps towards reformulating its policies so that they are more coherent and unified, more deeply engaged with Russia across a wide spectrum of issues, and also more coordinated with our European allies. This means that we must forego the idea that good relations between presidents suffice, or that we have no leverage on Russia, or that human rights should not be a major part of our concern. While Russian interests and concerns must be engaged with seriousness and respect, they cannot be allowed to overshadow our own interests and concerns. The need for permanent ongoing bureaucratic engagement with Russia remains a challenge for Washington, but it is one that can and must be met by means of a long-term strategically conceived policy. And that policy must engage Moscow across all the issues of topical concern to Washington.

Chapter 3- The Russian economy has grown impressively since 1999 and, by some measures, has been one of the fastest growing economies in the world. The growth has brought an improvement in the standard of living of the average Russian citizen and has brought economic stability that Russia had not experienced in at least a decade. This strong performance is a major factor in the popular support that former President (now Prime Minister) Putin enjoys– some 70%-80% of the population view him favorably. The improvement in the Russian economy is also arguably a factor in the boldness with which the Putin leadership has reasserted Russia's status as a world power, challenging the United States, Europe, the other former Soviet states in economic and national security areas.

The Russian economy is highly dependent on the production and export of oil, gas, and other natural resources. Its success has largely been the result of record- breaking world energy prices, although prudent fiscal policies have also helped to promote economic stability. However, oil dependence could prove to be a double- edged sword. The Putin regime's failure to complete important economic reforms and its penchant for re-asserting government control over key economic sectors also loom among the possible roadblocks down the road. How Putin' s successor, President Dmitriy Medvedev, will proceed is still a matter of speculation.

Although its influence has been greatly diminished since the Soviet period, Russia remains a formidable force on the global stage, and its influence seems to be growing. Russia's economy is large enough to influence global economic conditions. Many European countries and former Soviet states are highly dependent on Russian natural gas. Russia is a significant player on a number of issues critical to the United States, for example, nuclear proliferation by Iran and North Korea. Russia's perceived national interests do not always match those of the United States, creating an environment for disagreement if not conflict.

While U.S. exports to Russia are still relatively small, for some producers, such as poultry, energy equipment, and technology, Russia is an important market. Russia is also an important supplier of a number of raw materials that are critical to U.S. manufacturers. These links have drawn the attention of some Members of Congress. Hearings have recently been held on Russian economic performance and policies. Congress may consider in the near future whether to extend permanent normal trade relations (PNTR) status to Russia as Russia pursues accession to the World Trade Organization (WTO). This report on Russian economic conditions and policies will be updated as events warrant.

Chapter 4- In 1993, Russia formally applied for accession to the General Agreement on Tariffs and Trade (GATT). Its application was taken up by the World Trade Organization (WTO), the successor organization of the GATT, in 1995. Russia's application has entered into its most significant phase as Russia negotiates with WTO members on the conditions for accession.

Accession to the WTO is critical to Russia and its political leadership. President Vladimir Putin has made it a top priority. He views accession as an important step in integrating the

Russian economy with the rest of the world and in fostering economic growth and development by attracting foreign investment and by lowering trade barriers. For the United States, the European Union (EU) and other trading partners, Russia's accession to the WTO could increase stability and predictability in Russia's foreign trade and investment regime.

Differences over some critical issues remain, making the time for Russian accession to the WTO uncertain. The European Union and the United States have raised concerns about Russian energy pricing policies which allow natural gas, oil, and electricity to be sold domestically far below world prices providing, they argue, a subsidy to domestic producers of fertilizers, steel, and other energy-intensive goods. Russia counters that the subsidies are not illegal under the WTO. Concerns regarding Russian trade barriers in the services sector, high tariffs for civil aircraft and autos, intellectual property rights protection, and agriculture subsidies, have also slowed down the process. On November 19, 2006, U.S. and Russian officials signed a bilateral agreement on Russia's accession to the WTO, thus completing a major step in the accession process. Russia still needs to complete negotiations with working party members.

Congressional interest in Russia's accession to the WTO is multifaceted. Members of Congress are concerned that Russia enters the WTO under terms and conditions in line with U.S. economic interests, especially gaining access to Russian markets as well as safeguards to protect U.S. import-sensitive industries. Some Members also assert that Congress should have a formal role in approving the conditions under which Russia accedes to the WTO, a role it does not have at this time. A number of Members of Congress and members of the U.S. business community have advised the Bush Administration not to agree too quickly to Russia's accession to the WTO and to ensure that U.S. concerns are met. The Congress has a direct role in determining whether Russia receives permanent normal trade relations (NTR) status which has implications for Russia's membership in the WTO and U.S.-Russian trade relations. Without granting permanent NTR (PNTR) to Russia, the United States might not benefit from the concessions that Russia makes upon accession. Issues regarding Russia's accession to the WTO may arise during the second session of the 1 10th Congress. This report will be updated as events warrant.

Chapter 5- On May 13, 2008, President Bush submitted to Congress a proposed agreement for nuclear cooperation with the Russian Federation. The Atomic Energy Act (AEA) prescribes that the text of such an agreement be submitted to the Senate Committee on Foreign Relations and the House Committee on Foreign Affairs for at least 30 days of consultation. Also, the agreement itself is to be submitted to Congress for 60 days, during which the committees consider it and report recommendations. The agreement goes into effect unless a joint resolution of disapproval is enacted by the end of the 60-day period. This report will be updated to reflect congressional action.

The President's letter of transmittal states that the May 13 action meets all requirements for both submissions, and stipulates that the 60-day period start immediately upon conclusion of the 30-day period. Both periods are measured in "days of continuous session," which the AEA defines to include all days except recesses of either house of more than three days, with "continuity" broken only by the sine die adjournment of a Congress. By this definition, the 60-day period may begin on June 24. If both houses take recesses as scheduled, the projected sine die adjournment on September 26 may be only the 78th day of continuous session. In this case, the statutory period for disapproval would have to start over again when Congress reconvenes in January, 2009. On the other hand, if both houses hold pro forma sessions during scheduled recesses, as they did in some recent instances, the disapproval period could end, and the agreement take effect, as early as August 11.

The AEA prescribes the text for a disapproval resolution and directs House committee leaders and Senate floor leaders (or designees) to introduce it when the 60-day period starts (in addition, a House Member introduced such a resolution at the start of the 30-day period). The AEA also requires the President to state his approval of the agreement before the 60-day period begins, but he did so in his initial transmission letter, perhaps rendering moot the consultive purpose of the 30-day period. Yet both committees of referral met with State Department officials on the agreement during the 30-day period, which may constitute the consultations the AEA directs during that period, but might also be taken as the hearings mandated during the 60-day period.

The AEA prescribes an expedited procedure for Senate floor consideration of a disapproval resolution, including a non-debatable motion to take up the measure, a 10-hour limit on consideration, and a prohibition on amendments. For House consideration, the AEA invites the Committee on Rules to prescribe similar terms. Congress could also disapprove the agreement, or approve it with conditions, by enacting an alternative measure under its general rules. The President, however, might likely veto any disapproval or conditional approval, in which case the agreement would go into effect unless Congress overrides the veto before the end of the disapproval period. Inasmuch as the President may take 10 days for his action, the timely enactment of a disapproval resolution may be feasible only if Congress initially passes it with more than 10 days remaining in the disapproval period.

In: Russian Political, Economic and Security Issues
Editor: Harold J. Kowen

ISBN 978-1-60692-407-5

Chapter 1

RUSSIAN POLITICAL, ECONOMIC, AND SECURITY ISSUES AND U.S. INTERESTS*

Stuart D. Goldman
Foreign Affairs, Defense, and Trade Division

ABSTRACT

Dmitry Medvedev, Putin' s chosen successor and long-time protege, was elected President of the Russian Federation on March 2, 2008 with about 70% of the vote. Medvedev, formerly First Deputy Prime Minister, announced during the campaign that if elected, he would propose Putin as Prime Minister. Medvedev was inaugurated as President on May 7; Putin was confirmed as Prime Minister the next day. The Kremlin's Unified Russia party had previously swept the parliamentary election (December 2, 2007), winning more than two-thirds of the seats in the Duma. U.S. and EU observers criticized both elections as unfairly controlled by the governing authorities. Nevertheless, Putin's widespread popularity in Russia led many to conclude that the election results corresponded to Russian public opinion.

The economic upturn that began in 1999 is continuing. The GDP, domestic investment, and the general living standard have been growing impressively after a decade-long decline, fueled in large part by profits from oil and gas exports. There is a budget surplus, and the ruble is stable. Some major problems remain: 15% of the population live below the poverty line; foreign investment is relatively low; inflation is rising; and crime, corruption, capital flight, and unemployment remain high.

Russian foreign policy has grown more self-confident, assertive and anti- western, fueled by its perceived status as an "energy superpower." Russia's drive to reassert dominance in and integration of the former Soviet states is most successful with Belarus and Armenia but arouses opposition in Georgia, Ukraine, Azerbaijan, and Moldova. The Commonwealth of Independent States as an institution is failing. Washington and Moscow have found some common ground on the Iranian and North Korean nuclear concerns, but tension is rising on other issues such as NATO enlargement, Kosovo, and proposed U.S. missile defenses in Eastern Europe.

* Excerpted from CRS Report RL33407, dated July 28, 2008.

The military has been in turmoil after years of severe force reductions and budget cuts. The armed forces now number about 1.2 million, down from 4.3 million Soviet troops in 1986. Readiness, training, morale, and discipline have suffered. Russia's economic revival has allowed Putin to increase defense spending. Major weapons procurement, which virtually stopped in the 1990s, has begun to pick up. Some high-profile activities such as multinational military exercises, Mediterranean and Atlantic naval deployments, and strategic bomber patrols, have resumed.

After the Soviet Union's collapse, the United States sought a cooperative relationship with Moscow and supplied over $14 billion to encourage democracy and market reform, for humanitarian aid, and for WMD threat reduction in Russia. Direct U.S. foreign aid to Russia under the Freedom Support Act fell in the past decade, due in part to congressional pressure. U.S. aid in the form of WMD threat reduction programs, and indirect U.S. aid through institutions such as the IMF, however, was substantial. The United States has imposed economic sanctions on the Russian government and on Russian organizations for exporting nuclear and military technology and equipment to Iran and Syria. There are restrictions on aid to Russia in the FY2008 foreign aid bill. This CRS report will be updated regularly.

On March 2, 2008, First Deputy Prime Minister Dmitry Medvedev, President Putin' s chosen successor, was elected President with about 70% of the vote.

On March 3, Russia voted with the United States, France, the U.K. and China in the UN Security Council to impose a third, but more limited, round of sanctions against Iran in response to that country's continued defiance of UN calls to suspend its uranium enrichment activities.

On March 11, the State Department's annual report on human rights criticized Russia's "centralization of executive branch power," compliant legislature, corrupt and selective law enforcement, harassment of NGOs, and media restrictions, all of which "continued to erode the government's accountability to its citizens."

On April 4, at the Russia-NATO Council meeting in Bucharest, Romania, Putin warned that accession of Georgia and/or Ukraine to the Alliance would constitute a direct and serious threat to Russia's security.

On April 6, at the final Bush-Putin summit (in Sochi, Russia), Putin continued to oppose U.S. missile defense deployments in Poland and the Czech Republic, but expressed "cautious optimism" that the two sides could eventually reach agreement and that proposed U.S. confidence-building measures would be "important and useful" if implemented.

On April 16, Putin signed a decree authorizing direct official relations between Russian government bodies and the secessionist authorities in Georgia's Abkhazia and South Ossetia. The decree also called for providing economic, social, and other assistance to those "republics," most of whose people already hold Russian passports.

On May 7, Dmitry Medvedev was inaugurated as President of the Russian Federation. Putin was confirmed as Prime Minister the next day.

Most Recent Developments

On July 10, Russia's oil pipeline monopoly Transneft announced that oil deliveries to the Czech Republic would be cut from the contracted monthly volume of 500,000 tons down to 300,000 tons, for "technical reasons." Some suggest it iot a coincidence this move came two days after the U.S. and Czech governments signed an agreement to deploy a U.S. missile defense radar system on Czech territory.

Post-Soviet Russia and its Significance for the United States

Russia was by far the largest republic of the former Soviet Union. Its population of 142 million (down from 149 million in 1991) is about half the old U.S.S.R. total. Its 6.6 million square miles comprises 76.2% of the territory of the former Soviet Union and it is nearly twice the size of the United States, stretching across Eurasia to the Pacific, across 11 time zones. Russia also has the lion's share of the natural resources, industrial base, and military assets of the former Soviet Union.

Russia is a multinational, multi-ethnic state with over 100 nationalities and a complex federal structure inherited from the Soviet period. Within the Russian Federation are 21 republics (including Chechnya) and many other ethnic enclaves. Ethnic Russians, comprising 80% of the population, are a dominant majority. The next largest nationality groups are Tatars (3.8%), Ukrainians (3%), and Chuvash (1.2%). Furthermore, in most of the republics and autonomous regions of the Russian Federation that are the national homelands of ethnic minorities, the titular nationality constitutes a minority of the population. Russians are a majority in many of these enclaves. During Yeltsin's presidency, many of the republics and regions won greater autonomy. Only the Chechen Republic, however, tried to assert complete independence. President Putin has reversed this trend and rebuilt the strength of the central government vis-a-vis the regions.

The Russian Constitution combines elements of the U.S., French, and German systems, but with an even stronger presidency. Among its more distinctive features are the ease with which the president can dissolve the parliament and call for new elections and the obstacles preventing parliament from dismissing the government in a vote of no confidence. The Constitution provides a four-year term for the president and no more than two consecutive terms. The president, with parliament's approval, appoints a prime minister who heads the government. The president and prime minister appoint government ministers and other officials. The prime minister and government are accountable to the president rather than the legislature. Dmitry Medvedev was reelected president on March 2, 2008 and inaugurated on May 7. On May 8, Putin was confirmed as Prime Minister.

The bicameral legislature is called the Federal Assembly. The Duma, the lower (and more powerful) chamber, has 450 seats. In previous elections, half the seats were chosen from single-member constituencies and half from national party lists, with proportional representation and a minimum 5% threshold for party representation. In May 2005, Putin's proposal that all 450 Duma seats be filled by party list election, with a 7% threshold for party representation, became law. In the December 2007 parliamentary election, the pro-Kremlin

United Russia Party won 315 seats, more than the two-thirds majority required to amend the constitution. The upper chamber, the Federation Council, has 166 seats, two from each of the 83 regions and republics of the Russian Federation. Deputies are appointed by the regional chief executive and the regional legislature.

2001 and trial by jury is being introduced, although it is not yet the norm. The Supreme Court is the highest appellate body. The Constitutional Court rules on the legality and constitutionality of governmental acts and on disputes between branches of government or federative entities. Federal judges, who serve lifetime terms, are appointed by the President and must be approved by the Federation Council. The courts are widely perceived to be subject to political manipulation and control.

Russia is not as central to U.S. interests as was the Soviet Union. With the dissolution of the U.S.S.R. and Russia substantially diminished, much of the Soviet military threat has disappeared. Yet developments in Russia are still important to the United States. Russia remains a nuclear superpower. It will play a major role in determining the national security environment in Europe, the Middle East, and Asia. Russia has an important role in the future of arms control, nonproliferation of weapons of mass destruction, and the fight against terrorism. Such issues as the war on terrorism, the future of NATO, and the U.S. role in the world will all be affected by developments in Russia. Also, Russia's economy is recovering and it is a potentially important trading partner. Russia is the only country in the world with more natural resources than the United States, including vast oil and gas reserves. It is the world's second largest producer and exporter of oil (after Saudi Arabia) and the world's largest producer and exporter of natural gas. It has a large, well-educated labor force and a huge scientific establishment. Also, many of Russia's needs — food and food processing, oil and gas extraction technology, computers, communications, transportation, and investment capital — are in areas in which the United States is highly competitive, although bilateral trade remains relatively low.

POLITICAL DEVELOPMENTS

Former President Boris Yeltsin's surprise resignation (December 31, 1999) propelled Vladimir Putin (whom Yeltsin had plucked from obscurity in August 1999 to be his fifth Prime minister in three years) into the Kremlin as Acting President. Putin' s meteoric rise in popularity was due to a number of factors: his tough policy toward Chechnya; his image as a youthful, vigorous, sober, and plain-talking leader; and massive support from state-owned TV and other mass media. In March 2000, Putin was elected president in his own right. He won a second term four years later.

Putin, who was a Soviet KGB foreign intelligence officer for 16 years and later headed Russia's Federal Security Service (domestic component of the former KGB), is an intelligent, disciplined statist. His priorities appear to be strengthening the central government and restoring Russia's status as a great power.

Putin won early victories over regional leaders, reclaiming authority for the central government that Yeltsin had allowed to slip away. First, Putin created seven super-regional districts overseen by presidential appointees. Then he pushed legislation to change the composition of the Federation Council, the upper chamber of parliament — a body that was comprised of the heads of the regional governments and regional legislatures, giving those leaders exclusive control of that chamber and also parliamentary immunity from criminal prosecution. With Putin's changes, Federation Council Deputies are appointed by the regional leaders and legislatures, but once appointed, they are somewhat independent. In 2005, the Kremlin-controlledparliament gave Putin the power to appoint (previously elected) regional governors.

Under Putin, the government took nearly total control of nation-wide broadcast media. A key target was the media empire of Vladimir Gusinsky, which included Russia's only independent television network, NTV, which had been critical of Putin. Gusinsky was arrested in June 2000 on corruption charges and was later released and allowed to leave the country. The state-controlled gas monopoly Gazprom then took over NTV and appointed Kremlin loyalists to run it. The government then forced the prominent oligarch Boris Berezovsky to give up ownership of his controlling share of the ORT TV network. TV-6, the last significant independent Moscow TV station, was shut down under government pressure in 2002. The government has also moved against the independent radio network, Echo Moskvuy and other electronic media. In 2006, the Russian government forced most Russian radio stations to stop broadcasting programs prepared by the U.S.-funded Voice of America (VOA) and Radio Liberty (RL). Threats to revoke the stations' broadcasting licenses forced all but 4 or 5 of the more than 30 radio stations that had been doing so to stop broadcasting VOA and RL programs. Journalists critical of the government have been imprisoned, attacked, and in some cases killed, with impunity. The highly respected journalist and Chechen war critic Anna Politkovskaya was murdered in October 2006.

In the summer of 2003, the Russian government launched a campaign against Mikhail Khodorkovski, CEO of Yukos, then the world's fourth largest oil company. Khodorkovski, then the wealthiest man in Russia, had become a multi-billionaire in the 1 990s in the course of the often corrupt privatization of state-owned assets under former president Yeltsin. Khodorkovski, however, subsequently won respect in the West by adopting open and "transparent" business practices while transforming Yukos into a major global energy company. Khodorkovski criticized some of Putin' s actions, financed anti-Putin political parties, and hinted that he might enter politics in the future. After numerous searches and seizures of Yukos records and the arrest of senior Yukos officials, police arrested Khodorkovski in October 2003. Prosecutors then froze Yukos stock worth some $12 billion.

Khodorkovski's arrest was seen by many as politically motivated, aimed at eliminating a political enemy and making an example of him to other Russian tycoons. Many observers also saw this episode as the denouement of a long power struggle between two Kremlin factions: a business-oriented group of former Yeltsin loyalists and a group of Putin loyalists drawn mainly from the security services and Putin' s home town of St. Petersburg. A few days after Khodorkovski' s arrest, Presidential Chief of Staff Aleksandr Voloshin, reputed head of the Yeltsin-era group, resigned, as did several of his close associates, leaving the Kremlin in the hands of "the policemen." Khodorkovski went on trial in June 2004 on multiple criminal charges of tax evasion and fraud. In May 2005, he was found guilty, sentenced to nine years in prison, and later sent to a penal camp in Siberia.

Yukos was broken up and its principal assets sold off to satisfy tax debts allegedly totaling $28 billion. Yuganskneftegaz, the main oil production subsidiary of Yukos, was sold at a state-run auction, ostensibly to satisfy tax debts. The wining, and sole, bidder, Baikalfinansgrup, paid $9.7 billion, about half of its market value, according to western specialists. The previously unheard-of Baikalfinansgrup is a group of Kremlin insiders headed by Igor Sechin, Deputy Head of the Presidential Administration and a close Putin associate. Baikalfinansgrup was soon purchased by Rosneft, a wholly state-owned Russian oil company. Sechin is Chairman of Rosneft' s Board of Directors. The de-facto nationalization of Yuganskneftegaz was denounced by Andrei Illarionov, then a senior Putin economic advisor, as "the scam of the year." Since then, the government has re-nationalized or otherwise brought under its control a number of other large enterprises that it characterizes as "strategic assets." These include ship, aircraft, and auto manufacturing, as well as other raw material extraction activities. At the same time, the Kremlin has installed senior officials to head these enterprises. For example, former First Deputy Prime Minister Dmitry Medvedev (now president) was the Chairman of the Board of Gazprom, Russia's giant natural gas monopoly. Sergei Ivanov, another First Deputy Prime Minister and close Putin confidant, is the Chairman of the Board of Autovaz, Russia's largest auto manufacturer. This phenomenon of political elites taking the helm of many of Russia's leading economic enterprises has led some observers to conclude that "those who rule Russia, own Russia."

On September 13, 2004, in the aftermath of the bloody Beslan school hostage crisis (see below), President Putin proposed a number of changes to the political system, promptly approved by the legislature, that further concentrated power in his hands, necessitated, he said, by Russia's intensified war against international terrorism. He proposed, inter alia, that regional governors no longer be popularly elected, but instead that regional legislatures confirm the president's appointees as governors and that all Duma Deputies be elected on the basis of national party lists, based on the proportion of votes each party gets nationwide. The first measure makes regional governors wholly dependent on, and subservient to, the president, undermining much of what remained of Russia's nominally federal system. The second measure eliminates independent deputies, further strengthening the pro- presidential parties that already controlled an absolute majority in the Duma. Putin and his supporters argued that these measures would help reduce corruption in the regions and "unify" the country, the better to fight against terrorism. Critics saw the proposals as further, major encroachments on the fragile democratic reforms of the 1980s and 1990s that had already suffered serious setbacks under Putin. They warned of Putin' s growing authoritarianism. President Bush, Secretary of State Powell, and many members of Congress voiced concern that Putin' s September 13 proposals threatened Russian democracy. A few months later, parliament passed a controversial Kremlin-proposed law regulating non-government organizations (NGOs), which Kremlin critics charge gives the government leverage to shut down NGOs that it views as politically troublesome. The U.S. and many European governments expressed concern about the NGO law.[1]

On November 14, 2005, President Putin announced major high-level changes in the government. Presidential Administration head Dmitry Medvedev was named First Deputy Prime Minister and put in charge of high-level "national priority projects." Defense Minister Sergei Ivanov was promoted to Deputy Prime Minister and retained his Defense Ministry post. In February 2007, Ivanov was elevated to First Deputy Prime Minister. These two men were widely seen as the front runners to succeed Putin in March 2008.

On September 10, 2007, Putin made a surprise announcement dismissing Prime Minister Mikhail Fradkov — whom he had plucked from obscurity to take that post in 2005 — and nominated in his place the even more obscure Victor Zubkov, who had previously headed the Financial Monitoring Service, an arm of the Finance Ministry that investigates money-laundering. The 65 year-old Zubkov had no political power base or constituency of his own — other than Putin' s backing. Putin explained this move as necessary to "prepare the country" for forthcoming elections, which immediately triggered speculation that Zubkov might be Putin' s choice for president in 2008, perhaps as a "place holder," a mechanism that would allow Putin to retain control and/or return to the presidency after a brief interregnum. This brought the issue of the "Putin succession," which had been heating up since 2006, to a full boil.[2]

But in Russia's election cycle, the vote for president is preceded by the parliamentary election, which is seen as a harbinger of the presidential contest. The Kremlin decided to make the December 2007 parliamentary election a referendum on Putin and Putinism. And despite Putin' s apparent genuine popularity, they were determined to take no chances on the outcome. In the run-up to the Duma election, the authorities used myriad official and unofficial levers of power and influence to assure an overwhelming victory for United Russia, the main Kremlin party. Putin's October 1, 2007 announcement that he would run for parliament at the head of the United Russia ticket made the outcome doubly sure. The state-controlled media heavily favored United Russia and largely ignored or disparaged the opposition. Opposition party literature was seized and their rallies often shut down or harassed. Potentially popular opposition candidates were bought off, intimidated, or barred from running on "legal technicalities." In March 2007, for example, the Supreme Court ruled that Vladimir Ryzhkov' s Republican Party — one of the few remaining liberal democratic parties — must be disbanded because it violated the 2004 law requiring parties to have at least 50,000 members and 45 regional offices. Russian authorities effectively prevented the main election observing body of the Organization for Security and Cooperation in Europe (OSCE) from sending an observer team, first by limiting their number to 70 (compared to 450 OSCE observers for the previous Duma election) and then delaying issuance of visas until the last minute, thus blocking normal monitoring of the election campaign

The preordained result of the December 2, 2007 balloting for the Duma was a sweep by United Russia, which reportedly won 64.3% of the popular vote and 315 of the 450 seats — more than the two-thirds majority required to amend the constitution. A second pro-kremlin party, A Just Russia — widely believed to have been created by Kremlin "political technologists" in 2007 to draw leftist votes away from the Communists — won 7.74 percent of the vote and 38 seats. The platforms of United Russia and A Just Russia consisted of little more than "For Putin!" Vladimir Zhirinovsky' s misnamed Liberal Democratic Party of Russia (LDPR), with 8.14% of the vote, won 40 seats. Despite Zhirinovsky's buffoonery and reputation for right-wing extremism, the LDPR is also a reliable supporter of Putin in the Duma. Thus, the Kremlin can count on the votes of 393 of the 450 Duma Deputies. The only opposition party in the Duma is the Communist Party, which, according to the official vote count, won 11.57% of the vote and 57 seats. The remaining parties failed to cross the 7% threshold required to win seats in the legislature. The traditional liberal democratic parties, Yabloko and the Union of Rightist Forces, reportedly received 1.59% and 0.96% of the vote, respectively. The officially declared voter turnout was 63%.[3]

Despite some allegations of ballot-box stuffing, voter intimidation, and other "irregularities,"[4] there is little doubt that by dint of Putin' s genuine popularity, an honest vote count would still have given United Russia a resounding victory. The main problem with the election was not the vote count, but the entire process leading up to the balloting. In the words of an OSCE Parliamentary Assembly official, "the executive branch acted as though it practically elected the parliament itself."

On December 10, barely a week after the Duma election, Putin announced his choice for president: Dmitry Medvedev. One day after his anointment, Medvedev announced that, if elected, he would ask Putin to serve as Prime Minister. One week later, Putin formally accepted this offer. This carefully choreographed arrangement presumably was meant to assure political continuity for Putin and those around him.

On March 2, 2008, Medvedev easily won election as Russia's next president, with 70% of the vote. The Kremlin made sure that the outcome was never in doubt. News coverage was skewed overwhelmingly in Medvedev's favor, especially TV news, the principal source of political news for most Russians. The previous format of "all-Putin, all the time" was shifted to Medvedev.[5] Like Putin before him, Medvedev refused to participate in public debates with any of his rivals. Moscow also imposed the same restrictions on the OS CE's election observers as during the Duma election, with the same result: the OSCE refused to send election observers under the conditions imposed by Moscow. Election commissions in the United States, the United Kingdom, Spain, France, and Germany all officially informed Moscow that they would not observe the presidential ballot.[6]

The Putin regime manipulated election laws and regulations to block "inconvenient" candidates such as former Prime Minister Mikhail Kasyanov and former chess champion Gary Kasparov from getting onto the ballot. In the end there were three candidates besides Medvedev. The LDPR's Vladimir Zhironovsky and the Communists' long-time leader, Gennady Zyuganov. The fourth was the little- known Andrei Bogdanov, leader of the tiny Democratic Party.[7]

Dmitry Medvedev, the 42 year-old long-time Putin protégé, was inaugurated as President on May 7, 2008. Like Putin and many of the Kremlin inner circle, Medvedev is a native of St. Petersburg (formerly Leningrad). But unlike so many of the inner circle, he does not have a background in the security services. His academic training is as a lawyer. He is viewed by many in Russia and the West as one of the most liberal of the generally illiberal cadre surrounding Putin. All agree that he is a Putin loyalist.

Although there was no doubt that Medvedev would win the election, there is considerable uncertainty about the future relationship between President Medvedev and Prime Minister Putin. Competing scenarios and rumors abound. Some speculate that Putin' s obedient Duma majority may amend the constitution to shift power from the president to the prime minister. But Russia's super-presidential constitution would require a major re-write to implement that. Others suggest that President Medvedev may voluntarily cede substantial power to Prime Minister Putin, allowing the mentor to continue wielding real power. But such a "dual power" arrangement is viewed by some observers as inherently unstable. Another scenario envisions Medvedev resigning after a "decent interval," necessitating a new presidential election in which Putin would be eligible to run, since he would not have served more than two consecutive terms. Alternatively, Putin might remain as prime minister for a year or two while making sure that Medvedev is an able and loyal successor — and presumably be prepared to push Medvedev aside if the younger man proved unsatisfactory. The future is murky.

CHECH NYA

In 1999, Islamic radicals based in Russia's break-away republic of Chechnya launched armed incursions into neighboring Dagestan, vowing to drive the Russians out and create an Islamic state. At about the same time, a series of bombing attacks against apartment buildings in Moscow and other Russian cities killed some 300 people. The new government of then-Prime Minister Putin blamed Chechen terrorists and responded with a large-scale military campaign. Russian security forces may have seen this as an opportunity to reverse their humiliating 1996 defeat in Chechnya. With Moscow keeping its (reported) military casualties low and Russian media reporting little about Chechen civilian casualties, the conflict enjoyed strong Russian public support, despite international criticism. After a grinding siege, Russian forces took the Chechen capital, Grozny, in February 2000 and in the following months took the major rebel strongholds in the mountains to the south. Russian forces killed tens of thousands of civilians and drove hundreds of thousands of Chechen refugees from their homes.

In March 2003, Russian authorities conducted a referendum in Chechnya on a new Chechen constitution that gives the region limited autonomy within the Russian Federation. Moscow claims it was approved by a wide margin. In October 2003, the Moscow-appointed head of the Chechen Administration, Akhmad Kadyrov, was elected President of the republic. Russian hopes that these steps would increase political stability and reduce bloodshed were disappointed, as guerilla fighting in Chechnya and suicide bomb attacks in the region and throughout Russia continued. On May 9, 2004, Kadyrov was assassinated by a bomb blast in Grozny, further destabilizing Chechnya. On August 29, Alu Alkhanov, Moscow's preferred candidate, was elected President of Chechnya, replacing Kadyrov.

Many foreign governments and the U.N. and Organization for Security and Cooperation in Europe (OSCE), while acknowledging Russia's right to combat separatist and terrorist threats on its territory, criticized Moscow's use of "disproportionate" and "indiscriminate" military force and the human cost to innocent civilians and urged Moscow to pursue a political solution. Although Moscow has suppressed large-scale Chechen military resistance, it faces the prospect of prolonged guerilla warfare. Russia reportedly has lost over 15,000 troops in Chechnya (1999-2006), comparable to total Soviet losses in Afghanistan (1979-1989). Russian authorities deny there is a "humanitarian catastrophe" in the North Caucasus and strongly reject foreign "interference" in Chechnya. The bloodshed continued on both sides. Russian forces regularly conduct sweeps and "cleansing operations" that reportedly result in civilian deaths, injuries, and abductions. Chechen fighters stage attacks against Russian forces and pro-Moscow Chechens in Chechnya and neighboring regions and terrorist attacks against civilian targets throughout Russia.

On September 1, 2004, a group of heavily armed fighters stormed a school in the town of Beslan, taking some 1,150 children, teachers, and parents hostage and demanding the withdrawal of Russian forces from Chechnya. Two days later, in a chaotic and violent battle, 330 hostages and nearly all the pro-Chechen fighters were killed by explosives set by the hostage-takers and by gunfire from all sides. Radical Chechen field commander Shamil Basaev later claimed responsibility for the Beslan school assault. However, Aslan Maskhadov, the nominal political leader of Chechnya' s separatist movement, denounced the school attack and suicide bombings against civilian targets as unjustifiable acts of terrorism.

Maskhadov, who was elected President of Chechnya in 1997, was seen by some as a relatively moderate leader and virtually the only possible interlocutor if Moscow sought a political resolution to the conflict. Putin' s government labeled Maskhadov, like all Chechen rebels, as a terrorist and refused to negotiate with him. On March 8, 2005, Russian authorities announced that they had killed Maskhadov in a shoot-out in Chechnya, apparently extinguishing what little hope remained for a political settlement. Chechen rebel field commanders named Abdul-Khalim Sadulaev President and vowed to continue their struggle for independence.

In succeeding months, Russian forces eliminated many Chechen rebel field commanders. On June 17, 2006, Chechen rebel president Sadulaev was killed in a fire fight by Russian federal forces. Three weeks later, Basaev, the most prominent and notorious Chechen rebel field commander, was killed in an explosion. Moscow's success in eliminating so many Chechen rebel leaders and inflicting losses n rebel bands leads some to speculate that the back of the resistance has been broken. Nevertheless, sporadic attacks against Russian forces and pro-Moscow officials continue in Chechnya and neighboring regions.[8]

Economic Developments

After the collapse of the Soviet Union, Russia experienced widespread economic dislocation and a drop of close to 50% in GDP. Conditions worse than the Great Depression of the 1930s in the United States impoverished much of the population, some 15% of which is still living below the government's official (very low) poverty level. Russia is also plagued by environmental degradation and ecological catastrophes of staggering proportions; the near-collapse of the health system; sharp declines in life expectancy and the birth rate; and widespread organized crime and corruption. The population has fallen by about 6 million since 1991, despite net in-migration of 5 million mostly ethnic Russians from other former Soviet republics.

Against this background of near collapse, in 1999, macroeconomic indicators began a remarkable, and sustained, recovery. This was due partly to the sharp increase in the price of imports and increased price competitiveness of Russian exports caused by the 74% ruble devaluation in 1998. The surge in the world price of oil and gas also buoyed the economy. From 1999 to 2007, Russia's GDP, in current dollars, quintupled from $200 billion to $1.2 trillion, an average growth rate of 25% per year. In inflation-adjusted real terms, economic growth was a less astounding, but still impressive, 6.7%. In addition, Russia virtually eliminated its public foreign debt which, in 1999, had grown to 100% of GDP. Russia's hard currency reserves exceed $450 billion, the third largest in the world after China and Japan. And Russia has also established a "rainy day" stabilization fund of more than $150 billion. Although some of Putin's early economic reforms (see below) contributed to this reversal of fortune, Putin is more the beneficiary than the cause of Russia's economic revival.[9] Nevertheless, in Russia Putin generally gets credit for the recovery, which is a major factor in his popularity.

Not everything is bright in this picture, however. While Russia is not a "petrostate" in the classic sense, its economy is very heavily dependent on oil and gas, which account for 63% of Russia's exports and 50% of total state revenues. Manufacturing has not recovered from the

Soviet collapse and agriculture remains moribund. Investment in the energy sector is not keeping pace with requirements and oil and gas production are stagnating. At the same time, inflation is increasing, from 7% at the beginning of 2007 to 11% by years's end, and appears headed toward 15% in 2008.[10]

ECONOMIC REFORM

In January 1992, Yeltsin launched a sweeping economic reform program developed by Acting Prime Minister Yegor Gaidar. The Yeltsin-Gaidar program wrought fundamental changes in the economy. Although the reforms suffered many setbacks and disappointments, they are widely believed to have carried Russia beyond the point of no return as far as restoring the old Soviet economic system is concerned. The Russian government removed controls on the vast majority of producer and consumer prices in 1992. Many prices have reached world market levels. The government also launched a major program of privatization of state property. By 1994, more than 70% of industry, representing 50% of the workforce and over 62% of production, had been privatized, although workers and managers owned 75% of these enterprises, many of which have not still been restructured to compete in market conditions. Critics charged that enterprises were sold far below their true value to "insiders" with political connections.

Putin initially declared reviving the economy his top priority. His liberal economic reform team formulated policies that won G-7 (now G-8, with Russia as a full member) and IMF approval in his first term. Some notable initiatives include a flat 13% personal income tax and lower corporate taxes that helped boost government revenue and passage of historic land privatization laws. In May 2004, Russia reached agreement with the EU on Russian accession to the WTO. EU leaders reportedly made numerous economic concessions to Moscow. Russia agreed to sign the Kyoto Protocol and roughly double the price of natural gas domestically by 2010. In November 2006, U.S. and Russian officials signed a bilateral agreement on Russia's accession to the WTO, thus completing a major step in the accession process. Russia still needs to complete negotiations with working party members.[11]

In Putin' s second term, massive profits from oil and gas exports and related revenues made it easier for the government to put off politically difficult, but necessary, decisions on structural economic reform. Reform was further undermined by the Kremlin's take-over of oil giant Yukos, and subsequent re-nationalizations, which increased inefficiencies and corruption and darkened the investment climate. Putin appeared to turn away from market reform toward greater government control of "strategic sectors" of the economy, with top government officials being put into leadership positions in many of Russia's largest economic enterprises.

FOREIGN POLICY

Russia and the West

In the early 1990s, Yeltsin's Russia gave the West more than would have seemed possible. Moscow cut off military aid to the Communist regime in Afghanistan; ordered its combat troops out of Cuba; committed Russia to a reform program and won IMF membership; signed the START II Treaty that would have eliminated all MIRVed ICBMs (the core of the Soviet Strategic Rocket Forces); and radically reduced Russian force levels in many other categories. The national security policies of Yeltsin and Foreign Minister Andrei Kozyrev came to be strongly criticized at home, not only by hardline communists and ultra nationalists but also by many centrists and prominent democrats, who came to agree that the Yeltsin/Kozyrev foreign policy lacked a sense of national interest and was too accommodating to the West — at Russia's expense.

In 1995, Yeltsin replaced Kozyrev as Foreign Minister with Yevgeny Primakov, who was decidedly less pro-Western. Primakov opposed NATO enlargement, promoted integrating former Soviet republics under Russian leadership, and favored cooperation with China, India, and other states opposed to U.S. "global hegemony." When Primakov became Prime minister in September 1998, he chose Igor Ivanov to succeed him as Foreign Minister. Ivanov kept that position until March 2004, when he was replaced by career diplomat Sergei Lavrov, formerly Russia's U.N. Ambassador.

During Putin' s first year as president he continued Primakov' s policies, but by 2001, even before September 11, he made a strategic decision to reorient Russian national security policy toward cooperation with the West and the United States. Putin saw Russia's economic revitalization proceeding from its integration into the global economic system dominated by the advanced industrial democracies — something that could not be accomplished in an atmosphere of political/military confrontation or antagonism with the United States. After 9/11, the Bush Administration welcomed Russia's cooperation against Al Qaeda and the Taliban regime in Afghanistan, which paved the way for broader bilateral cooperation.

Moscow remained unhappy about NATO enlargement in Central and Eastern Europe, but reconciled itself to that. NATO and Russian leaders meeting in Rome signed the "NATO at 20" agreement, in which Russia and NATO members were to participate as equals on certain issues. Russia reacted relatively calmly to NATO's admission of seven new members (May 2004), including the former Soviet Republics of Estonia, Latvia, and Lithuania.

During Putin' s second term, relations with the West grew more strained. The status of Kosovo became a very contentious issue, with the United States, NATO, and the EU supporting Kosovo's independence from Serbia, while Russia strongly backed Belgrade's insistence that Kosovo remain part of Serbia.[12] Two other disputes between Russia and the West are so highly charged they threaten, according to some analysts, to revive Cold War era enmity: proposed U.S. missile defense deployments in Poland and the Czech Republic, and Russia's troubled relations with – and possible NATO accession by – Georgia and Ukraine. These issues are discussed below.

RUSSIA AND THE SOVIET SUCCESSOR STATES

After the collapse of the Soviet Union, a consensus emerged in Moscow on reestablishing Russian dominance in this region as a very high priority. There has been little progress toward overall CIS integration. Russia and other CIS states impose tariffs on each others' goods in order to protect domestic suppliers and raise revenue, in contravention of an economic integration treaty. Recent CIS summit meetings have ended in failure, with many of the presidents sharply criticizing lack of progress on common concerns and Russian attempts at domination. The CIS as an institution appears to be foundering, and in March 2005, Putin called it a "mechanism for a civilized divorce."

On the other hand, in October 2000, the presidents of Russia, Belarus, Armenia, Kazakhstan, Kyrgyzstan, and Tajikistan upgraded their 1992 Collective Security Treaty, giving it more operational substance and de jure Russian military dominance. In February 2003, the presidents of Russia, Ukraine, Belarus, and Kazakhstan agreed in principle to create a "single economic space" (SES) among the four countries. They signed a treaty to that effect in September 2003 but failed to agree on fundamental principles and terms of implementation. The December 2004 election of western-oriented Viktor Yushchenko as President of Ukraine seemed to kill the SES agreement, but Yushchenko's political reverses in 2005-2006 and the appointment of a more pro-Russian Prime Minister in Kyiv in August 2006 put this matter in play again for a time.

Russia and Belarus have taken some steps toward integration. Belarusian President Aleksandr Lukashenko may have hoped for a leading role in a unified state during Yeltsin's decline. Lukashenko unconstitutionally removed the parliamentary opposition in 1996 and strongly opposes market reform in Belarus, making economic integration difficult and potentially very costly for Russia. In April 1997, Yeltsin and Lukashenko signed documents calling for a "union" between states that were to remain "independent and sovereign," and a year later, they signed a Union Charter. Lukashenko minimized his and his country's political subordination to Moscow. Yeltsin avoided onerous economic commitments to Belarus. After protracted negotiations, the two presidents signed a treaty on December 8, 1999, committing Russia and Belarus to form a confederal state. Moscow and Minsk continue to differ over the scope and terms of union, and Putin repeatedly has sharply criticized Lukashenko' s schemes for a union in which the two entities would have equal power. The prospects for union seem to be growing more distant, especially after the sharp oil price dispute between the two governments in January 2007 that temporarily disrupted Russian oil deliveries to Belarus.

Russian forces remain in Moldova against the wishes of the Moldovan government (and the signature of a troop withdrawal treaty in 1994), in effect bolstering a neo-Communist, pro-Russian separatist regime in the Transnistria region of eastern Moldova. Russian-Moldova relations warmed, however, after the election of a communist pro-Russian government in Moldova in 2001, but even that government became frustrated with Moscow's manipulation of the Transnistrian separatists. The United States and the EU call upon Russia to withdraw from Moldova. Russian leaders have sought to condition the withdrawal of their troops on the resolution of Transnistria' s status, which is still manipulated by Moscow.

Russian forces intervened in Georgia's multi-faceted civil strife, finally backing the Shevardnadze government in November 1993 — but only after it agreed to join the CIS and allow Russia military bases in Georgia. Russia tacitly supports Abkhazian and South Ossetian separatism in Georgia and delayed implementation of a 1999 OSCE-brokered agreement to withdraw from military bases in Georgia. In 2002, tension arose over Russian claims that Chechen rebels were staging cross- border operations from Georgia's Pankisi Gorge, near the border with Chechnya. In 2002, the Bush Administration sent a small contingent of U.S. military personnel to Georgia to help train and equip Georgian security forces to combat Chechen, Arab, Afghani, Al Qaeda, and other terrorists who had infiltrated into Georgia. Tension between Moscow and Tbilisi sharpened further after Georgia's "Rose Revolution" catapulted U.S.-educated Mikhiel Saakashvili into the presidency in November 2003. Saakashvili is an outspoken critic of Moscow and seeks to bring Georgia into NATO. Nevertheless, in July 2005, Russia concluded an agreement with Georgia to withdraw its forces from military bases it had occupied in Georgia since the Soviet era. The base withdrawal was completed in 2007, although the continued presence of Russian "peacekeepers" in Abkhazia and South Ossetia is strongly objected to by the Georgian government.[13] In September 2006, Georgian authorities arrested four Russian army officers on charges of espionage. Although the Georgian government soon released the officers, Moscow imposed a broad economic embargo against Georgia and expelled hundreds of Georgians from Russia.

Escalating tension between Moscow and Tbilisi over Abkhazia and South Ossetia has led some observers to warn that the danger of war exists in the North Caucasus. In March-April 2008, Russia lifted trade sanctions against Abkhazia, established broad-ranging government-to-government ties with the regions, and sent more "peacekeeping" troops into Abkhazia. Russian forces also reportedly shot down at least one unmanned aerial vehicle sent over Abkhazia by the Georgians for reconnaissance. Putin adamantly opposes NATO membership for Georgia, arguing that it would threaten Russia's security. Some Russian politicians have argued that since the United States and most NATO and EU members supported Kosovo' s independence, Russia should recognize the independence of Abkhazia, South Ossetia, and the Transnistrian region of Moldova.

Moscow has used the Armenian-Azerbaijani conflict over Nagorno-Karabakh to pressure both sides and win Armenia as an ally. Citing instability and the threatened spread of Islamic extremism on its southern flank as a threat to its security, Moscow intervened in Tajikistan' s civil war in 1992-93 against Tajik rebels based across the border in Afghanistan.

A major focus of Russian policy in Central Asia and the Caucasus has been to gain more control of natural resources, especially oil and gas, in these areas. Russia seeks a stake for its firms in key oil and gas projects in the region and puts pressure on its neighbors to use pipelines running through Russia. This became a contentious issue as U.S. and other western oil firms entered the Caspian and Central Asian markets and sought alternative pipeline routes. Russia's policy of trying to exclude U.S. influence from the region as much as possible, however, was temporarily reversed by President Putin after the September 11 attacks. Russian cooperation with the deployment of U.S. military forces in Uzbekistan, Kyrgyzstan, and Tajikistan would have seemed unthinkable before September 11. More recently, however, Russian officials have voiced suspicions about U.S. motives for prolonged military presence in Central Asia.

On July 5, 2005, the Shanghai Cooperation Organization (comprising China, Russia, Kazakhstan, Kyrgyzstan, Tajikistan, and Uzbekistan), approved a Moscow- backed initiative calling for establishing deadlines for the withdrawal of U.S. and coalition military bases from the Central Asian states. On July 29, 2005, the Uzbek government directed the United States to terminate its operations at the Karshi-Khanabad (K2) airbase within six months. Tashkent is believed to have acted not only in response to Russian and Chinese urging but also out of anger over sharp U.S. criticism of the Uzbek government's massacre of anti-government demonstrators in Andijan in May 2005.[14]

A Russian-Estonian political crisis erupted in April-May 2007 in connection with the Estonian government's relocation of a WW II Soviet war memorial from central Tallinn to a suburban military cemetery. The Russian government denounced this act as "fascistic" and "blasphemous." On the night of April 27, ethnic Russians in Tallinn — with Moscow's seemingly tacit encouragement — rioted, ransacking many commercial establishments. One Russian youth was stabbed to death. Moscow denounced Estonian "repression" of "peaceful Russian demonstrators," made numerous demands of the government in Tallinn, and called upon the EU to protest Estonia's actions. This was accompanied by extensive cyber attacks against Estonian government and commercial websites. The Russian state railway monopoly announced that due to a sudden scarcity of railway cars, all shipments of coal and oil to and through Estonia would be halted. The EU (of which Estonia is a member) backed Estonia and criticized Russia's political and economic pressure.[15]

Of all the Soviet successor states, Ukraine is the most important for Russia. Early on, the Crimean Peninsula was especially contentious. Many Russians view it as historically part of Russia, and say it was illegally "given" to Ukraine by Khrushchev in 1954. Crimea's population is 67% Russian and 26% Ukrainian. In April 1992, the Russian legislature declared the 1954 transfer of Crimea illegal. Later that year Russia and Ukraine agreed that Crimea was "an integral part of Ukraine" but would have economic autonomy and the right to enter into social, economic, and cultural relations with other states. There was tension over Kyiv' s refusal to cede exclusive use of the Sevastopol naval base in Crimea to Russia. Finally, in May 1997, Yeltsin and Ukrainian President Leonid Kuchma signed a Treaty resolving the dispute over Sevastopol and the Black Sea Fleet and declaring that Russian-Ukrainian borders cannot be called into question. This agreement, widely viewed as a major victory for Ukrainian diplomacy, was ratified in April 1999. However, as tension rose between Moscow and Kyiv after the 2004 "Orange Revolution" (see below), some Russian politicians have revived the issue of Crimea's sovereignty. Ukrainian leaders are seeking to assure the departure of the Russian Navy from Sevastopol by the treaty-stipulated date of 2017.

Ukraine's October 31, 2004, presidential election pitted the openly pro-Moscow Prime Minister, Viktor Yanukovych, against an independence and reform-minded candidate, Viktor Yushchenko. Putin strongly and openly backed Yanukovych and lent much material support to his campaign. Nevertheless, Yushchenko narrowly out-polled Moscow's man in the first round. In the disputed run-off election on November 21, Yanukovych initially claimed victory and was publically congratulated by Putin. Evidence of widespread election fraud, however, sparked massive Ukrainian street demonstrations and strong U.S. and EU criticism, pitting Russia against the West in a way reminiscent of the Cold War. After Ukraine's parliament and Supreme Court threw out the results of the November 21 election, the re-run on December 26 was won by Yushchenko (52% vs. 44%). Many observers in Russia, Ukraine, and the West, saw this outcome (hailed as the "Orange Revolution") as a powerful blow to perceived Russian hopes of reasserting dominance over Ukraine. Yushchenko declared integrating Ukraine economically and politically into Europe as his top priority, with NATO membership an ultimate goal.

Under Yushchenko, Ukraine opted out of the SES agreement promoted by Moscow. Ukraine, however, is economically dependent on Russia, especially for energy, although Kyiv also has some leverage in this area, as the main pipelines carrying Russian gas and oil to Europe pass through Ukraine. This troubled relationship leapt to prominence on January 1, 2006, when Russia stopped pumping natural gas to Ukraine after the two sides had failed for months to reach agreement on Russia's proposed quadrupling of the price of gas. This led to a sharp reduction in Russian gas supplies to Central and Western Europe, which pass through Ukraine. In response to strong European protests, Russia resumed pumping gas to and through Ukraine on January 3. The next day, Russia and Ukraine announced agreement on a complicated deal that doubled the price Ukraine paid for gas. Many analysts saw the outcome as strengthening Russian influence in Ukraine and politically weakening Yushchenko prior to parliamentary elections (March 26, 2006), in which Yushchenko's party won only 13% of the vote, finishing third among five major parties. After four months of political deadlock in Kyiv, Yushchenko appointed his 2004 arch-enemy, Yanukovych, Prime Minister in August 2006. Yanukovych, however, signed an agreement pledging to continue Yushchenko' s policy of integration with the West, and Yushchenko was able to have pro-western members of his own party head the Ministries of Foreign Affairs and Defense. This arrangement broke down and in April 2007 Yushchenko triggered a political showdown by dissolving the pro-Yanukovych parliament and calling for snap parliamentary elections. After a prolonged standoff, the two sides agreed on elections in September, which resulted in a narrow victory for the old Orange Revolution Yushchenko-Timoshenko coalition. Yulia Timoshenko became Prime Minister. The Yushchenko-Timoshenko government put NATO accession high on its agenda, which aroused vehement Russian opposition. At the NATO summit in Bucharest, April 2-4, 2008, Russia was relieved that the Alliance did not to offer Ukraine (and Georgia) immediate Membership Action Plans, despite President Bush's strong backing for MAPs. But NATO's decision to review Ukraine's and Georgia's requests for MAPs in December 2008 keeps the issue very much alive. It remains to be seen how these Ukrainian political developments ultimately will affect the country's relations with Russia, the EU, NATO, and the United States.[16]

Defense Policy

Fundamental Shakeup of the Military

The Russian armed forces and defense industries have been in turmoil since 1992. Their Soviet-era privileged position in the allocation of resources has been broken, as has their almost sacrosanct status in official ideology and propaganda. Hundreds of thousands of troops were withdrawn from Eastern Europe, the former Soviet Union, and the Third World. Massive budget cuts and troop reductions forced hundreds of thousands of officers out of the ranks into a depressed economy. Present troop strength is about 1.2 million men. (The Soviet military in 1986 numbered 4.3 million.) Weapons procurement virtually came to a halt in the 1990s and is only slowly reviving. Readiness and morale remain low, and draft evasion and desertion are widespread. Yeltsin and later Putin declared military reform a top priority, but fundamental reform of the armed forces and the defense industries is a difficult, controversial, and costly undertaking. The Chechen also conflict delayed military reform.

Putin has pledged to strengthen and modernize the armed forces, and has taken some steps in that direction. At the same time, he appears to be aware of Russia's financial and material limitations. The decisions announced in August and September 2000 to greatly reduce Russia's strategic nuclear forces (from 6,000 to 1,500 deployed warheads), to shift resources from strategic to conventional forces, and to shift from a conscript to a volunteer force suggest possibly serious intent to effect military reform.

Putin made some changes in the military leadership that may lead to policy changes. In 2001, Putin named Sergei Ivanov, a former KGB general and close confidant, to be Defense Minister. Ivanov had resigned his nominal intelligence service military rank and initially had headed Putin' s Security Council as a civilian. Putin explained that the man who had supervised the planning for military reform (Ivanov) should be the man to implement reform as Defense Minister. In May 2004, the General Staff was taken out of the direct chain of command and given a more advisory role, a move that appears to strengthen civilian control.

The improvement of Russia's economy since 1999, fueled in large part by the cash inflow from sharply rising world oil and gas prices, enabled Putin to reverse the budgetary starvation of the military during the 1990s. Defense spending has increased substantially in each of the past few years. The 2007 defense budget was 821 billion rubles ($31.6 billion), a fourfold increase since 2002. If one adds the funds allotted in 2007 for the nuclear, security, and defense-related law-enforcement activities to the total defense expenditures, total budget spending on defense reaches around $58 billion.[17] According to Russian press reports, defense spending in 2008 will be 20% higher than 2007. Even factoring in purchasing power parity, Russian defense spending still lags far behind current U.S. or former Soviet, levels. But Russia is beginning to resume serial production of major weapons systems, albeit at rates very far below Soviet Cold-War levels. Some high-profile military activities have been resumed, such as large-scale multi-national military exercises, show-theflag naval deployments to the Mediterranean and the Atlantic, and strategic long- range bomber patrols that approach U.S. and NATO airspace.

Despite its difficulties, the Russian military remains formidable in some respects and is by far the largest in the region. Because of the deterioration of its conventional forces, however, Russia relies increasingly on nuclear forces to maintain its status as a major power. There is sharp debate within the Russian armed forces about priorities between conventional vs. strategic forces and among operations, readiness, and procurement. Russia is trying to increase security cooperation with the other CIS countries. Russia has military bases on the territory of all the CIS states except Azerbaijan and is seeking to take over or share in responsibility for protecting the external borders of the CIS. In the proposed Russia-Belarus union, President Lukashenko pointedly emphasizes the military dimension. On the other hand, Georgia, Ukraine, Moldova, and Azerbaijan are shifting their security policies toward a more western, pro-NATO orientation.

CONTROL OF NUCLEAR WEAPONS

When the U.S.S.R. collapsed in 1991, over 80% of its strategic nuclear weapons were in Russia. The remainder were deployed in Ukraine, Belarus, and Kazakhstan. Those three states completed transfer of all nuclear weapons to Russia and ratified the Nuclear Non-Proliferation Treaty as non-nuclear-weapon states by 1995-1996. All Soviet tactical nuclear weapons, which had been more widely dispersed, reportedly were moved to Russia by 1992. The command and control system for strategic nuclear weapons is believed to be tightly and centrally controlled, with the Russian president and defense minister responsible for authorizing their use. The system of accounting and control of nuclear (including weapons grade) material, however, is much more problematic, raising widespread concerns about the danger of nuclear proliferation. There are growing concerns about threats to Russian command and control of its strategic nuclear weapons resulting from the degradation of its system of early warning radars and satellites. At the June 2000 Clinton-Putin summit, the two sides agreed to set up a permanent center in Moscow to share near real-time information on missile launches, but this has yet to be implemented.[18]

U.S. POLICY

U.S.-Russian Relations

The spirit of U.S.-Russian "strategic partnership" of the early 1990s was replaced by increasing tension and mutual recrimination in succeeding years. In the aftermath of the September 11, 2001 attacks, the two nations reshaped their relationship on the basis of cooperation against terrorism and Putin' s goal of integrating Russia economically with the West.[19] Since 2003, however, tensions have reemerged on a number of issues that again strain relations. Although cooperation continues in some areas, and Presidents Bush and Putin strove to maintain at least the appearance of cordial personal relations, there is now more discord than harmony in U.S.-Russian relations. This was highlighted by Putin's increasingly sharp criticism of the United States in 2007-2008.[20]

Russia's construction of nuclear reactors in Iran and its role in missile technology transfers to Iran have been critical sources of tension with the United States. Despite repeated representations from the White House and Congress, which argue that Iran will use the civilian reactor program as a cover for a covert nuclear weapons program, Russia refused to cancel the project, which is nearly completed. Revelations of previously covert Iranian nuclear developments revived this issue, and some Russian political leaders criticized the policy of nuclear cooperation with Iran, giving rise to policy debate on this issue in Moscow. Moscow's position is that it intends to continue its civilian nuclear power projects in Iran, while demanding that Tehran halt its uranium reprocessing and enrichment activities.

In late 2005, Moscow proposed a compromise plan to avert a showdown between Iran and the United States and the EU over Iran's insistence on its right to reprocess uranium. The Russian proposal, which won luke-warm Bush Administration support, would allow Iran to reprocess uranium, in facilities on Russian territory, presumably subject to international inspection. After prolonged talks, Iran's Foreign Ministry in March 2006 rejected the Russian proposal. The United States and an EU group (France, Germany, and the U.K.) won Russian (and Chinese) agreement to move the issue to the UN Security Council. After months of negotiations, during which Russia argued that diplomacy with Iran would yield greater results than would sanctions, the Security Council agreed to U.N. Security Council (UNSC) Resolution 1737, passed unanimously on December 23, 2006, to impose some modest sanctions on trade with Iran's nuclear infrastructure and a freeze on trade with and the assets of ten Iranian entities and twelve individuals.[21] In response to Iran's continued intransigence on the uranium reprocessing issue, on March 24, 2007 Russia voted with the United States in the UNSC to toughen sanctions against Iran. Perhaps more significantly, Moscow also withdrew most of its technicians and scientists from the unfinished Bushehr reactor project, citing alleged Iranian arrears in payments for the project — a claim that Iranian officials denied. An attempt by the Bush Administration to win Russian (and Chinese) approval for a third round of UNSC sanctions in late 2007 proved unsuccessful. Administration hopes were further dimmed by the publication in December 2007 of Key Judgements of the National Intelligence Estimate on Iran that cast doubt on earlier U.S. assertions that Iran was unquestionably pursuing a clandestine nuclear weapons program. On March 3, 2008, Russia again voted with the United States, France, the U.K. and China in the UNSC to impose a third round of sanctions against Iran, but these "watered down" sanctions mostly called for voluntary application by UN members. More significant was Russia's decision to resume construction and shipment of nuclear fuel to Bushehr. Fuel delivery was completed in January 2008. The reactor is expected to begin operation in late 2008 or 2009.

Since the mid-1990s, U.S. and Russian interests have clashed over Iraq. Russia strongly opposed military action against Iraq in connection with the U.N. inspection regime. After September 11, Moscow moved away from blanket support of Iraq. Some Russian officials suggested that under certain circumstances, U.S. military action against Iraq might not seriously strain U.S.-Russian relations — provided it was not unilateral and Russia's economic interests in Iraq were protected. As the United States moved toward military action against Iraq, Putin tried to balance three competing interests: protecting Russian economic interests in Iraq; restraining U.S. "unilateralism" and global dominance; and maintaining friendly relations with the United States. In February-March 2003, Putin aligned Russia with France and Germany in opposition to U.S. military action and threatened to veto a U.S.-backed UNSC resolution authorizing military force against Iraq. The U.S.-led war in Iraq further strained U.S.-Russian relations, but the senior leadership in both countries said that this would not be allowed to jeopardize their overall cooperation. On May 22, 2003, Russia voted with other members of the UNSC to approve a U.S.-backed resolution giving the United States broad authority in administering post-war Iraq.

A sharp U.S.-Russian clash of interests over missile defense, the ABM Treaty, and strategic arms reductions flared in the first year of the Bush Administration. These problems were substantially reduced, but not entirely resolved, at the BushPutin summit in May 2002. The Bush Administration declared its disinterest in START II and the ABM Treaty and its determination to pursue robust missile defense. This approach was met with resistance from Moscow, but the Administration stuck to its policies and, despite skepticism from some Members of Congress and many European allies, gradually won Russian acquiescence on most elements of its program.

Moscow reacted negatively to early Bush Administration determination to press ahead vigorously with missile defense, although the atmospherics, at least, improved after the Bush-

Putin summit in Slovenia on June 16, 2001. In December 2001, the Bush Administration gave Moscow official notification of its intention to renounce the ABM Treaty within six months. Russia's official response was cool but restrained, calling the U.S. decision a mistake, but saying that it would not cause a major disruption in relations. Similarly, in January 2002, Moscow reacted negatively to the Bush Administration's proposed plans to put in storage many of the nuclear warheads it planned to withdraw from deployment, rather than destroy them. Again, however, Russian criticism was relatively restrained, while the two sides continued intensive negotiations.

The negotiations bore fruit in mid-May, when final agreement was announced. Moscow won U.S. agreement to make the accord a treaty requiring legislative approval. The terms of the treaty, however, achieved all the Administration's key goals: deployed strategic nuclear warheads are to be reduced to 1,700-2,200 by 2012, with no interim timetable, no limits on the mix or types of weapons, and no requirement for destroying rather than storing warheads. The so-called Treaty of Moscow was signed by the two presidents on May 24, 2002. On June 13, the United States became free of all restraints of the ABM Treaty. On the same day, Moscow announced that it would no longer consider itself bound by the provisions of the (unratified) START II Treaty, which has become a dead letter. In June 2002, the commander of Russia's Strategic Rocket Forces announced that in response to the U.S. withdrawal from the ABM Treaty, Russia would prolong the life of its MIRVed ICBM force, which, he said, could be extended another 10-15 years. On June 1, 2003, Presidents Bush and Putin exchanged instruments of ratification allowing the Treaty of Moscow to enter into force. They also agreed to cooperate in missile defense. In November 2004, Putin announced that Russia was developing a new strategic nuclear missile superior to any in the world. The SS-27 reportedly combines a hypersonic boost phase and a maneuverable warhead, characteristics designed to defeat (U.S.) ballistic missile defenses.

A sharp new disagreement on missile defense emerged in 2007 in the form of Russian objections to Bush Administration plans to deploy a ground-based midcourse missile defense system (GMD) in Europe to help defend U.S. forces and allies in Europe against a possible long-range ballistic missile threat from Iran. The proposed GMD system would include 10 silo-based interceptors in Poland and a radar installation in the Czech Republic.[22]

Russian objections include the following arguments: a) the proposed GMD, situated close to Russia's borders, poses a threat to Russia's strategic nuclear deterrent and retaliatory capability and is really directed against Russia, not against some non-existent Iranian or North Korean threat; b) Russia was not adequately consulted about the GMD deployment; c) the GMD system, if deployed, will spur a renewed nuclear arms race; d) the proposed deployments in Poland and the Czech Republic violate earlier U.S./NATO pledges to Moscow not to establish new military bases in those countries; e) the missiles deployed in Poland could have offensive capability to strike targets in Russia; f) the radar in the Czech Republic could be used to "spy" on Russia.

Supporters of the GMD deployment dismiss these arguments as misinformed, spurious, or malicious. It is not clear to what extent, if any, competent Russian authorities believe these arguments, although there is deep underlying resentment of U.S. military deployments on the territory of Moscow's former Warsaw Pact allies. Many U.S. and European observers believe, however, that Russia's objections to GMD have other motives: a) to drive a wedge between the United States and its European allies; b) to drive a wedge between new NATO members such as Poland and the Czech Republic, which view Russia as unfriendly and potentially threatening, and West European NATO members such as Germany and France, which seek cooperation and partnership with Russia; c) to use GMD as an excuse to renounce certain arms control agreements that Moscow now finds militarily constraining, and; d) to use GMD to “change the subject” from western criticism of various Russian domestic and foreign policies to criticism of U.S. “militarism” and “unilateralism.”

Russian officials have threatened that Russia might “target” the GMD facilities in Poland and the Czech Republic. Russia has threatened to abrogate the 1987 Intermediate-Range Nuclear Forces (INF) Treaty if the GMD system is deployed in Europe. In his annual address to parliament on April 26, 2007, Putin cited the proposed GMD deployment as part of the justification for a “moratorium” on Russian compliance with the Treaty on Conventional Forces in Europe (CFE). In late May 2007, Putin warned that the U.S. GMD deployments threatened to spark a new arms race in Europe and called for an emergency European security conference in June to consider GMD and the CFE Treaty. This conference, in Vienna, Austria, ended in deadlock.

In a surprise move during the G8 summit in Germany (June 2007), Putin appeared to take up Bush’s offer to partner with the United States on missile defense. Putin suggested that Russia would not object to U.S. interceptor missiles in Iraq, Turkey, or at sea, and also floated the idea of using a Soviet-era radar facility in Azerbaijan, leased and operated by Russia, to help track and target hostile missiles that might be launched from the Middle East. Bush welcomed Putin’ s shift on missile defense that reduced tensions on the issue. At a July 1-2 meeting in Kennebunkport, Maine, Putin expanded on his counterproposal by recommending that missile defense be coordinated through offices in Brussels and Moscow. He also suggested the possible use of a radar in south Russia and said that cooperation could be expanded to other European countries through the use of the NATO-Russia council — thus eliminating the need for facilities in Poland and the Czech Republic.[23] President Bush responded positively to Putin’s new proposal, but insisted on the need for the Eastern European sites.

On October 12, 2007, Secretaries Rice and Gates met with Putin and other senior Russian officials in Moscow and brought with new proposals aimed at defusing Russian opposition to GMD. These proposals reportedly included expanded opportunities for Russian cooperation in building the missile defense system and for Russian inspections of, and observers at, GMD sites. These proposals appear to have elicited some interest in Moscow, but not a break through. Talks have continued intermittently, with another Rice-Gates trip to Moscow and a Bush-Putin meeting in Sochi, Russia on April 6, 2008. At Sochi, Putin continued to oppose U.S. missile defense deployments in Poland and the Czech Republic, but expressed "cautious optimism" that the two sides could eventually reach agreement and that proposed U.S. confidence-building measures would be "important and useful" if implemented.[24] Meanwhile, Russian officials alternate between harsh criticism of GMD and demands for clarification and more concessions on the U.S. proposals.

Moscow and Washington are cooperating on some issues of nuclear weapons reduction and security. Since 1992, the United States has spent over $7 billion in Cooperative Threat Reduction (CTR or “Nunn-Lugar”) funds and related pr weapons-grade plutonium by fifty metric tons. In June 1999, U.S. and Russian officials extended the CTR program for another seven years. The two sides also agreed to each dispose of an additional 34 tons of weapons-grade plutonium, with the U.S. to seek international funding to help finance the $1.7 billion Russian effort. The planned U.S.-Russian joint missile early warning information center in

Moscow, however, has yet to be established. In April 2002, the Bush Administration decided not to certify that Russia was fully cooperating with U.S. efforts to verify its compliance with agreements to eliminate chemical and biological weapons. This could have blocked U.S. funding for some CTR programs, but President Bush granted Russia a waiver.

In September 2006, the United States and Russia resolved a long-standing dispute over liability issues that had threatened to disrupt an important bilateral nuclear nonproliferation program. The Elimination of Weapons-Grade Plutonium Production Program — designed to convert 68 tons of excess weapons-grade plutonium (enough for 16,000 nuclear weapons) into mixed oxide fuel for use in nuclear reactors, a form that cannot be used for weapons by terrorists or others — is now on track to continue. In November 2007, U.S. Secretary of Energy Bodman and Russian Federal Atomic Energy Agency Director Sergei Kiriyenko signed a joint statement outlining a plan to dispose of the 68 tons of plutonium. The U.S. Department of Energy and Russian counterpart agencies also conduct joint training exercises to deal with the possibility of civilian nuclear accidents.

On August 4, 2006, the U.S. State Department announced sanctions against the Russian state arms export agency, Rosoboroneksport, and the aircraft manufacturer Sukhoi, for alleged violations of the Iran Nonproliferation Act of 2000, thereby barring U.S. companies from dealing with those Russian entities for two years. Russian officials denounced the action as retaliation for their Venezuelan arms sales. In December 2006, the sanctions against Sukhoi were lifted, but those against Rosoboroneksport were reconfirmed for two more years, over Russian protests.

Despite continued tension between Washington and Moscow over Iran, Iraq, missile defense, and the future status of Kosova, both governments seek to preserve mutually advantageous elements of the cooperative relationship they built following the September 11 attacks. In March 2003, Senator Lugar introduced legislation to exempt Russia from the Jackson-Vanik amendment to the Trade Bill of 1974, action which would grant Russia permanent normal trade relations (PNTR) status and facilitate Russian accession to the WTO, but it received no further action. After years of difficult negotiations, U.S. and Russian officials concluded a U.S.-Russian trade agreement in November 2006, paving the way for Russian accession to the WTO. This means that the 111th Congress may address the issues of PNTR for Russia and the Jackson-Vanik Amendment. But approval of these measures is by no means assured. On February 21, 2007, Representative Lantos, then-Chairman of the House Foreign Affairs Committee, said in a Moscow press conference that he would work to "end the Jackson-Vanik process," which he called a "relic of the Cold War." As of mid-2008, no legislation to this end has been introduced.

U.S. ASSISTANCE

From FY1992 through FY2007, the U.S. government obligated more than $16 billion in assistance to Russia, including over $3.7 billion in Freedom Support Act (FSA) aid for democratization, market reform, and social and humanitarian aid. Most of the rest went for CTR (Nunn-Lugar) and other security-related programs. But Russia's share of the (shrinking) NIS foreign aid (FSA) account fell from about 60% in FY1993-FY1994 to 17% in FY1998 and has been between 15%-22% since then. The Administration requested $148 million for

Russian FSA programs in FY2003, $93.4 million in FY2004, $85 million in FY2005, $48 million in FY2006 (which was raised by Congress to $80 million), and $58 million in FY2007. The Administration's request for FSA aid to Russia in FY2008 is $50 million.[25]

Both the FSA and the annual foreign operations appropriations bills contain conditions that Russia is expected to meet in order to receive assistance. A restriction on aid to Russia was approved in the FY1 998 appropriations and each year thereafter, prohibiting any aid to the government of the Russian Federation (i.e., central government; it does not affect local and regional governments) unless the President certifies that Russia has not implemented a law discriminating against religious minorities. Presidents Clinton and Bush have made such determinations each year.

Since FY1996, direct assistance to the government of Russia has hinged on its continuing sale of nuclear reactor technology to Iran. As a result, in most years as much as 60% of planned U.S. assistance to the federal Russian government has been cut. The FY2001 foreign aid bill prohibited 60% of aid to the central government of Russia if it was not cooperating with international investigations of war crime allegations in Chechnya or providing access to NGOs doing humanitarian work in Chechnya. Possibly as a result of Russian cooperation with the United States in its war on terrorism, the war crime provision was dropped.

REFERENCES

[1] See CRS Report RL32662, Democracy in Russia: Trends and Implications for U.S. Interests, by Jim Nichol.

[2] See CRS Report RL34392, Russia's 2008 Presidential Succession, by Stuart D. Goldman

[3] See CRS Report RS22770, Russia's December 2007 Legislative Election: Outcome and Implications, by Jim Nichol.

[4] The embattled North Caucasus regions of Chechnya, Ingushetia, and Dagestan reported heroically Soviet-era voter turnout of 99%, 98% and 92% respectively, with United Russia gaining 99% of the vote in Chechnya and Ingushetia and 89% in Dagestan.

[5] "Study Shows Medvedev Benefits from Massive Media Advantage," RFE/RL, Newsline, January 23, 2008; Peter Finn, "Prime Time for Putin's Anointed," Washington Post, January 30, 2008.

[6] RFE/RL, Newsline, February 5, 20, 2008.

[7] This party, seen by many as a Kremlin-backed pseudo-opposition group, won fewer than 90,000 votes nation-wide in the December 2007 Duma election.

[8] See CRS Report RL3 2272, Bringing Peace to Chechnya? Assessments and Implications, by Jim Nichol.

[9] Anders Aslund, "The Russian Economy Facing 2017," in Alternative Futures for Russia to 2017, by Andrew C. Kuchins, Center for Strategic and International Studies, Washington, D.C., November 2007.

[10] Ibid.

[11] See CRS Report RL3 1979, Russia's Accession to the WTO, by William Cooper.

[12] See CRS Report RL3 1053, Kosovo and U.S. Policy: Background to Independence, by Julie Kim and Steven Woehrel.

[13] See CRS Report RL33453, Armenia, Azerbaijan, and Georgia: Political Developments and Implications for U.S. Interests, by Jim Nichol.

[14] For more on Russian policy in these regions, see CRS Report RL3 3458, Central Asia: Regional Developments and Implications for U.S. Interests by Jim Nichol, and CRS Report RL33453, Armenia, Azerbaijan, and Georgia: Political Developments and Implications for U.S. Interests, also by Jim Nichol.

[15] See CRS Report RS22692, Estonia: Current Issues and U.S. Policy, by Steven Woehrel.

[16] 16 See CRS Report RL33460, Ukraine: Current Issues and U.S. Policy, by Steven Woehrel; and CRS Report RL34415, Enlargement Issues at NATO's Bucharest Summit, by Paul Gallis, Paul Belkin, Carl Ek, Julie Kim, Jim Nichol, and Steven Woehrel.

[17] "Russia: Reviving The Army, Revising Military Doctrine," RFE/RL, March 12, 2007.

[18] See CRS Report RL32202, Nuclear Weapons in Russia: Safety, Security, and Control Issues, by Amy F. Woolf.

[19] For the change in Russian policy toward integration with the West and cooperation with the United States, see CRS Report RL3 1543, Russian National Security Policy After September 11, by Stuart D. Goldman, last updated August 20, 2002.

[20] See, for example, speech at the annual Munich security conference on February 10, 2007 and his annual address to parliament on April 26, 2007

[21] See CRS Report RL32048, Iran: U.S. Concerns and Policy Responses, by Kenneth Katzman.

[22] See CRS Report RL34051, Long-Range Ballistic Missile Defense in Europe, by Steven A. Hildreth, and Carl Ek.

[23] "Putin Expands On His Missile Defense Plan," New York Times. July 3, 2007; "Putin Proposes Broader Cooperation On Missile Defense," Washington Post, July 3, 2007.

[24] RFE/RL, Newsline, April 7, 2008.

[25] See CRS Report RL32866, U.S. Assistance to Russia and the Former Soviet Union, by Curt Tarnoff.

In: Russian Political, Economic and Security Issues
Editor: Harold J. Kowen

ISBN 978-1-60692-407-5

Chapter 2

TOWARDS A NEW RUSSIA POLICY

Stephen J. Blank
Air University, Maxwell AFB, Alabama, United States of American
University of Texas, San Antonio, United States of American
University of California, Riverside, United States of American

ABSTRACT

East-West relations have noticeably deteriorated, and Russia's behavior has become commensurately more self-assertive. Key arms control achievements are in jeopardy, and Russia claims to be facing an array of growing threats, most prominently from America. In fact, Russia demands more respect from and equality with Washington and a free hand in world politics. In key respects, Moscow's new foreign policy grows out of the logic of its ever more autocratic and neo-imperial political structure. As analyzed in the monograph, this structure reinforces the long-standing Russian tendency to view other states as being inherently adversarial, i.e., it has a disposition to see world politics in terms of a presupposition of a priori enemies. Thus it views arms control issues from the standpoint of deterring enemies not working with strategic partners.

The danger of a foreign policy that relies on truculent rhetoric, inflated and aggressive threat assessments, and an autocratic and neo-imperial political structure based on the ideology of Russia's desire for a free hand in world politics and ingrained belief that others are inherently the same is that it will stimulate precisely the adversarial behavior in Washington that it claims to see. There are already growing signs that certain sectors of the policymaking community are increasingly inclined to view Russia as a question mark, if not a rival of American policy. This is particularly the case regarding issues of arms control and nuclear policy. Thus the current rhetorical belligerence seen in Russian policy and the increasing amount of interest in higher defense spending and inflated threat assessments could bring about exactly what Russian elites already claim to observe.

Accordingly, it is necessary for the United States to understand the scope of the challenge posed by Russia and to take steps towards reformulating its policies so that they are more coherent and unified, more deeply engaged with Russia across a wide spectrum of issues, and also more coordinated with our European allies. This means that we must forego the idea that good relations between presidents suffice, or that we have no leverage on Russia, or that human rights should not be a major part of our concern. While Russian interests and concerns must be engaged with seriousness and respect, they cannot be allowed to overshadow our own interests and concerns. The need for permanent ongoing bureaucratic engagement with Russia remains a challenge for Washington, but it is one that can and must be met by means of a long-term strategically conceived policy. And that policy must engage Moscow across all the issues of topical concern to Washington.

INTRODUCTION: THE ADVERSARIAL EAST- WEST RELATIONSHIP

Today speculation about a new cold war or arms race between Moscow and Washington is rampant, easy to come by, and even permeates official discourse. Indeed, Russian Foreign Minister Sergei Lavrov characterized Russo-American relations as “alarming” in June 2007.[1] Similarly, at least some senior officials in the Bush administration now believe that, far from merely craving respect (although that certainly is the case), Russia has provided “overwhelming evidence” that it seeks to weaken America. Thus “wherever possible internationally,” they say, “Moscow will work to stop America from achieving success.”[2] And at the same time North Atlantic Treaty Organization (NATO) Secretary-General Jaap de Hoop Sheffer is calling on Moscow to clarify its views on ties with NATO, and there are moves afoot in both Moscow and Washington to restrict foreign investment in their economies by tightening national security reviews of such proposed investments.[3]

Although Lavrov and Deputy Prime Minister (and former Defense Minister) Sergei Ivanov both explicitly rule out “Cold War” as a label for Russo-American relations, their subordinates are not so soothing.[4] Thus Deputy Foreign Minister Aleksandr’ Losyukov, speaking in Tehran, said that Washington was using Korea and Iran’s prolfieration as an issue to consolidate its global strategic position, i.e., invoking those two states to justify its missile defense program. If this issue cannot be resolved by diplomatic means, he warned, Russia will carry out a series of military acts to balanceand establish security. And this could prompt an arms race.[5] This frosty warning, rather than the calculated, insincere, and misleading efforts to invoke Russo- American partnership, more accurately characterizes the present state of Russo-American relations even if they are far from the Cold War.

Recent Russian actions include two overflights of Great Britain, Finland, and Norway; flights to Guam of Tu-95s; the resumption of armed aerial patrols; repeated overflights and bombings of Georgia; suspension of compliance with the Conventional Forces in Europe (CFE) Treaty; threats to renounce the Intermediate nuclear Forces in Europe (INF) Treaty; threats to target the Czech Republic and Poland if missile defense installations are placed there; announcement of plans to refurbish the Navy’s Mediterranean squadron; calls for a gas cartel; continuing regression towards ever more authoritarian political practices; arms sales to Iran and Syria, and recognition of Hamas; and the launching of an information war attack against Estonia for removing a Soviet war monument in Tallinn. All these imply the consolidation of a fundamentally adversarial position towards the West, not just the United States.

Russian President Vladimir Putin’s speeches to the Munich Wehrkunde Conference in February 2007 and to the Russian Federal Assembly in April highlighted this trend and outlined many of Russia’s grievances against the West and Washington in particular.[6] Subsequently in his V-E day speech on May 9, 2007, he explicitly compared the United

States to Nazi Germany.[7] In the speech to the Federal Assembly, he confirmed that adversarial quality of bilateral relations when he announced the suspension of Russia's compliance with the CFE Treaty.[8] Indeed, Russian Chief of Staff General Yuri N. Baluyevsky subsequently warned that this treaty is on the verge of collapse.[9] Since that treaty has no provisions for a moratorium, Baluyevsky's warning probably presages Russia's withdrawal from the CFE treaty.[10] Thus Putin's decree of July 14, 2007, suspending Russian participation in the treaty, should not have surprised us, although apparently it did surprise some in Washington.[11]

We and the West as a whole were clearly surprised as well by Putin's speech at Munich and by many other recent Russian policies. This complacency and unpreparedness is unwarranted as Russian unhappiness with U.S. policy has been growing since 2002-03. Neither should we be so complacent as to think that some high-level meetings, like presidential summits, can paper over this rift. Such meetings cannot substitute for a sound strategy and/or policy even when officials claim that Presidents Putin and Bush are confident that enough has been done to keep the positive momentum of the relationship going.[12] Russian analysts certainly do not make this mistake. Instead, they rightly point to the issue at stake, i.e., Moscow's insistence upon Russia's standing or status as a great power that demands Washington take its interests into account. Thus Ivan Safranchuk of Moscow's Office of the Center for Defense Information told U.S. reporters that,

> In the United States there is an underestimation of how serious Putin and his team are. This team is ready to spoil relations with the United States as far as necessary. There are no limitations. Putin is doing this not because he wants a new Cold War, but because he wants the Russian state to be seriously revived.[13]

This demand lies at the heart of the issue because Moscow at the very least believes that the West as a whole, and particularly America, do not take it or its interests seriously enough. And, as suggested above by a U.S. official, it is possible that we have an outright rivalry over the entire or most of the two states' bilateral political agendas whereby Russia's purpose is simply to fight American policy. Thus what is at stake in the Russo-American relationship is Russia's resentment of American power and the way it is displayed, particularly in regions that Moscow wants to dominate. In other words, Russia, like the late comedian Rodney Dangerfield, constantly laments that it doesn't get any or enough respect from America. Putin's presidential envoy for relations with the European Union (EU), Sergei Yastrzhembskiy, stated that this was Russia's main objection to recent developments in world politics.[14] Similarly Russian Ambassador to America Yuri Ushakov recently echoed that statement.[15]

So while East-West relations have become essentially adversarial, the most visible stresses are in Russo-American relations. Baluyevsky said that cooperation with the West has not helped Russia; instead the situation has become more difficult. In fact, "the U.S. military leadership's course aimed at maintaining its global leadership and expanding its economic, political, and military presence in Russia's traditional zones of influence" is a top threat to its national security.[16] However, rhetoric aside, there is no tangible military threat to Russia.[17] Yet Moscow has issued endless complaints that America does not take Russia sufficiently seriously, i.e., at Moscow's own self-serving and inflated valuation of itself.

What Russia wants, though, is clear enough— enhanced status and a completely free hand vis-à-vis Washington and Europe on issues vital to it. Lavrov, in a televised address denounced U.S. unilateralism and demanded "total equality, including equality in the analysis of threats, in finding solutions, and making decisions." Likewise, Russia sees itself (or at least professes to see itself) as a sovereign, i.e., wholly independent, actor in world politics that should be regarded as a superpower equal to America and be able to constrain its policies while remaining free from such constraints on what matters most to it, i.e., the Commonwealth of Independent States (CIS). Indeed, Putin at this Munich speech (and even earlier as well) called for a new "architecture of global security" and his actions before and after that speech indicate that Russia is acting to bring such a structure—which it deems to be a multipolar one—into being.[18] Alternatively Russia argues that a multipolar world where Russia is a free standing independent actor is already taking shape.

Lavrov has also presented an elaborate assessment of America's declining power and moral standing in the world as indicating and justifying the failure of the unipolar project.[19] Thus Washington's hoped for unipolar world cannot be achieved. Yastrzhembskiy echoed this by claiming that Washington faces growing international isolation due to the growing disparity between its views and those of other governments.[20]

Putin's litany of complaints in speeches going back to 2006 specified Russia's complaints in greater detail. Putin specifically charged that,

- America is a unipolar hegemon which conducts world affairs or aspires to do so in an undemocratic way (i.e., it does not take Russian interests into account).
- America has unilaterally gone to war in Iraq, disregarding the United Nations (UN) Charter, and demonstrating an "unconstrained hyper use of force" that is plunging the world into an abyss. It has therefore become impossible to find solutions to conflicts. (In other words, American unilateralism actually makes it harder to end the wars in Iraq and Afghanistan—hardly an incontestable proposition.) Because America seeks to decide all issues unilaterally to suit its own interests in disregard of others, "no one feels safe" and this policy stimulates an arms race and proliferation of weapons of mass destruction (WMD).
- Therefore we need a new structure of world politics, i.e., multipolarity and nonintervention in the affairs of others. Here Putin cited Russia's example of a peaceful transition to democracy! Of course, Russia hardly has a spotless record with regard to nonintervention as Estonia, Moldova, Ukraine, and Georgia illustrate.
- Putin expressed concern that the Moscow Strategic Offensive Arms Reduction Treaty of 2002 (SORT) may be violated or at least undermined by America which is holding back several hundred superfluous nuclear weapons for either political or military use. America is also creating new destabilizing high-tech weapons, including space weapons.
- Meanwhile the CFE treaty is not being ratified, even though Russian forces are leaving Georgia and only carrying out peacekeeping operations in Moldova. Similarly, U.S. bases are turning up "on our border." (Here Putin revealed that for him the border of Russia is, in fact, the old Soviet border since Russia no longer borders either on Romania or Poland.)

- America is also extending missile defenses to Central and Eastern Europe even though no threat exists that would justify this. In regard to this program, Putin replied to a question at the Wehrkunde Conference by saying that,

> The United States is actively developing and already strengthening an anti-missile defense system. Today this system is ineffective but we do not know exactly whether it will one day be effective. But in theory it is being created for that purpose. So, hypothetically, we recognize that when this moment arrives, the possible threat from our nuclear forces will be completely neutralized. Russia's present capabilities, that is. The balance of powers will be absolutely destroyed and one of the parties will benefit from the feeling of complete security. That means that its hands will be free not only in local but eventually also in global conflicts.[21]

Thus he has bought the General staff's habit of thinking exclusively in terms of worst-case scenarios to justify a policy of threats and military buildup. Moreover, Baluyevsky and the General Staff all regularly argue that because there is allegedly no threat from Iran, these missile defenses can only be aimed at Russia and at threatening to neutralize its deterrent.[22]

- NATO expansion (the Russian term in opposition to the Western word enlargement) therefore bears no relationship to European security but is an attempt to divide Europe and threaten Russia.
- Finally, America seeks to turn the Organization for Security and Cooperation in Europe (OSCE) into an anti-Russian organization, and nongovernment organizations (NGOs) are also being used by individual governments for such purposes despite their so called formal independence. Thus, revolutions in CIS countries are fomented from abroad, and elections there often are masquerades whereby the West intervenes in their internal affairs.[23] Obviously this view projects Russia's own politics and policies of interference in these elections (e.g., the $300 million it spent and the efforts of Putin's "spin doctors" in Ukraine in 2004) onto Western governments and wholly dismisses the sovereign internal mainsprings of political action in those countries, another unconscious manifestation of the imperial mentality that grips Russian political thinking and action.

It is hardly surprising, then, that Russian commentators regularly say that "Russia's strategic worldview is fundamentally at odds with the American one and perhaps with American perspectives on international security."[24] Indeed, Lavrov recently stated that the United States was perhaps Moscow's "most difficult" partner and should learn from its mistakes in world politics.[25] In that context, Russia's independence is the primary achievement of Russian foreign and defense policy.[26] Lavrov also observed in 2005 that "We can come to the conclusion that the whole complex of our [foreign] relations, the weight of existing military and strategic links between Russia and the [United States] . . . will be constantly declining. We will never separate, but drifting away from each other could have irreversible consequences."[27]

But beyond that, Lavrov contended that while America seeks to secure its global leadership status based on military power, it lacks the financial, trade, economic, "and—last but not least—moral resources to do so. [Thus], the West is losing the monopoly on establishing rules of the game."[28] So, aligned to this adversarial relationship is Russia's growing belief that its star is ascending, while the West and America are in steady decline. Consequently, Russia is, or should be, taking part in the formation of a new architecture of international relations and playing a role as a "system forming" power.[29] Yet, simultaneously, Russia's ruling elite regime paradoxically regards itself and Russia as being under constant threat from within and without despite this ascent. This marriage of paranoia and truculent boastfulness is unfortunately a Soviet, if not tsarist, heritage of Russian diplomacy, especially when things are going well for Moscow, and contains more than a little imperial arrogance.[30]

Neither is this expectation of tension in the bilateral relationship a uniquely Russian one. Russian truculence towards America increases the likelihood of comparable U.S. reactions over a broad range of issues. Director of National Intelligence Vice Admiral John McConnell (U.S. Navy Ret.), recently told the Senate Armed Services Committee that,

> Russian assertiveness will continue to inject elements of rivalry and antagonism into U.S. dealings with Moscow, particularly our interactions in the former Soviet Union, and will dampen our ability to cooperate with Russia on issues ranging from counterterrorism and nonprolif eration to energy and democracy promotion in the Middle East. As the Litvinenko murder demonstrates, the steady accumulation of problems and irritants threatens to harm Russia's relations with the West more broadly.[31]

Department of Defense (DoD) Secretary Robert Gates' testimony to the Senate Armed Services Committee in February 2007 about "the uncertain paths of China and Russia, which are both pursuing sophisticated military modernization programs" and Putin's overly alarmist reply to it at Munich, already reflects the danger of this element of rivalry and of reciprocal irritation that McConnell warned about.[32]

Moscow's argument that Russia does not get enough respect, whatever its validity, also omits those elements of Russian policy which have caused its image to suffer in the West. Putin's speeches omitted mentioning the state-sponsored decline of Russian democratic tendencies and institutions; Chechnya; Russian intervention in Ukraine's election in 2004; its habitual use of the energy weapon to intervene in Baltic, CIS, and East European governments' policies, threaten Transcaucasian regimes, and limit Central Asian sovereignty; the fact that the expansion of the U.S. military presence in Europe and missile defenses were briefed extensively to Moscow since 2004-05; the fact that Russia has tested intercontinental ballistic missiles (ICBMs) (both the stationary and mobile version of the Topol-M or SS-27, as well as the short- range Iskander missile) that, according to Putin and Former Defense Minister Sergei Ivanov, can beat any missile defense; and the fact that these missiles are now being mass produced.[33 These Russian charges also omit Moscow's military intervention in Georgia's ethnic conflicts, Moldova, and Nagorno-Karabakh; and its arms sales and nuclear technology transfer to states like China, Iran, Syria, and Venezuela.[34]

Perhaps worse and more disheartening is that Putin's speeches and those of his subordinates reflect that they still have a woefully incomplete and distorted understanding of the West despite 15 years of supposed democracy and freedom. Indeed, they are prone to accept the worst-case scenarios of Russian intelligence services and elites who are notorious for presenting distorted and utterly mendacious threat and policy assessments. Either that or they share a wholly cynical, materialistic, virtually exclusively self-referential, and misconceived notion of Western weakness, Russophobia, and disunity. To partisans of this mindset, America does not count anymore as a partner because Iraq has distracted it and diverted its interest from Russia.[35] It also is quite probably the case, as defense correspondent Pavel Felgenhauer reports, that,

> Russia has a Prussian-style all-powerful General Staff that controls all the different armed services and is more or less independent of outside political constraints. Russian military intelligence — GRU, as big in size as the former KGB and spread over all continents—is an integral part of the General Staff. Through GRU, the General Staff controls the supply of vital information to all other decision-makers in all matters concerning defense procurement, threat assessment, and so on. High-ranking former GRU officers have told me that in Soviet times the General Staff used the GRU to grossly, deliberately, and constantly mislead the Kremlin about the magnitude and gravity of the military threat posed by the West in order to help inflate military expenditure. There are serious indications that at present the same foul practice is continuing.[36]

For example, Putin complained that American politicians are invoking a nonexistent Russian threat to get more money for military campaigns in Iraq and Afghanistan. Putin's remarks represent a wholly fabricated analysis of Secretary Gates' testimony to Congress, but signify that he wants to believe the worst For example, Putin complained that American politicians are invoking a nonexistent Russian threat to get more money for military campaigns in Iraq and Afghanistan. Putin's remarks represent a wholly fabricated analysis of Secretary Gates' testimony to Congress, but signify that he wants to believe the worst about American intentions as do the General Staff, intelligence agencies, and like-minded Russian political leaders.[37] For example, in his press conference before the annual G-8 conference in Heiligendam, Germany in June 2007, Putin told reporters that Russia and the West were returning to the Cold War and added that,

> Of course, we will return to those times. And it is clear that if part of the U.S. nuclear capability is situated in Europe and that our military experts consider that they represent a potential threat, then we will have to take appropriate retaliatory steps. What steps? Of course, we must have new targets in Europe. And determining precisely which means will be used to destroy the installations that our experts believe represent a potential threat for the Russian Federation is a matter of technology. Ballistic or cruise missiles or a completely new system. I repeat that it is a matter of technology.[38]

Similarly, despite dozens of statements and briefings to the contrary, Russian generals and politicians insist that 10 missile defense radars and interceptors stationed in the Czech Republic and Poland represent a strategic threat to Russia and its nuclear deterrent not because of what they are but because of what they might be, just as Putin said above.[39] Russia also charges that rotational deployments of no more than 5,000 army and air force troops in Bulgaria and Romania represents an imminent threat to deploy forces to the Caucasus.[40] Russian spokesmen view these new bases and potential new missions of U.S. and NATO forces, including missile defense and power projection into the Caucasus or Central Asia, as anti-Russian threats, especially as NATO has stated that it takes issues like pipeline security in the Caucasus and its members' energy security increasingly seriously.[41] Yet actually U.S. "bases" in Romania and Bulgaria are nothing more than periodic rotational deployments of a small number of Army and Air forces whose mission is primarily the training of the forces of their host countries. They are anything but a permanent base for strike forces in the CIS and Moscow knows it.[42] Indeed, in 2004 Defense Minister Sergei Ivanov publicly accepted the reasons behind America's realignment of its forces and global basing structure and did not find it alarming.[43]

No less consequential than the observation about returning to the Cold War is that Putin's statements indicate his full acceptance of the General Staff's vision and version of ubiquitous a priori American and Western threats expressed in a worst-case scenario. Worse yet, he openly conceded their power to define and formulate those threats and on that basis formulate requirements for defense policy and strategy. Indeed, here he openly invited the General Staff—these military experts—to determine Russia's threat assessment and announced that the government would accept it. These actions seriously jeopardize any hope for effective civilian, not to mention, democratic control over the armed forces.

Since Moscow neither faces an urgent or imminent strategic or military threat nor does it claim to face one, the threat it perceives is psychological, one of influence and diminished status abroad. Thus when Putin proposed in June 2007 that Washington share the Russian radar at Gabala, Azerbaijan, with it as a compromise, Yastrzhembskiy stated that, "We consider this issue not a military question, but a political one."[44] Similarly the so-called threat from NATO enlargement, for all the Russian complaints about it, was and remains a psychological rather than strategic issue. The innumerable statements by Russian generals that their weapons could beat any missile defense confirm this point. This gap between rhetoric and reality suggests not just a desire to ratchet up threat assessments for political and economic benefits for the military and political elites doing so within Russia, or a search for foreign policy gains, but also a deliberate mis or disinformation of the leadership and the population as Felgenhauer suggests.

Certainly Russian charges that there is no Iranian missile threat are unsustainable because Moscow's own analysts and Russian officials like Ivanov and Baluyevsky acknowledge it.[45] Commenting on Iran's launch in early 2007 of a suborbital weather rocket, Lieutenant General Leonid Sazhin stated that "Iran's launch of a weather rocket shows that Tehran has not given up efforts to achieve two goals—create its own carrier rocket to take spacecraft to orbit and real medium-range combat missiles capable of hitting targets 3,000-5,000 miles away."[46] Although he argued that this capability would not fully materialize for 3-5 years, it would also take that long to test and deploy the American missile defenses that are at issue. Equally significantly, Major-General Vitaly Dubrovin, a Russian space defense expert, said flatly "now Tehran has a medium-range ballistic missile, capable of carrying a warhead."[47] Naturally, both men decried the fact that Iran appears intent on validating American threat assessments.[48]

Arguably Russia has accepted a threat perception for which ultimately there is no solution but an arms race. To take Russia at its own inflated self-valuation means to privilege its interests and security above those of every other state with which it either interacts or with which it has a border. While Moscow obviously wants that outcome, it is equally obvious that it would have strongly negative consequences for many issues in international affairs. Certainly doing so reinforces Russian temptations towards autocracy and neo-imperial foreign policies for as the Russian philosopher Sergei Gavrov writes,

> The threats are utopian, the probability of their implementation is negligible, but their emergence is a sign. This sign — a message to "the city and the world"—surely lends

> itself to decoding and interpretation: we will defend from Western claims our ancient right to use our imperial (authoritarian and totalitarian) domestic sociocultural traditions within which power does not exist to serve people but people exist to serve power.[49]

Taking these inflated threat assessments at Russia's self-valuation and acting accordingly would therefore have calamitous consequences throughout Eurasia. Doing so only stimulates still more aggressive and overbearing Russian behavior, while not getting anything in return. This does not mean disrespecting or gratuitously provoking Russia, but it does mean that we should understand that its threat perceptions and pretensions are greatly inflated, and we should therefore defend our legitimate ground. While there are actual areas where Russia might legitimately feel that its interests are adversely affected by U.S. policies and that such an assessment might be justified (see below), most of what we have recently heard about threats should not be included among them.

Indeed, numerous commentators have observed that for some time Russia has cast itself as a "besieged fortress," charging Washington with imperialism, launching an arms race, interfering in the domestic policies of CIS states (including Russia), expanding NATO, unilateralism, disregard for international law when it comes to using force, and resorting to military threats against Russian interests, etc.[50] This wide-ranging threat perception also embraces Russia's domestic politics as well. Regime spokesmen, e.g. Vladislav Surkov, also openly state that Russia must take national control of all the key sectors of the economy lest it be threatened by hostile foreign economic forces and so called "offshore aristocrats."[51] In other words, this threat perception links both internal and external threats in a seamless whole (as did Leninism) and represents the perception that Western democracy as such is a threat to Russia. Therefore U.S. and Western military power, even if it is not actually a threat, is a priori perceived as such.

Thus the problem is not that Russia is insufficiently respected abroad but rather that it defines its interests in ways that postulate an intrinsically adversarial relationship with the West, particularly Washington. Russian policy operates, as the German philosopher Carl Schmitt would have said, on the basis of the "presupposition of enemies." Consequently, Moscow cannot accept that its problem lies not in Washington or in the stars but in itself as much, if not more than, in American policy. Indeed, the student of the Russian press would have no trouble discerning this besieged fortress mentality that permeates it and that can only be triggered from above.[52] As in the Soviet past, Moscow, like Washington, remains wholly ethnocentric and self-absorbed in its attitudes and relationship to the external world. Russia's single-minded pursuit of its own concept of its interests also shows little respect for or understanding of the reality of other governments' policies or their opinions. Much of this syndrome is traceable not to American policy, but to the nature of the Russian political system. Hence the growing standoff with Washington.

Potential Consequences

While (rightly or wrongly) nobody expects a resurrection of the intense Cold War global geopolitical, military, and ideological rivalry replete with the ever- present specter of nuclear war, the consequences of this rift are profound. First, this rift has already begun to stimulate renewed strategic arms buildups by both sides. Second, this rift highlights the failure to transcend the traditional agenda of past efforts at Russo-American (or Soviet-American) partnership—i.e., international security, strategic arms control, nonproliferation of WMD, and energy cooperation—to a true strategic partnership.[53] Therefore issues of regional security in Europe, the Middle East, and Asia have become enmeshed with horizontal or vertical proliferation threats in these regions, making them more intractable and complicating the situation within which Eurasian governments must operate.

At the same time, issues of regional security throughout the CIS borderlands and in areas like the Black Sea have also become a subject of Russo-American, if not East-West, contention. Some commentators, like American conservative Bruce Jackson, proclaim that Russia wages a "soft war" against Western influence in Eastern Europe, including the Black Sea zone.[54] But the soft war also partakes of a classical geopolitical East- West rivalry, e.g., Moscow's attacks on the Amer-ican military presence in and around the Black Sea and concern about Bulgaria's and Romania's overall pro- Western foreign and defense policies. Similar rivalries occur throughout the entire post-Soviet periphery, the Middle East, and Northeast Asia.

Finally, there is a significant ideological dimension to this struggle. If it is not as intense as the Cold War was, it is still a meaningful struggle over the issue of democracy and its expansion. This "values gap" is expressed in Russian attacks on the OSCE and NGOs, and in the deliberately widely-disseminated official belief that Washington somehow is or was behind all the color revolutions and is now seeking to undermine other CIS governments, including Russia's. As Robert Kagan has recently noted, "If two of the world's largest powers [Russia and China-author] share a common commitment to autocratic government, autocracy is not dead as an ideology."[55]

The consequences of this adversarial relationship go beyond America, Russia, and their bilateral relations. They also encompass ties with other parties in Europe, the CIS, the Middle East, and Northeast Asia. Therefore this growing antagonism has significant global implications. And as it takes place in a less structured world than during the Cold War where both sides, to survive, had to acknowledge the other's red lines, today neither side needs each other. As the natural deterring factors of the Cold War have evaporated, the resulting situation is potentially more volatile, if not dangerous.[56] Moreover, as this adversarial relationship grows in scope and in its multiple dimensions, those consequences are already making themselves felt among Russia's neighbors, interlocutors, and peripheries: Europe, Asia, and the Middle East. Therefore, this rift possesses potentially significant strategic implications for both Russia and the United States.

One view of these frictions is that they are tactical not strategic. Consequently,

> It is not that Moscow and Washington have strategic interests that are directly opposed to one another. In fact, leaders in both capitals see eye-to-eye on the pressing issues of nuclear proliferation and terrorism, and on more long-term goals, such as managing a peaceful rise of achieving these strategic aims. Russian leaders have a hard time conceding global leadership to Washington; likewise many in the United States still harbor ingrained prejudices against the longtime adversary in Moscow.[57]

However, that viewpoint clashes with the fact that the repercussions of the bilateral tensions in this relationship encompass so much of today's global security agenda. Second, this line of analysis plays down the truly serious differences between the parties and actually condescends towards Russian demands. After all, it is precisely American leadership that Russia is challenging. Third, this view also clashes with the fact that the differences between both states are not only strategic ones, they are also growing. Thus there is a hardening conviction among Russian elites that American policy in many of its dimensions, both strategic and ideological—i.e., its rhetoric of democratization—represents a fundamental threat to the integrity and sovereignty of Russia. Or at least they believe that no improvement in those relations is possible in the foreseeable future.[58]

While we may regard such talk as an unmerited manifestation of a well-developed and long-cultivated Russian paranoia, Russia's elite increasingly professes that America resents Russia's recovery, and attempts to weaken it in order to ultimately undermine it. This pervasive and unfounded view in Moscow triggers the well-developed and long-cultivated psychological armory of Russian responses, including the growing truculence and resort to bullying of its neighbors that we have seen in the Soviet, if not Imperial, past. However, psychoanalyzing this relationship should not lead us to discount the profound and immediately tangible consequences of this rift for Russia's neighbors or interlocutors.

For example, in 2005 Lithuanian Foreign Minister Antanas Valionis observed that the issue of Russia's democratization was connected with key issues like the provision of energy supplies to the Baltic states as a whole; the inclusion of new members, e.g., Ukraine, in NATO; and, most of all, with security throughout the region. He stated that,

> Finally, the strengthening or weakening of democracy in Russia itself will have a pivotal influence on the region. If Russia is democratic, Lithuania will find itself in the epicenter of very interesting events. If Russia will be non-democratic, it is possible that after a certain time period, something resembling the iron curtain will be recreated. If we do not succeed in preventing that, we will end up on the periphery of events. That is the essence of things—to make sure that the gas pipeline is not exchanged for silence about human rights and democracy in Russia. Finally, the geopolitical fate of the world in 15 to 20 years depends upon the question of Russia's democratization.[59]

Similarly, Walter Slocombe, Under Secretary of Defense for Policy during the Clinton Administration, testified to Congress in 1995 that "Russia's development, both internal and external, is perhaps the central factor in determining the overall fate and future of European security."[60] However, this argument's validity is not confined to one man, or one government, or even to one continent—Europe—alone. What is true for the Baltic littoral pertains with equal force throughout Eurasia: As stated by Dr. Andrew Michta of the Marshall Center in Garmisch, i.e., "the extent to which regional security will balance between old and new tasks will hinge on domestic political developments in Russia as well as the progress of the current Russian military modernization program to be completed in 2010."[61]

The intersection of numerous and overlapping global developments and crises—the war on terrorism, Iraq, the energy crisis, and the rise of China and India in Asia—enhances the significance of geostrategic trends in Russia and its peripheries. And these trends certainly include regression towards autocracy for it encourages and allows the aggressive tendencies so visible in contemporary Russian foreign policy. As Kagan observes,

> It certainly would be a strategic error to allow Putin and any possible successor to strengthen their grip on power without outside pressures for reform, for the consolidation of

> autocracy at home will free the Russian leadership to pursue greater nationalist ambitions abroad. In these and other autocracies, including Iran, promoting democracy and human rights exacerbates internal political contradictions and can have the effect of blunting external ambitions as leaders tend to more dangerous threats from within.[62]

The common thread of perceiving America as a threat in both geopolitical and ideological terms has also united Moscow and Beijing in a common cause.[63] Already in the 1990s, prominent analysts of world politics like Richard Betts and Robert Jervis, and then subsequent Central Intelligence Agency (CIA) studies, postulated that the greatest security threat to American interests would be a Russian-Chinese alliance.[64] Arguably, that is happening now and occurs under conditions of the energy crisis that magnifies Russia's importance to China beyond providing diplomatic support, cover for China's strategic rear, and arms sales.[65]

Several analysts of trends in East Asia see the confluence of the energy and other current international crises contributing to a Russo-Chinese alliance that has already formed in opposition to American power and ideas. That alliance would encompass points of friction with Washington: strategic resistance to U.S. interests in Central and Northeast Asia; resistance to antiproliferation and pressures upon the regimes in Iran and North Korea; an energy alliance; an ideological counteroffensive against U.S. support for democratization abroad; and the rearming of both Russia and China, if not their proxies and allies, with a view towards conflict with America.[66]South Korean columnist Kim Yo'ng Hu'i wrote in 2005 that,

> China and Russia are reviving their past strategic partnership to face their strongest rival, the United States. A structure of strategic competition and confrontation between the United States and India on the one side, and Russia and China on the other is unfolding in the eastern half of the Eurasian continent including the Korean peninsula. Such a situation will definitely bring a huge wave of shock to the Korean peninsula, directly dealing with the strategic flexibility of U.S. forces in Korea. If China and Russia train their military forces together in the sea off the coast of China's Liaodong Peninsula, it will also have an effect on the 21st century strategic plan of Korea. We will now need to think of Northeast Asia on a much broader scale. The eastern half of Eurasia, including Central Asia, has to be included in our strategic plan for the future.[67]

Since then, Lyle Goldstein and Vitaly Kozyrev have similarly written that,

> If the Kremlin favors Beijing, the resulting Sino-Russian energy nexus—joining the world's fastest growing energy consumer with one of the world's fastest growing producers—would support China's growing claim to regional preeminence. From Beijing's point of view, this relationship would promise a relatively secure and stable foundation for one of history's most extraordinary economic transformations. At stake are energy reserves in eastern Russia that far exceed those in the entire Caspian basin. Moreover, according to Chinese strategists, robust Sino-Russian energy links would decrease the vulnerability of Beijing's sea lines of communication to forms of "external pressure" in case of a crisis concerning Taiwan or the South China Sea. From the standpoint of global politics, the formation of the Sino-Russian energy nexus would represent a strong consolidation of an emergent bipolar structure in East Asia, with one pole led by China (and including Russia) and one led by the United States (and including Japan).[68]

Russia's tie to China certainly expresses a deep strategic identity or congruence of interests on a host of issues from Korea to Central Asia and could have significant military implications. Those implications are not just due to Russian arms sales to China which are clearly tied to an anti-American military scenario, most probably connected with Taiwan. They also include the possibility of joint military action in response to a regime crisis in the Democratic People's Republic of Korea (DPRK) as suggested by the joint maneuvers of the Russian and Chinese militaries in 2005 and 2007.[69] Thus we could be on the verge of a new strategic bipolarity that bifurcates Europe and Asia and places Washington and Moscow on opposite sides in both peacetime and times of crises.[70] Equally disquieting is that many analysts in both Russia and America expect bilateral relations to worsen in the foreseeable future, not least because Russian observers expect the current Congress to be more anti-Russian than its predecessor.[71]

Despite occasional U.S. and European efforts to soften the rhetoric, chances are that this forecast of worsening relations will actually materialize. Even though Putin has stated that the United States is a major, if not the only, partner for Russia on issues of disarmament and global security, nonproliferation, global health, combating poverty, and trade, and that this partnership could soon expand in ways not yet foreseen, Putin's visible contempt for Western policy at the 2006 G-8 meeting in St. Petersburg and afterwards, has manifested itself in even more sarcastic fashion than was previously the case.[72] And the systematic flooding of the Russian media with anti-American propaganda certainly adds to the likelihood of longterm estrangement.

Since Russia is now experiencing a succession scenario which is the achilles heel of its political system but which will also drive all Russian politics even further in an anti-Western direction, Russian elites have every incentive to keep stoking this fire. But they and we must remember that the consequences of intensifying this adversarial quality of the bilateral relationship could be very negative for international security. In previous cases, Russian rulers have resorted to violence and fomented crises so as to secure domestic popularity and legitimacy, e.g., Yeltsin's war with Chechnya in 1994.[73] Likewise, several Western scholars, including this author, believe that the 1999 succession crisis was managed in such a way as to tie Putin's ascension to power to the incitement of the war in Chechnya.[74] The seizure of Yukos and the arrest of its chief executives, Platon Lebedev and Mikhail Khodorkovsky, in 2003- 04 represent another example of the resort to direct force and the fomenting of a crisis to further narrow the possibilities for democratization and strike at Westernizing forces in Russia.[75] It is entirely possible, then, that this discernibly enhanced aggressiveness and threat-mongering are intended, as Gavrov and many other Russian analysts suggest, to create a favorable domestic environment for the succession.[76]

Under the most favorable explanation for recent political violence and assassinations directed against regime critics like Anna Politkovskaya and Alexnader Litvinenko, alleged "rogue elements" of the FSB are trying to impose one or another's political scenario upon Russia and destabilize the Putin regime. If this is true, it hardly furnishes evidence of Russia's reliability or stability with regard to world politics. And if the state committed those assassinations, then we are dealing with what truly is a criminalized and rogue state. This last charge is not as surprising as it may seem, for Russian and foreign observers have long pointed to the integration of criminal elements with the energy, intelligence, and defense industrial sectors of the economy.[77]

Second, every succession since 1991 has been the result of violence or electoral fraud, if not both phenomena.[78] Consequently Russia's importance as a major energy and military (and recovering military) power, its function as the sponsor of anti-democratic movements or trends and alibi of last resort throughout the CIS for such tendencies, its ability to block nonproliferation or to provide arms, nuclear reactors, know how, and substantial political support for anti-Western and anti- American regimes, e.g., Iran and Myanmar, and even for terrorist movements, and, finally, the link between its fundamental domestic instability and its foreign policy, leads it to figure prominently in many different potential threat scenarios. As one recent American assessment observes,

> The central puzzle of Russian politics is that 15 years after the collapse of the USSR, the country still lacks any stable and legitimate form of state order. The result is continuing pervasive political and social uncertainty— concretized in the palpable official fear that independent civil society organizations might promote additional "color revolutions" in Russia or other post-Soviet states and the endless rumors about various unconstitutional or semi constitutional schemes Putin might employ to stay in power after his formal second term ends in March 2008. Bearing in mind that Russia remains the world's largest country by territory and still possesses thousands of nuclear warheads as well as large stockpiles of chemical and biological weapons of mass destruction, such uncertainty could quickly become a major international problem as well.[79]

These political conditions duly represent some of the reasons why even Russian analysts admit that Russia remains "a risk factor" in world politics, not the reliable pole of world politics that it claims to be.[80]

Although some, including U.S. officials, may believe that Russia's hostile rhetoric is connected with the upcoming succession to Putin, at best that is only partly the case.[81] Russia's adversarial posture towards America and the West is not just a ploy to mobilize support for the regime, though it is that. Rather, this policy is intrinsically linked to and grows out of Russia's regression towards a police state, where the police rule through the state and the state enforces a stifling tutelage over the citizenry.[82] In other words, as both foreign and domestic observers have written, this systematically inculcated authoritarian, anti-American line and gravitation towards China are systemically and structurally driven.[83] Or, as Lilya Shevtsova has written, anti-Westernism is the new national idea.[84] Thus Vladimir Shlapentokh has shown that an essential component of the Kremlin's ideological campaign to maintain the Putin regime in power and extend it (albeit under new leadership) past the elections of 2008 is anti-Americanism. As he wrote,

> The core of the Kremlin's ideological strategy is to convince the public that any revolution in Russia will be sponsored by the United States. Putin is presented as a bulwark of Russian patriotism, as the single leader able to confront America's intervention in Russian domestic life and protect what is left of the imperial heritage. This propaganda is addressed mostly to the elites (particularly elites in the military and FSB) who sizzle with hatred and envy of America.[85]

Similarly, Minxin Pei of the Carnegie Endowment for International Peace observes that,

> The rapid improvement in ties and growing cooperation between China and Russia owes, to a great extent, not to any Chinese new initiative, but to Russia's changing relationship with the West under Vladimir Putin's rule. As President Putin became increasingly authoritarian, he needed China as an ally in counterbalancing the West. The net strategic effect of Russia's reorientation of its policy toward the West has been tremendously positive for China.[86]

Russia's threat perceptions are either oriented towards terrorism from the south, as was generally the case even until 2006, or more recently primarily to the West.[87] Key Russian officials now proclaim that the greatest threats to Russia come from the West, supposedly in the form of NATO's enlargement (although NATO is a shadow of its past military strength); American military power in both its conventional and nuclear aspects; or as President Bush himself has now recognized, in the form of demands for greater democratization.[88] Recently Putin himself, stated that,

> You know, I think that the problem in international relations today is that there is increasingly less respect for the basic principles of international law. There is an ever growing desire to resolve this or that issue based on the political considerations and expediency of the moment. This is very dangerous, and it is precisely this that leads to small countries not feeling secure. It is also this that fuels the arms race in large countries.[89]

Lavrov has duly echoed this assessment.[90] It is unlikely, though, that either he or Putin had Russian policy towards Chechnya, Ukraine, Georgia, Belarus, Moldova, the Baltic states, or Russian domestic policy in mind when they made these statements.

Military and Nuclear Issues

The repercussions of this rift with the West are particularly visible in Russian military policy. Indeed, in the military, we find the threat assessments claiming that Russia faces a threat situation comparable to that of the 1930s America stated in Ministry of Defense and General Staff journals as a matter of course.[91]

Obviously this argument invokes the traditional specter of a large-scale continental or even intercontinental war and Western invasion of Russia to elicit more resources from the government. Yet it is not an inaccurate representation of Russian defense thinking. Putin's statements above (and below), as well as those by other key spokesmen and/or analysts, display the growing belief in a Western threat. Russian political and military literature abounds with charges that Washington seeks to "crush" Russia and is organizing secret plans to undermine or overthrow the Russian government by fomenting new "color revolutions" to follow Georgia, Ukraine, and Kyrgyzstan.[92] Neither are these apprehensions intended only for domestic consumption because they influence policy and force deployments in Russia and possibly in the United States as well, especially with regard to nuclear weapons. For example, Russian officials have blocked discussions of reducing tactical nuclear weapons (TNW) in Europe, not least because they see them as weapons to stop a NATO or American conventional offensive and restore intrawar stability and escalation control.[93] Thus Ivanov's remarks about Russia's capability to launch mass production of missiles apply to them as well.[94]

Regarding strategic nuclear weapons and missile defenses, the situation is no better. Moscow regards Washington's policies of leaving the Antiballistic Missile (ABM) treaty, building missile defenses in Poland and the Czech Republic, seeking to militarize space, and conventional and nuclear force modernization as posing a combination of threats to it. Thus beyond its own urgent, long overdue, and ongoing conventional modernization, it has announced plans for qualitative modernization of its strategic and tactical nuclear systems through 2020.[95] Evidently Moscow expects a confrontation involving the threat or even use of nuclear or space weapons and a concomitant urgent necessity of rebuilding its conventional and nuclear forces.[96] The program outlined below, according to Ivanov, will allow Russia to replace 45 percent of its existing arsenals with modern weapons by 2015.

Thus, Ivanov has recently unveiled plans to build by that date: 50 new Topol-M ICBM complexes on mobile launchers, 34 new silo-based Topol-M missiles and control units, 50 new bombers, 31 ships; and to fully rearm 40 tank, 97 infantry, and 50 parachute battalions.

Forty Topol-M silo-based missiles have already been deployed. In 2007 alone, the military would get 17 new ballistic missiles rather than 4 a year, as has recently been the case, and 4 spacecraft and booster rockets. It would overhaul a long-range aviation squadron, 6 helicopter and combat aviation squadrons, and 7 tank and 13 motor rifle battalions. In 2007 alone, 11 billion dollars will be spent on new weapons, and 31 new ships will be commissioned, including 8 fleet ballistic missile submarines (SSBNs) carrying ICBMs (presumably the forthcoming Bulava missile). And in 2009-10, Russia will decide whether or not to build a new shipyard for the construction of aircraft carriers, and 50 Tu-160 Blackjack and Tu-95 Bear Strategic Bombers will operate over this period as well. Doctrinally, Russia will also retain its right of launching preemptive strikes.[97]

In and of itself, this program does not necessarily revive the Cold War confrontation or an inherently anti- American program of arms racing; the modernization of Russia's weapons is desperately needed. But this program does betray a heightened threat assessment and the growing strategic importance and even utility attached by Moscow to nuclear weapons. The latter point, of course, is one for which America is often blamed, but has figured prominently in official Russian doctrine and strategy at least since 1993.[98] Indeed, it appears that Russia has unilaterally violated President Boris Yeltsin's commitment for disarmament of Russian attack or multipurpose submarines so that they would not carry tactical nuclear weapons (TNW) and is deploying these weapons on attack submarines "on combat patrols."[99] Moscow now advocates a legally binding treaty saying that U.S. and Russian nuclear arsenals do not target each other in order to dispel this alleged threat.[100] This request appears to be purely propagandistic since Presidents Yeltsin

and Clinton agreed to this over a decade ago, and the required computer programs for targeting could be reinstated at a moment's notice. So it appears that we will see what Putin calls an "asymmetrical but highly efficient" Russian response, perhaps in its new Bulava or Topol missiles that supposedly can avoid or spoof missile defenses.[101] But this reply also suggests the potential return of the competitive procurement spiral that featured so prominently during the Cold War.

This intensified threat assessment contradicts earlier statements by Ivanov and Putin dating back to 2001 that the U.S. withdrawal from the ABM treaty may have been a mistake but not a threat to Russia. Alarmist threat briefings that these missile defenses, America's conventional force modernization, or its nuclear programs reflect an urgent and growing threat, display either a misunderstanding (whether deliberate or unintentional) of U.S. policy or an apprehension that the cherished dream of a closed bloc in the former Soviet Union and great power status are at risk.[102]

Thus the outbreak of this rhetoric reflects deeper political exigencies that drive Russian policy, not some major change in what the Soviets used to call the correlation of forces. For example, the Strategic Offensive Reductions Treaty (SORT) of 2002, also known as the Moscow treaty, essentially uncoupled U.S. and Russian strategic force modernization programs from each other. The treaty stipulated that both sides can build whatever nuclear forces they need within the treaty's limits without referring to the other side's programs or directly countering them in their own force building programs.[103] However, thanks to the controversy on missile defense, Russia now insists that if the United States unilaterally installs missile defenses in Eastern Europe, it will affect Russo-NATO relations, create confrontations in Europe, and in general end civilization as we know it. Therefore, Washington must first involve Russia before it makes any such deployment.[104] At the same time, Putin and his minions say that if America accepts his proposals for missile defense cooperation based on the system at Gabala or alternatively on a new one being built at Armavir in the North Caucasus, then the bilateral relationship can become once again a strategic one and lead to a "revolution" in world politics. But if we do not accept this, then, of course, the regression to a neoCold War situation is implicit in those statements.[105]

As part of this recent proposal for use of the Gabala installation and in the overall controversy over missile defense, Russia evidently again wants a veto or at least a "droit de regard" (right of regard) over U.S. and NATO military programs, particularly ones within what Russia calls the vicinity of its borders or interests. But these demands also show that with regard to Washington, Moscow operates its policies from the presupposition of enemies.

Given the several years of briefings and consultations involved among all the parties including Russia, American unilateralism is not the issue here. Rather, it is an attempt by Russia to force America to give Russia a veto over its policies and trigger further dissension in NATO. Thus Baluyevsky argued that "In our opinion, military activity by the alliance close to Russia's borders should be comprehensible to Russia and commensurate with the new challenges and threats that are rising. At the same time Russia has an interest in having a predictable partner in the shape of NATO."[106] This demand is, in fact, a tried, tested, but also tired Soviet and post-Soviet refrain. Obviously this is unacceptable to Washington, NATO, and its members.

Even though there is no military threat as Russian military men admit, and as did Putin in 2001, Russia, especially its armed forces and political leaders, cannot relinquish the belief in NATO and America as an a priori enemy. They are still tied to the presupposition of an enemy and to a relationship based on the expectation of a threat, i.e., a relationship of deterrence rather than of defense. Lavrov recently underscored this point. He told an interviewer for Rossiyskaya Gazeta that,

> Our main criterion is ensuring the Russian Federation's security and maintaining strategic stability as much as possible. . . . We have started such consultations already. I am convinced that we need a substantive discussion on how those lethal weapons could be curbed on the basis of mutual trust and balance of forces and interests. We will insist particularly on this approach. We do not need just the talk that we are no longer enemies and therefore we should not have restrictions for each other. This is not the right approach. It is fraught with an arms race, in fact, because, it is very unlikely that either of us will be ready to lag behind a lot.[107]

Thus he emphasized that in an atmosphere of political mistrust and where both sides' deployments are still based on the philosophy of deterrence and mutual assured destruction, strategic unilateralism is both unacceptable and indeed dangerous to all because it stimulates arms races across the world. In other words, American unilateralism is inherently a threat to Russia wherever it appears because Russia cannot but proceed from the a priori assumption of hostile American interest, i.e., the presupposition of an enemy.

Thus the problem and the threats that we face as this relationship erodes are not due to Russia's military modernization but rather to the overall deterioration of Russo-American relations or to the failure to break out of past cognitive paradigms. And here Russia, precisely because it has reverted to previous policies, structures, and mentalities, is as much to blame as is the United States. Whereas the United States is moving or has sought to move toward a strategic relationship based on partnership with Russia, defense against and dissuasion of enemies, and lessened reliance on nuclear weapons and deterrence vis-à-vis Russia and other states, Russia cannot overcome the past.[108] It remains committed to a strategy and posture of deterrence that postulates an inherently adversarial relationship with the United States. Russian analysts recognize the continuing conformity of Russian policy with Schmitt's notion of the presupposition of the enemy as an approach to national security policy in Russia.[109] That failure to break out of past paradigms, however it is understood, inevitably heightens the impact of geostrategic rivalry across the entire Russo-American agenda and in international relations more broadly.

Thus Lavrov complains that "we are being called upon to fight a hypothetical threat (i.e., intermediate range missiles from Iran that could hit Europe) while a real threat to our security is looming." This statement falsely negates what Russian military men and Lavrov know to be a real and growing threat from Iran's missile, nuclear, and space programs.[110] But the threat that really alarms Lavrov here, a nonmilitary one it should be noted, is one that has frightened Russian statesmen for centuries, namely the idea of a unified Europe from which it is isolated. So Lavrov went on to warn that NATO, the OSCE, and the CFE Treaty, the pillars of the European security system, are being converted into a bloc policy which would fold up the reform of Europe's security architecture that Russia desires and bifurcate Europe.[111] That Moscow's policy toward Europe

aspires to strategic bipolarity throughout Eurasia, as described below, seems to have eluded Lavrov here, but underscores the fundamentally psychological resentment of lost power and craving for status with America that drives Russian policy.

POTENTIAL U.S. THREATS TO RUSSIA AND INFLATED RUSSIAN THREAT PERCEPTIONS

To say this is not to deny that possible changes in U.S. force structures and deployments could provide a threat or threats to Russia. Indeed, the best available studies of American nuclear policies, including modernization of those weapons, highlight the fact that these policies, including the introduction into practice of new concepts like dissuasion and preemptive, if not preventive, war, could, if they have not already done so, develop into perceived potential threats to Russia in the near future.[112] Oddly enough, though, these potential threats are hardly ever mentioned in Russian commentary. This suggests, once again, that it is internal Russian perceptions as much as actual realities that are driving policy. As an example of these potential threats, although the United States has upgraded its naval and other strategic forces and is gradually shifting them to the Pacific Ocean largely to meet potential North Korean or Chinese contingencies, those deployments also could threaten Russian forces.[113] But Moscow has said little or nothing about these forces.

A second, equally negative possible outcome is that American policymakers will come to perceive Russia not just as a recalcitrant independent actor that does not want to cooperate with America, but as a potential or even active threat in its own right. As this potential inheres primarily in Russia's nuclear capability, the developments cited here are already creating a climate among government circles in which Russia can quickly come to be seen as a potential military threat due to its political differences with America. For example, the recent Report of the Defense Science Board on Nuclear Capabilities stated openly that nuclear reductions agreed to in the Moscow treaty of 2002 and recommended in the Nuclear Posture Review of 2001 pointed to a new and benign strategic relationship with Russia after the end of the Cold War and the desire to forge a new bilateral strategic relationship that no longer was based on the principles of Mutual Assured Destruction.

Today, the Report observes, that presumption of a new benign strategic relationship with Russia is increasingly open to doubt. This is because, "Although United States relations with Russia are considered relatively benign at the moment [December 2006], Russia retains the capacity to destroy the United States in 30 minutes or less." Moreover, its reliance on nuclear weapons to compensate for a weakened conventional military has led it to emphasize nuclear weapons for purposes of maintaining superpower status, deterrence, and potentially warfighting. Russia's regression from democracy, and rivalry with America over Iraq, Iran, and Central Asia [other issues may well be added since then to the mix—author], suggest that the assessment of 2003 that nothing had changed since 2001 to justify revising the Nuclear Posture Review's (NPR) presumption of a benign strategic relationship with Russia needs to be revised.[114] Therefore, the Report recommends the creation of a permanently standing assessment "Red Team" "to continuously assess the range of emerging and plausible nuclear capabilities that can threaten the United States and its allies and friends with potentially catastrophic consequences."[115] This team would monitor Russian, Chinese, and North Korean developments because,

> Despite the desire for improved relations with Russia, the direction, scope, and pace of the evolution of U.S. capabilities must be based on a realistic recognition that the United States and Russia are not yet the reliable, trusted friends needed for the United States to depart from a commitment to a robust nuclear deterrent. Intentions can change overnight; capabilities cannot."[116]

Other examples of a growing wariness about Russian intentions can also be cited.[117] Thus there is a real danger that these perceptions can grow on both sides into self-fulfilling threat perceptions that will drive conventional and nuclear defense acquisitions and foreign policy decisions as well until they influence formal doctrinal and strategic pronouncements. Some Russian military observers have already openly postulated that Russia and America (or NATO) are still enemies. For example, Colonel Anatoly Tsyganok, a noted military commentator speaking about the increase in large-scale and regular Russian military exercises, observed that apart from the need to conduct such exercises as part of the Army's regular routine, they are necessary to respond to American deployments in places like Hungary and Bulgaria. Both sides, he says, remain enemies, and these exercises are hardly antiterrorist ones but rather something else (i.e., he hints at their being intended to be anti-NATO).[118] Certainly and similarly, the so-called "Ivanov doctrine" of 2003, formalized in a Russian white paper that did not name NATO, was oriented nonetheless to the primacy of a NATO/American threat.[119]

Nevertheless for such threats to be actualized and formalized in official state papers like defense doctrines, the political climate between Moscow and Washington would have to decline still further. Consequently, while we should not rush to restore the Cold War, the present trends on both sides are disturbing and destabilizing, not only for what they mean to each other but also because of their impact on regional security throughout Eurasia and how they affect the calculations of other nuclear states or states that seek nuclear weapons like Iran and North Korea. In other words, these tensions cannot be confined to discussions of bilateral strategy and politics but deeply impinge upon the problems of regional security, global proliferation, and deterrence.

In fact, in the context of charges raised in 2006 that the United States now has and has been striving for a usable first-strike nuclear capability against Russian forces—an argument that ignited a firestorm of polemics in Russia—such interactive Russian and American deployments of both conventional and nuclear forces do, in fact, raise the prospect of real as opposed to notional threats of an arms race where Washington seems to move for a supposed first-strike capability in both Russian and Western strategic analyses.[120] Thus David McDonough's analysis of U.S. nuclear deployments in the Pacific Ocean states that,

> The increased deployment of hard-target kill weapons in the Pacific could only aggravate Russian concerns over the survivability of its own nuclear arsenal. These silo- busters would be ideal to destroy the few hundred ICBM silos and Russia's infamously hardened command-andcontrol facilities as well as help reduce any warning time for Russian strategic forces, given their possible deployment and depressed trajectory. This is critical for a decapitation mission, due to the highly centralized command-and-control structure of the Russian posture, as well as to preempt any possible retaliation from the most on-alert Russian strategic forces. The Pacific also has a unique feature in that it is an area where gaps in Russian early-warning radar and the continued deterioration of its early-warning satellite coverage have made it effectively blind to any attack from this theatre. This open-attack corridor would make any increase in Pacific-deployed SLBMs appear especially threatening.[121]

Similarly, already in 2003 when the first reports of the Pentagon's interest in new low-yield and bunker- busting nuclear weapons became public, Russian analysts warned that even if such programs are merely in a research stage, they would add to the hostile drift of Russo-American relations.[122] Events since then have only confirmed this assessment and their warning. Meanwhile, the trend continues towards increasing Russian reliance upon nuclear weapons against a perceived growing American threat. This threat perception and reliance upon nuclear weapons takes place despite American assertions that charges of excessive U.S. reliance on nuclear forces; that the United States is either not reducing nuclear forces or doing so fast enough; that the United States is building new and more dangerous nuclear weapons; that the United States is lowering the threshold for nuclear weapons use by emphasizing preemption; and that these alleged failures and the supposed failure to sign new arms control treaties are encouraging proliferation are myths.[123] So if we may paraphrase a famous movie line, "What we have here is a failure to communicate," while both sides appear to be sinking deeper into their self-justifying perceptions.

For example, even less plausibly, Russian spokesmen regularly and increasingly decry the U.S. intention to build missile defenses bases in Poland and in the Czech Republic as threats to Russian security because they will really be used, so they say, against Russia, and not Iran, so as to render Russia's first or second strike capability impotent or to threaten such outcomes.[124] The ensuing nuclear blackmail would allegedly then be used to further reduce Russia's foreign policy and military capabilities, standing, and security. Lavrov and other officials have now frequently reiterated that "the military presence of the United States in Europe is becoming a strategic factor."[125]

Baluyevsky too attacked this deployment because it could touch off an arms race in many countries (the hidden idea being that Russia could not keep up with the pace of America and China), and that these defenses are not needed because neither Iran nor North Korea has the capability to strike at Europe or America. Thus these missile defenses are there to threaten Russia and deprive it of access to key zones along its frontier— perhaps the real threat in political terms. Missile launchers could be converted to interceptors that strike throughout European Russia; the missiles will not actually defend against all incoming attacks (which is strange since he said there were no attacks to be expected); they create possible ecological nightmares or even wars in Europe, etc.[126] These rhetorical salvos are coming fast and furious even though dispassionate and thorough Russian analyses, e.g., by Alexei Arbatov of the Carnegie Endowment in Moscow, demonstrate that these missile defenses cannot possibly threaten Russia.[127] Hence the demand for more American transparency concerning those missiles and their purpose as well as some kind of binding agreement that Russia cannot be and is not a target of those missiles.[128] Furthermore, the internal contradictions among them, e.g., that Iran simultaneously is and is not a threat or that Russian missiles could spoof defenses, etc., indicate just how seriously these threat assessments should be taken.

Thus, this demand for suspending the program, along with multiple complaints that Washington has not answered Russia's questions, etc., are one large bluff inasmuch as Russia also received over 10 technical briefings on this program.[129] The artificiality, not to mention systematic mendacity, of this campaign is all too redolent of Soviet tactics and suggests another attempt to divide Washington and Europe from each other by frightening the latter even as it reflects the abiding status insecurity that underlies so much of Russian foreign policy. And, of course, the other critical goal of this campaign is to prevent any American military presence in the former Warsaw Pact states, not to mention the former Soviet Union, so as to leave open the possibility of their remaining a Russian sphere of influence.

At the same time, this campaign also illustrates the Russian military-political elite's inability to reconcile themselves to a diminished budget and status, and finally their consistent belief that America and NATO are enemies of Russia. As Nikolai Sokov recently wrote, in regard to the study by Keir Lieber and Daryl Press about U.S. strategic capabilities that generated so much heat in Russia,[130]

> The reason why hardliners in Russia pay so much attention to the state of the U.S.-Russian strategic balance (and why they continue to discuss it in terms of "parity" rather than retaliatory capability) is that they conceive of U.S.-Russian relations today in the same terms as during the Cold War. The underlying unspoken assumption of the Lieber-Press study is that

> a systematic fundamental conflict either exists or could emerge in the future; this assumption is not lost on Russian hardliners.[131]

Other implications of the growing antagonism between Washington and Moscow have also made themselves felt in military affairs. Coordination with NATO has turned out to be much less than what was hoped for once it began in 2002.[132] Indeed, Sergei Ivanov admitted that Russo-NATO cooperation in fighting terrorism has not reached the desired level, and that development of medium-term plans for cooperation in countering security threats in general is needed. Thus the NATO-Russia Council has been only a political factor with limited effectiveness in shaping military outcomes or a fundamental change in international relations.[133] Similarly U.S.-Russian and NATO-Russian planned exercises in Russia were suddenly cancelled just before they were supposed to start in September 2006.[134]

Russian military writers likewise regularly inveigh against what they consider to be NATO and American plans to encircle Russia with both conventional and nuclear weapons at bases either in the Baltic, Poland, and Eastern Europe, or from attempts to place U.S. military bases within the CIS.[135] Lavrov, for example, warned that the failure of NATO members and the Baltic states to ratify the CFE treaty (which they will not do because of Russian deployments in Moldova and Georgia in violation of the OSCE's Istanbul accords of 1999) plus the enlargement of NATO, the resulting conventional imbalance, and the U.S. military presence in Europe all constitute a strategic factor, i.e., threats to Russia.[136] In addition,

> Perceived foreign threats also include military buildup(s) changing the balance near the borders of Russia and its allies, anti-Russian policies of certain neighboring governments, and the US withdrawal from the 1972 ABM Treaty announced by the G. W. Bush [Administration].[137]

As we have seen above, these so-called threats do not exist. Indeed, Sergei Ivanov as Defense Minister said as much in 2004.[138] Therefore these claims are essentially phantoms for justifying Russia's foreign and domestic policy goals as well as the military's campaign for more money and high-tech weapons against NATO and America. But because the real threats facing Russia are internal in nature, this perception of Russia as a besieged fortress and the primary global counterpole to America and the West demonstrate that Moscow's inability to find a point of domestic stability and legitimacy carries over into its foreign and defense policies. These facts also suggest that a fundamental problem in the Russo- NATO relationship is the unyielding opposition of the MOD and the government to genuine defense reform and strategic cooperation which would entail, among other things, eliminating the ingrained presupposition of enemies and policies deriving from that posture.[139]

All these trends highlight an increasing Russian ambivalence about the arms control treaties of the 1980s and 1990s like the CFE Treaty of Paris of 1990 and the Intermediate Nuclear Forces (INF) Washington Treaty of 1987. Ivanov has frequently called all of these treaties, including the START I Treaty, relics of the Cold War.[140] Since then Lavrov, Baluyevsky, and Putin have threatened to withdraw from the CFE treaty, called it meaningless, and blamed NATO for not ratifying it (even though Moscow refuses to pull its forces out of Moldova) and for deploying forces in the states of new members.[141] Clearly, the Russian debate over these treaties is closely linked to the issue of NATO's enlargement and their impact and continuation are seen in the context of that expansion. This debate also reveals the persistence of Cold War thinking in Moscow. But this debate over existing arms treaties also reveals that Moscow is unwilling to reveal or confront its true threat perceptions and instead blames Washington for its failure to take Russian interests into account.

Much evidence also suggests that various political forces in Russia, particularly in the military community, are urging withdrawal from those treaties, not least because of NATO enlargement towards the CIS and U.S. foreign and military policy in those areas. In March 2005 Sergei Ivanov raised the question of withdrawal from the INF Treaty with the Pentagon.[142] More recently, Ivanov has stated that the INF treaty was a mistake.[143] And since then Baluyevsky followed suit, threatening to pull out of the treaty unless Washington ceased its missile defense plans.[144]

Indeed, withdrawal from the INF treaty makes no sense unless one believes that Russia is genuinely— and more importantly—imminently threatened by NATO, or Iran and China, but most of all by U.S. superior conventional military power, and cannot meet or deter that threat except by returning to the classic Cold War strategy of holding Europe hostage to nuclear attack to deter Washington and NATO. Similarly with regard to China and Iran, absent a missile defense, the only applicable strategy would be to use nuclear weapons to deter them, but this means admitting that these supposed partners of Russia actually constitute a growing threat to it. Since it is by no means clear that Russia can or should reply to any such threat by producing intermediate range ballistic missiles (IRBMs), the desire to leave the INF treaty and reactivate missile production of IRBMs represents only the interests of the defense and defense industrial sectors, not necessarily Russia's state interest.

As part of this debate, General Vladimir Vasilenko also raised the issue of withdrawal from the treaty after Ivanov did so in 2005, though it is difficult to see what Russia gains from withdrawal from that treaty.[145] Vasilenko, anticipating Baluyevsky, also stated that the nature and composition of any future U.S./NATO missile defense would determine the nature and number of future Russian missile forces and systems even though admittedly any such missile defense systems could only defend against a few missiles at a time. Therefore,

> Russia should give priority to high-survivable mobile ground and naval missile systems when planning the development of the force in the near and far future. . . . The quality of the strategic nuclear forces of Russia will have to be significantly improved in terms of adding to their capability of penetrating [missile defense] barriers and increasing the survivability of combat elements and enhancing the properties of surveillance and control systems.[146]

Obviously such advocacy represents a transparent demand for new, vast, and unaffordable military programs, similar to the demand for reactivating production of IRBMs regardless of consequences. But in that case, Russia's government and military, are, as Sokov suggested, thereby postulating an inherent East- West enmity that is only partially and incompletely buttressed by mutual deterrence.[147] That posture makes no sense in today's strategic climate, especially when virtually every Russian military leader repeatedly proclaims, as did Baluyevsky through 2006, that no plan for war with NATO is under consideration, and that the main threat to Russia is terrorism, not NATO and not America.[148] At the same time, that posture also is an open sign to Beijing and Tehran of Russian suspicions concerning their ambitions and capabilities. Still, Russian generals do not raise these issues unless told to do so. Thus it would appear, as it does to Secretary Gates, that the real threat is the rise of neighboring states' short and medium-range missile capabilities, e.g., Iran and China.[149] This is a fine irony inasmuch as Russia was instrumental in providing the wherewithal for these states' military development. If Moscow withdrew from the INF treaty, that would allow NATO to station INF missiles in the Baltic and Poland as well as lead China and Iran to step up their production of intermediate range missiles as well. Furthermore, it is by no means clear that Moscow could regenerate production for both intermediate and ICBMs as their plant for such production systematically misses production goals. Thus withdrawal from the treaty could actually further diminish Russian security, not enhance it.[150] Yet Moscow dare not admit that the enemy of America is also its enemy lest its domestically based foreign and defense policy that postulates partnership with China and Iran be seen to be inherently contradictory and even dangerous.

Russia's Evolving Threat Assessment

Under the circumstances, we should not be surprised that Putin's and Ivanov's recent threat assessments suggest that Washington and NATO or their policies are becoming a growing if not the main threat.[151] Similarly, every account of Russia's forthcoming new defense doctrine similarly suggests that America and NATO are the main enemies and threats to Russia.[152] Putin's remarks to the Federal Assembly in his annual speech on May 10, 2006, presaged his remarks in Munich and merit extensive citation for they indicate the evolving threat assessment, on the basis of which he likely has given his defense and foreign policy team new strategic guidance towards postulating the source of threats to Russia and its interests.

Putin began this speech by stating that, as has been the case since 2001, the terrorist threat is the main one, but he then seamlessly linked it to what he perceives as a defining characteristic of much American foreign policy, i.e., the notion stated above that key American elites want to keep Russia tied down and weak.

> The terrorist threat remains very real. Local conflicts remain a fertile breeding ground for terrorists, a source of their arms and a field upon which they can test their strength in practice. These conflicts often arise on ethnic grounds, often with inter-religious conflict thrown in, which is artificially fomented and manipulated by extremists of all shades. I know that there are those out there who would like to see Russia become so mired in these problems that it will not be able to resolve its own problems and achieve full development.[153]

Putin then invoked the threat of nuclear proliferation, particularly to terrorists. Thus,

> The proliferation of weapons of mass destruction also represents a serious danger. If these weapons were to fall into the hands of terrorists, and they pursue this aim, the consequences would be simply disastrous. I stress that we unambiguously support strengthening the nonproliferation regime, without any exceptions, on the basis of international law. We know that strong-arm methods rarely achieve the desired result and that their consequences can even be more terrible than the original threat.[154]

He then went on to berate Washington for abandoning arms control and raising the threat of using nuclear weapons against Russia:

> I would like to raise another important issue today. Disarmament was an important part of international politics for decades. Our country made an immense contribution to maintaining strategic stability in the world. But with the acute threat of international terrorism now on everyone's minds the key disarmament issues are all but off the international agenda, and yet it is too early to speak of an end to the arms race. What's more, the arms race has entered a new spiral today with the achievement of new levels of technology that raise the danger of the emergence of a whole arsenal of so-called destabilizing weapons. There are still no clear guarantees that weapons, including nuclear weapons, will not be deployed in outer space. There is the potential threat of the creation and proliferation of small capacity nuclear charges. Furthermore, the media and expert circles are already discussing plans to use intercontinental ballistic missiles to carry non-nuclear warheads. The launch of such a missile could provoke an inappropriate response from one of the nuclear powers, could provoke a full-scale counterattack using strategic nuclear forces.[155]

Finally, he concluded his threat assessment with an attack on the anti-Russian thrust of American foreign policy:

> And, meanwhile, far from everyone in the world has abandoned the old bloc mentality and the prejudices inherited from the era of global confrontation despite the great changes that have taken place. This is also a great hindrance in working together to find suitable responses to the common problems we face.[156]

This kind of threat assessment has several critical consequences. First, it closely resembles the assessment published by the Chinese government in its White Papers of 2004 and 2006 on Defense.[157] Thus the shared perception of both the location and nature of the common threats they face helps cement an anti- American Russo-Chinese alliance on a host of issues in the contemporary agenda of world politics. Second, the results of this growing sense of threat from the West have not only restored the need for Russia to rearm with both conventional and nuclear weapons, they have all but undone the hopes for Russo-NATO cooperation after 9/11. As of 2003, the General Staff made clear its opposition to joint Russian-NATO exercises allegedly on the grounds of NATO enlargement and the improvement of missiles.[158] At the same time, both Ivanov and Baluyevsky made clear that if NATO remained a military organization, this could force Russia to make changes in its overall military doctrine and nuclear policies.[159] Baluyevsky went even farther by stating that "If the anti-terrorist direction of NATO continues, the threshold for using nuclear weapons will become lower and this will require a change of the principle for military planning of the Russian armed forces, including a change of military strategy."[160]

Since the military had already stated in 1999 that circumstances (among them NATO's Kosovo operation) had led Russia to argue for lowering the threshold for nuclear use and broaden the circumstances under which tactical nuclear weapons might be used against purely conventional attacks, such remarks must be taken quite seriously.[161] In fact, the military's enmity to NATO is not due to its policies but rather to the fact of its existence. As the Ministry of Defense stated in the so called Ivanov doctrine or White Paper of October, 2003,

> Russia . . . expects NATO member states to put a complete end to direct and indirect elements of its anti-Rus sian policy, both from military planning and from the political declarations of NATO member states.... Should NATO remain a military alliance with its

> current offensive military doctrine, a fundamental reassessment of Russia's military planning and arms procurement is needed, including a change in Russia's nuclear strategy.[162]

Therefore, it is not surprising that first Moscow has tried, and recently with some success, to interest Washington in negotiating what would in effect be a START III treaty to reduce nuclear weapons on both sides.[163] Neither should we be surprised that Putin and his subordinates see a deteriorating threat situation that is drawing ever closer to Russia. Putin, in his speech to the Foreign Ministry on June 27, 2006, emphasized the increasingly threatening nature of the international system, the unilateral American use of force and supposedly indiscriminate attacks on Islam, and the possibility of proliferation as major threats coming closer to Russia. Thus he said that,

> We need to be fully aware that, despite all our efforts, the potential for conflict in the world continues to grow. After the collapse of the bi-polar world order there exists a lot of unpredictability in global development. Perhaps this is why we continue to hear talk of an unavoidable conflict of civilizations that could become a long-term confrontation on the lines of the Cold War. I am convinced that we have reached a point today where the entire global security architecture is indeed undergoing modernization, and you have probably noticed this for yourselves. If we let old views and approaches continue to hold sway, the world will be doomed to further futile confrontation. We need to reverse these dangerous trends and this requires new ideas and approaches. Russia does not want confrontation of any kind. And we will not take part in any kind of "holy alliance." . . . I must say, too, that the causes fuelling the desire of a number of countries to acquire weapons of mass destruction and carry out other military programs include not just national ambitions but also the overblown importance given to force in international relations that is being foisted on us all. In this respect, the stagnation we see today in the area of disarmament is of particular concern. Russia is not responsible for this situation. We support renewed dialogue on the main disarmament issues. Above all, we propose to our American partners that we launch negotiations to replace the START Treaty, which expires in 2009.[164]

Again, Lavrov echoed this position.[165]

Arms Control and European Security

These strategic military issues extend as well into the conventional sphere and have direct impact on European security. We have already discussed the INF treaty above. The foundation stones of European and Eurasian security are the series of treaties beginning with the Helsinki treaty of 1975, its extension at Moscow in 1991, the 1987 Washington INF Treaty, the 1990 CFE Treaty, extended in 1999, the Paris and Rome treaties between NATO and Russia in 1997 and 2002, and the START and SORT treaties from 1991-2002. However, as noted above, some, if not all, of these treaties are apparently at risk.

Apart from Russian ambivalence about the INF treaty, we see the same thing happening with regard to the CFE treaty. Even before Putin suspended it and Baluyevsky warned that it might collapse, Ivanov and his subordinates said that Russia might withdraw from the CFE Treaty or that it might die a natural death.166 Russia has claimed that the Baltic States' failure to ratify this treaty makes the Baltic a "gray zone" from which potential threats to

Russian security could come even though they also admit that NATO's token forces there hardly represent a current threat.167 Russia has also raised the question as to whether the projected American restructuring of its basing posture in Europe, moving its forces to new bases in Romania and Bulgaria, violates the CFE treaty as well as the 1997 NATO-Russia agreement on the terms of NATO expansion.[168]

The West's reply is first that these new U.S. bases do not violate either of those accords:

> The Russia-NATO pact forbids the development of new bases in the territories of newly absorbed NATO members. However, the pact has no stipulations concerning the possibility of improving and expanding the existing military bases and infrastructures of new members, which is what the Pentagon is proposing to do. Additionally, the Pact limits the stationing of large military forces in new member countries, but Washington intends only to preposition equipment and rotate brigade-strength units (3,000 to 5,000 troops) through the bases. The planned basing of light forces, rather than heavy armor, also strengthens the Pentagon's argument that it is operating within the bounds of the CFE, which imposes limitations only on the amount of heavy military hardware and armor a state may possess. Therefore Washington has strong grounds to argue that its rebasing proposals are within the bounds of the established treaty framework.[169]

In addition, Western officials argue that at the Istanbul 1999 OSCE conference they stated that the Baltic States would ratify this treaty when Russia withdraws its forces from Moldova and Georgia as it promised to do then. Russia has since then refused either to withdraw the forces from Moldova or accept that it had any legal or political obligation to do so. Thus a standoff ensued. Recently, thanks partly to Western pressure, Russia agreed with Georgia that it would withdraw from its bases there by 2008. But meanwhile it refuses to leave Moldova. Indeed, it seeks a 20-year lease on a base there to perpetuate its intervention on behalf of a separatist and visibly criminalized Russian faction across the Dniester River.[170] Russian officials also talk of launching political gambits to formalize Russia's incorporation of Georgia's breakaway province South Ossetia into Russia.

These actions not only violate Russia's 1999 agreement, putting the lie to claims that Russia has no juridical obligation to leave Moldova and Georgia, they also would shatter the basis of European security as outlined in the aforementioned treaties. Incorporation of South Ossetia, Abkhazia, or Transnistria by force not only invokes Soviet and Tsarist precedents, those actions violate the Helsinki and Moscow treaties and the Istanbul accords, and shatter the post-Cold War accords with NATO. Like Moscow's 2004 and 2006 intervention in Ukrainian elections, such actions betray Russia's continuing inability to accept the end of empire in Eurasia even though a Russian empire there inherently threatens Eurasian and even Russian security.

The efforts to withdraw from the INF and CFE treaties are also connected to Russian fears that Western military-political pressure will be used to consolidate post-Soviet states' membership in NATO and/or the EU or to compel democratizing reforms in Russia or elsewhere in the CIS where Moscow supports the reigning authoritarians. Since Russia cannot compete militarily with the United States, let alone NATO, it has openly discussed using its strategic and/or tactical (or so-called nonstrategic) nuclear weapons in a first strike mode in the event of a threat by either of those parties against it or its interests in the CIS.[171] And Sergei Ivanov wrote in 2006 that Russia regards threats to the constitutional order of CIS regimes as the main threat to its security.[172] But it is hard to see how "the threat of democracy" or even of revolution in a CIS state is easily amenable to military reprisals from Moscow other than the use of Russian forces in a power projection and counterinsurgency mode. Even so, Moscow has tried to assert its unilateral security umbrella over the CIS. Indeed, it long ago gratuitously extended its nuclear umbrella to the CIS.

Accordingly, Russian military planners envision all kinds of potential military scenarios in Eurasia due to NATO's enlargement that would force Russia to rearm or retaliate, if necessary with nuclear weapons. For example, in July 2005 Konstantin Sivkov of the General Staff's Center of Military Strategic Studies stated that,

> The Alliance has achieved strategic depth of operations in Russia. U.S. tactical aircraft operating from NATO airfields may now reach Moscow, Tula, Kursk, and other cities of Central European Russia. This is an important factor from a geostrategic point of view. . . . It means that there are no more strategic barriers between Russia and NATO. What may it lead to? It may lead to escalation of border disputes with NATO countries (say because of certain territorial claims, or problems with oil production at sea, and fishing matters) into armed conflicts. Dangers of this sort exist in the Baltic region (Estonia claims the Pyatlov District of the Pskov Region) and in North Europe. . . . the situation is such that a local conflict may promptly become international. When it happens, it will be the alliance as such or the United States that will be putting forth demands, not the initiator of the conflict. Weapons may be used if Russia refuses to make concessions—space weapons first and foremost.[173]

Alternatively, informational weapons that were once thought of as science fiction weapons but are now usable might be deployed.[174] In any case, Russia must be prepared for what its sees as the threats to overturn the constitutional order in CIS states as its biggest threat and those efforts, pace Sivkov, could then escalate.[175] Not surprisingly, Ivanov demands full transparency from NATO about its actions and plans and raised the issue (or had his subordinates raise the issue) of withdrawal for these arms control treaties.[176] Contingency planning for these kinds of threats could only truly be taken to its logical culmination if Moscow frees itself from these two treaties that are pillars of arms control and security in Europe, and renounces its interest in European security.

However, such an outcome reignites an arms race in Europe and around the CIS that, as Putin and Company know, Russia cannot afford and which is in nobody's interest.[177] Ironically, Russia actually depends for its security on the restraints imposed by those treaties upon NATO's members including Washington. Moreover, it depends on them for subsidies like those through the Nunn-Lugar Act or Comprehensive Threat Reduction program to gain control over its nuclear, biological, and chemical weapons arsenals. Without that funding, the recent visible regeneration of the Russian armed forces would have been greatly impeded because at least some of those funds would have had to go to maintain or destroy decaying nuclear, biological, and chemical weapons. Russia also needs Western, and especially American help against terrorism emanating from Afghanistan, or Iranian and North Korean nuclearization, and is still interested, as recent agreements show, in curtailing those states or terrorists' access to these materials. [178] Therefore these efforts to withdraw from the relevant treaties are quite misguided even though Moscow's legal right to withdraw from a treaty is not at issue. But if Moscow persists in these gambits to weaken, eviscerate, or even leave these treaties, what does that signify concerning its goals and what then is the future of European and Eurasian security?

Therefore, an appropriate American response should be to maintain the validity of both the CFE and INF treaties, insist upon fulfillment of the former, and state U.S. willingness to reaffirm or extend the latter which is supposed to expire in 2009. Nobody, least of all Russia, benefits from a new arms race in a Europe that should be a model of security practices, not a case of a model gone bad. And Russia's announced desire to renegotiate the START I Treaty that is to expire in 2009 was rightly taken up as a new opportunity for further reducing the likelihood of nuclear weapons use or threats to use them among the two leading nuclear states.[179]

Still, despite the agreement to renegotiate nuclear arms reductions, there appears to be a fundamental difference in approach to these negotiations between Moscow and Washington. Hitherto the Bush administration has evaded getting into a negotiation, claiming it does not want to return to the Cold War relationship where both sides' nuclear arsenals were the defining factor in their relationship. In other words, the Bush administration is still chasing the will of the wisp of strategic unilateralism in nuclear matters.[180] Even if it has accepted in principle the idea of negotiating a new arms control treaty, it is likely to adhere as far as possible to its previous thinking on verification and arms control treaties, including thinking of Russia more as a partner than as a nuclear enemy. Lavrov's approach, cited above, shows that while the administration is and has been prepared to move beyond deterrence with regard to Russia, Moscow cannot move beyond its inherited anti-Western strategic paradigm that sees America as the main enemy. Therefore it can only contemplate a deterrence relationship with Washington which inherently, protestations of friendship aside, is based on Schmitt's concept of the presupposition of enemies. Thus unilateralism on one side encounters a posture grounded in that presupposition on the other that remains frozen in a hostile and deterrence posture. The results should not have been difficult to foresee.

Meanwhile, Russia's posture on other arms control treaties like the INF treaty, is no less dangerous. However, Washington's perceived quest for ever more credible options for deterrence, dissuasion, and even nuclear warfighting scenarios only stimulates everyone else's insecurities and desire to achieve their own means of deterring or dissuading America.[181] Doing so would also further stimulate the trend toward greater reliance on nuclear weapons as warfighting instruments that have been in effect at least since 2000, and also possibly enhance the attractiveness of such weapons to would- be proliferators.[182]

To say this however, is not to abandon the need to put pressure on Russia to fulfill the treaties it has signed whether they deal with nuclear arms control or conventional weapons and Eurasian security. Indeed, such a strategy is all the more necessary for our policy toward Russia because just as we seek to achieve our immediate defense and security goals by advocating democratization and the rule of law—albeit by chasing rhetorical abstractions or theological categories of good and evil and regime change vis-à-vis Iran and North Korea—so must we do so with regard to Russia. But we must not do so on the grounds that are commonly asserted, i.e., theological and liberal political universalism as interpreted by the particular administration in power at any given time. Rather, whatever our private beliefs might be about the justification for such pressure for reform, in political terms it is only sustainable on the grounds that the treaties to which Russia is party explicitly invoke these values and processes and thus represent Russia's solemn commitments as well as the constitutional foundation of our present world order from which Moscow as well as Washington benefit.[183] Abandoning those treaties therefore undermines world order and directly counters both American and Russian interests.

THE DOMESTIC BASIS OF ESTRANGEMENT

This increasing mutual estrangement grows out of both American and Russian domestic trends. Certainly the rhetoric, posture, policies, and activities of the Bush administration and of its domestic coalition, or the spokesmen thereof, reinforce long-standing Russian and other perceptions of a rogue American power unfettered by concern or respect for its interests or international institutions, and threatening both the integrity and the vital foundations of the Russian state, i.e., its pretensions to great power status. Similarly America's unilateral invasion of Iraq clearly and conclusively convinced many Russian policymakers that partnership with Washington led nowhere and that America was itself a kind of rogue elephant in international politics that had to be restrained by countervailing power.[184]

More recently there is an increasing belief that efforts to be America's partner are inherently unavailing because of America's fixed hostile position and that, in any case, America is in decline as Lavrov has now repeatedly stated.[185] The mounting Russian perception of increased military threats from America and NATO also plays no small role in this litany of grievances against Washington and the West.

While there is obviously no lack of foreign or domestic criticism of the Bush administration's policies or reasons for engaging in that practice, it is equally obvious that the administration now is hamstrung and isolated, largely due to Iraq and its repercussions. The outcome of a policy aiming to leave Washington with a free hand to act as it pleases in world affairs is that its hands are full, while its energies and legitimacy are depleted. This condition applies to U.S. policy in dealing either with North Korea, Iran, the Middle East in general, or, for that matter, Russia.

But the same relationship between domestic and foreign policy whereby the former profoundly conditions the latter in America holds true for Russian policy as well. Russian foreign policy grows out of the need to validate or legitimate both a revived autocracy and the accompanying neo-imperial pretext for it, and the mystique attached to the latter. Psychologically, it evidently is imperative for the Russian elite not only to believe that Russia is always a great power regardless of the actual reality, but apparently to internalize the belief of Soviet leaders dating back at least to Lenin that all world politics revolve around Russia and its trajectory.[186] Therefore foreign observers like Hryhoriy Nemyria, Director of the Kiev based Center for European and International Studies, has accurately stated that, "A significant part of Putin's legitimacy lies in his ability to control developments in Russia's near abroad."[187] The continuing existence of this and other associated convictions discussed below, is inextricably connected to the fact that the structure of the Russian state increasingly resembles that of late Tsarism with some Soviet or contemporary innovations.[188]

As Russian succession struggles illustrate, the recurrence of corruption, subversion, and force. deployed against internal "enemies" is among the most important indicators that Russia's elite refuses to be bound by or account to any system of laws or of legal-political institutions.[189] Western diplomats, including Secretary of State Condoleezza Rice, have publicly expressed concern that Putin observe the terms of the constitution and not succeed himself in 2008.[190] This kind of injunction need not be directed at a truly self-confident and legitimate state. In Russia, autocracy logically entails empire, an autarchic and patrimonial concept of a Russian state that is owned by the Tsar, controlled by his servitors, and which can only survive by expansion.[191] Therefore Nemyria's observations are perfectly consonant with the internal logic of the regime.[192] Similarly it is equally noteworthy that Russia now defines energy security as denoting its companies', i.e., the state's, access to Western firms while restricting Western access to its own firms. While Russia's main weapon is energy, it apparently is toying with enlarging its territory at Georgia's expense by fabricating grounds for annexing Abkhazia and South Ossetia, if not the Transnistrian Republic that it seized from Moldova.[193]

It logically follows that such a regime will have difficulty accepting the conventions of international life, including solemn treaties that it finds burdensome. Beyond that, just as autocracy means that the autocrat is not bound by or answerable to any institution or principle at home, it also means that in foreign policy, as often happened under the tsars, Russia feels free not to be bound by its own prior treaties and agreements.[194] As Lilia Shevtsova of the Carnegie Endowment for International Peace in Moscow observes,

> It is impossible not to see that Russia's foreign policy is the hostage of Russian internal systemic problems. Growing authoritarianism, redistribution of property, attempts to destroy political alternatives—all these elements result in Moscow's zig-zagging foreign policy. Quasi-democracy and quasi-market go hand in hand with Russia's quasi-partnership with the West. Attempts to preserve Russia's traditional system which strives to look modern, are likely to exhaust political pragmatism and increase the danger of unpredictability, especially when Russia discovers that the raw materials potential is more a weakness, than a source of power. The West, in turn, will have to decide what its partnership with Russia really means—an incentive to modernization or international legitimization of its slide towards traditionalism.[195]

But this point about the "autocratic" nature of Russian foreign policy is profoundly true in a more general sense. German analyst Heinrich Vogel has formulated this point in a deeper way, namely,

> Continuity of the kind [of leadership] described above also implies increasing volatility as the leadership has full sway in shifting political priorities in the agenda of foreign relations. Freed from any substantive balances or restrictions at home, Russian foreign policy is open in more than one direction.[196]

This insight has immediate ramifications in East-West relations. For example, Vogel also observes that,

> The partnership between [the] EU and Russia is shaped by the perceptions and ambitions of political elites on both sides who do not see eye to eye. Geopolitical analysts in Russia now even claim a chance to recoup political territory which was lost over the last 10 years. Any dialogue about a "common strategic vision" will therefore be particularly difficult if the leadership of one side, unconstrained by institutional balances, is hedging unclear or outright incompatible ideas about the rules of cooperation and competition in Europe. This is the case with Russian policies of "liberal imperialism": and the prevailing hegemonial approach of coaching and defending autocratic regimes in Belarus, Moldova, and Central Asia against any outside criticism. The unconditional support for antidemocratic practices and trends in Russia's near abroad dovetails with a distinct trend toward authoritarian regime justified by the Russian elites of all political shades as the "Russian way to democracy."[197]

RUSSIA AND THE POLICY OF THE FREE HAND

There can be little doubt that Russia pursues a policy of the free hand above all. In 2005 Lavrov announced that Russia refuses to be bound by foreign standards or conform to them.[198] Lavrov also insists that the West respect Russian interests in the CIS but makes no reciprocal statement of respect for the treaties Russia has signed and violated.[199] These statements and actions that comprise the actuality of Russian foreign policy confirm Trenin's warnings that Russia really does not want to belong to a larger institutional grouping and most of all wants a free hand in world politics, especially, but not only, in the CIS.

Russian observers fully understand that the demand for a free hand in world politics, and for a closed antidemocratic bloc in the CIS, is directly traceable to Russia's domestic politics. As Dmitry Furman wrote in 2006,

> Our system's democratic camouflage demands partnership with the West. However, the authoritarian, managed content of our system dictates the exact opposite. A safety zone for our system means a zone of political systems of the same kind of managed democracies that we are actively supporting in the CIS and, insofar as our forces allow, everywhere—in Serbia, the Middle East, even Venezuela. The Soviet Union's policy might seem quixotic. Why spend so much money in the name of "proletarian internationalism"? But if you do not ex-pand, you contract. The same could be said about our policy toward Lukashenko's regime [in Belarus-author]. The system of managed democracy in Russia will perish if Russia is besieged on all sides by unmanaged democracies. Ultimately it will once again be a matter of survival. The West cannot fail to support the establishment of systems of the same type as the West's, which means expanding its safety zone. We cannot fail to oppose this. Therefore the struggle inside the CIS countries is beginning to resemble the Russian-Western conflict.[200]

We should note here the explicit statement that spread of democracy in and of itself is a mortal threat to Russia's rulers. Hence the demand for a free hand. But the demand for a free hand means an unconstrained foreign policy based wholly on power and the interests of the state conceived of in the most atavistic and unbridled form of realpolitik, another example of Schmitt's presupposition of being encircled by enemies.[201] The only limit to the exercise of that autocratic power, as in tsarist times, is the conscience of the tsar, and in Putin's case, that is a weak reed. Unfortunately, Lavrov and Furman do not speak for themselves alone. Rather, they articulate a consolidated elite mentality that sees Russia as an independent, revisionist, even autarchic actor in world affairs which merits recognition as a self-sufficient pole, even empire, in Eurasia. Other analysts too have discerned the ideational elements of this stance in the peculiar but deep-rooted conviction that Russia is a separate civilization, neither wholly Western nor Eastern, and therefore it merits a special role in Eurasia as a great power. John Loewenhardt reported in 2000 that despite the fact that this status as a leading pole in global affairs was then understood to be increasingly more rhetorical than real,

> In one of our interviews a former member of the Presidential Administration said that the perception of Russia as a great power "is a basic element of the self-perception of high bureaucrats." If a political leader were to behave as if Russia was no longer a great power, there would be "a deeply rooted emotional reaction in the population."[202]

Six years of Putin's invigoration of authoritarianism and of Russia's imperial mystique have inevitably strengthened those tendencies, making them even more prominent in officialdom's mentality and self- reinforcing public propaganda.[203] And this ideological-political reinforcement has also created the basis for the perception of a perpetual Western or at least American ideological and domestic threat to Russia's integrity and form of government which are inextricably linked in both the elite and popular mind.[204] Since Russia still cannot accept its reduced status, its military- political elite still harbors unwarranted and unjustified assessments of Russia's status in world affairs and equally unjustified demands for tangible benefits. For example, a 2005 article in the General Staff journal, Military Thought, says that, "Russia's geopolitical situation enables it not only to effectively develop its own national economy but also to form a kind of geoeconomic region comprising the world's largest nations—Japan, China, India, and other countries." [205]

This concept also insists that none of the other former Soviet republics are genuinely capable of being self-standing truly independent states.[206] Certainly numerous statements by Russian ambassadors to former Soviet satellites or CIS governments conclusively show that they do not really accept the full sovereignty and independence of the states to which they are accredited.[207]

Logically, then, any bloc including those states is a strategic as well as ideological threat to Russia and a stalking horse for NATO and the EU and their supposedly openly anti-Russian policy.[208] The threat is not just to Russia's great power and imperial ambitions, but to its existence not only as autocracy but even as a state. Hence the flourishing of democratic states on its frontier is a constant threat to the survival of the state in the only form that its servitors can recognize it, i.e., an autocracy. This is one reason why Russian policymakers have evinced such panic and hysteria (not too strong a set of words) when confronted by "color revolutions" which they cannot believe originated in Georgia, Ukraine, and Kyrgyzstan due to their internal political developments. Hence much of Russian foreign policy has been directed toward preventing such revolutions, e.g., Russian intervention in Ukraine's 2004 presidential election and its policies toward Belarus and Georgia.[209]

The idea that these states on Russia's border or in its vicinity might choose NATO and the EU of their own volition or feel genuinely threatened by Russia's heavy-handed and unsubtle policies is never even considered. Not surprisingly, Russian spokesmen decry the formation of any such blocs and state that without Russia they will inevitably fail. Alternatively, they look forward to the reunification of the former Soviet republics of the CIS under Moscow's auspices.[210]

But what they always insist upon, i.e., their bottom line, is a unique and superior status for Russia above any kind of international political constraint. Thus Sergei Ivanov, Chizhov, and Yastrzhembskiy have publicly stated that Russia is economically, politically, and militarily self-sufficient and therefore really does not need partners.[211] Chizhov, speaking about Europe, argued further that,

> Russia has full rights and counts on participation in European affairs as an equal partner. It should not be isolated from the remaining part of the continent by new dividing lines and should not be the object of "civilizing influence" on the part of other countries or their unions but should be equal among equals.[212]

Similarly, in 2002 the publisher Vitaly Tretiakov wrote an article for the journal of the Ministry of Foreign Affairs where he stated that,

> We want to be regarded and treated as an ally of the West in all spheres, including export of energy and, probably, in the production of armaments. Otherwise, relations will follow a different pattern. This should apply to the security sphere. We also expect to be treated as equals in the sphere of economy and in cases of extending aid to us in the way this is done among allies.[213]

In other words, treat us as equals or we will make endless trouble for you, while at the same time we insist upon a free hand for ourselves. Not surprisingly, this kind of policy amounts to extortion, or in other words to a protection racket. Close examination of much of Russian foreign policy reveals that such blackmail or intimidation tactics feature prominently in Russia's diplomacy toward both the weaker states of the CIS and toward Europe and the United States.

However, great power status cannot be conferred exclusively by virtue of unilateral assertion or by the threat of raising a ruckus if your demands go unheeded. To be recognized as a great or superpower—and many Russian analysts and political figures now argue that Russia is an energy superpower — a state must be able to project its power effectively into neighboring regions to create a legitimate and/or durable order and be recognized as such by its interlocutors. Inasmuch as all projections of power abroad are "injections" into the world order and efforts to reshape it, we can see the fundamentally revisionist thrust of Russia's project from its activities in the near abroad or efforts to bully European states with regard to energy.[214] It also habitually uses the energy revenues accruing to it to buy politicians and subvert regimes in its neighborhood.[215]

Russia's attitude of imperial unilateralism might be a "post-imperial" mentality rather than an imperial one as Trenin argues.[216] But this attitude's practical implications as seen in ongoing demands for bases throughout the CIS; obstruction in CIS frozen conflicts; and the energy crises with Ukraine, Georgia, and Belarus in 2006-07, are unmistakably imperial in consequence and reflect a belief that Russia is an empire sufficient unto itself and thus above all of the other rules of international life; precisely what it attacks Washington for doing.[217] Certainly, Russian scholars know full well that Russia's elites have long continued to see the Russian state in imperial terms. As Alexei Malashenko observed in 2000, Russia's war in Chechnya is logical only if Russia continues to regard itself as an empire.[218] More recently Russian political scientist Egor Kholmogorov has observed that "'Empire' is the main category of any strategic political analysis in the Russian language. Whenever we start to ponder a full-scale, long-term construction of the Russian state, we begin to think of empire and in terms of empire. Russians are inherently imperialists."[219]

If Russia is such an empire, then it becomes clear why EU or NATO membership becomes a threat to Russian sovereignty. For as Deputy Foreign Minister Ivan Ivanov stated in 1999,

> Our country is not in need of affiliation with the EU. This would entail loss of its unique Euro-Asian specifics, the role of the center of attraction of the re-integration of the CIS, independence in foreign economic and defense policies, and complete restructuring (once more) of all Russian statehood based on the requirements of the European Union. Finally

> great powers (and it is too soon to abandon calling ourselves such) do not dissolve in international unions—they create them around themselves.[220]

Not only does he here anticipate Trenin's observations about a solar system around Russia, Ivanov also listed as a reason for not joining the EU the idea that empire preceded independence. Here he also implied or suggested the deeply rooted belief among Russian elites that if Russia is not an empire, it is not a state. But the quest for great power and empire is the fetish invoked by Russian statesman throughout the ages to ward off the nightmare of being marginalized and no longer being a great power. This nightmare haunts the imagination of Russia's political elites and undoubtedly is one of the most primordial psychological and cognitive drivers of Russian foreign policy, even if it postulates only two possible outcomes for Russia—great or even superpower status, or oblivion and marginalization.[221] Indeed, in pursuing this mirage of being a great power which can act unconstrained in world affairs, Putin has sought to copy the Bush administration's doctrine of preemption or preventive war to justify its unlimited right to military intervention in the CIS with rather less justification than did President Bush, for there have been no foreign based attacks upon Russia.[222]

Toward an American Response: Overcoming Western Internal Divisions

Notwithstanding these problems with Russia, it must be engaged, not ignored. Given the preoccupation with Iraq, it is by no means clear if our political class is paying sufficient attention to Russia. That the U.S. Government keeps being surprised by Putin is also a sign of insufficient attention to Russian issues or understanding of what is involved in them. Nevertheless as a recent study from the Congressional Research Office (CRO) observed,

> Yet developments in Russia are still important to the United States. Russia remains a nuclear superpower. It will play a major role in determining the national security environment in Europe, the Middle East, and Asia. Russia has an important role in the future of arms control, nonproliferation of weapons of mass destruction, and the fight against terrorism. Such issues as the war on terrorism, the future of NATO, and the U.S. role in the world will all be affected by developments in Russia. Also, although Russia's economy is distressed, it is recovering and potentially an important trading partner.[223]

Similar statements were also presented above, e.g., Slocombe's testimony in 1995 and the observations by Andrew Michta of the Marshall Center concerning regional security.[224] It should be noted that this balanced account by the CRO does not imply, as do many other statements on why Russia is important, that America's need for Russian support on these issues outweighs Russia's need for American support on these and many other issues. An essential requirement in getting Russia right, therefore, is a balance between what both sides need from the other and can reasonably expect of the other side.

For this reason, a policy that merely lectures Russia without credible counteractions to offensive (in both senses of the word) Russian policies or actions that advance American interests has no value. If U.S. policy is to advance towards the goals of defending U.S. security and then promoting a better world order, it must take account of the powers that be, not those that ought to be in a perfect world. Thus a credible Russia policy must aim to overcome these defects in Russian policy, but to do so, it must begin (but not end) by realizing where Russia currently is and sees itself.[225]

Even bearing this admonition in mind, an intelligent policy towards Russia cannot let Moscow's objections deter American actions in support of the national interest where those objections undermine our ability to reach those interests. This should be the case even though we might have to pay a higher price for doing so. But intelligent policymaking towards Russia requires a fine judgment of what interests can or must be secured, at what costs, and finally unremitting attention to that end. It requires a deeper assessment of Russian realities and trends than the habitual American tendency (that began long before this administration) of indulging in the idea that personal relationships with the Russian leader are either substitutes for or the purpose of U.S. policy towards Moscow.

Acknowledging Russian realities does not mean giving Moscow a veto on our policies or overlooking the intrinsicly self-seeking and opportunistic nature of the Russian regime that is structurally, not personally, determined. There are few "imagined" misdeeds in the record of the Putin government for which it is being attacked abroad. The Putin's regime's record is all too transparent in that regard. Rather, there are all too many real deeds that deserve consistent international censure. Instead, acknowledging Russian realities means that our calculation of interest and of the costs we can pay to reach them must be better than has hitherto been the case because on all too many issues, particularly those connected with the regression from democratization, we have given Russia a pass.

Thus a sound American policy must also mean that Moscow must be made to acknowledge other realities besides its own self-interest. We must realize, and do so despite the critics at home, that Moscow needs American support far more than Washington needs its support. Second, to the degree that U.S. power is limited by other states' interests, so must Russian power be limited accordingly. U.S. policy must see to it that Russia does not get a free hand to act as it pleases in world affairs or be allowed simply to make trouble so that its status or importance will then grow. Accepting Russia's demands for a free hand, either actively or tacitly, or giving it a free hand, especially in the CIS, only leads to greater autocratic behavior at home and belligerence abroad. For example, precisely because it seeks a free hand in Eurasia and was not countered by effective action, it is now threatening to leave the CFE treaty and thus be free to do what it wants with its armed forces in Eurasia, thereby achieving a unique status among every other signatory of that treaty.

While Russia cannot be ignored in American policymaking on the issues listed above, its negative impact can and should be countered and reduced. This applies equally to Russia's domestic policies. Indeed, the strategy outlined below aims at integrating Russia over time into the Eurasian constitutional and political order and treaties that it has signed which govern both domestic and foreign policy practices. In other words, our strategy must aim at integrating Russia into a world order that it has voluntarily accepted, and gradually eroding the possibilities for it to realize a free hand abroad. To the extent that we succeed in doing so, Russian governments will also then not be able to act with a totally free hand at home. Rather, they will be bound by the treaties and conventions to which they are a party. Over time, only that kind of policy will work to counter the authoritarian impulses that are so deeply rooted in Russian politics and culture. It must be realized that this is a patient, long-term policy, not one that seeks immediate gratification or is motivated by evangelical and theological beliefs about the superiority of democracy masquerading as certainties. And it also means that U.S. policies must be governed and thus restrained by the same constitutional order whose validity we seek to uphold and extend.

To achieve those goals, however, we must first dispel several myths and obstacles that obstruct coherent U.S. and Western policymaking and then take appropriate policy actions. The first obstacle is the widely accepted myth that we or the West as a whole have little or no leverage upon Russian policy and therefore must adjust to it or tolerate it silently. [226] This, of course, is a highly self-serving tactic when stated by Russians who love to insist that the United States or the West cannot sway their policies, and that foreign motives towards Russia are invariably hostile and self-serving. Or else they argue that such criticism is pushing to a return of the Cold War.[227] In the West, this precept amounts to a self-denying ordnance that paralyzes efforts to advance Western political objectives when it has the stronger hand in every dimension of international power. Moreover, obtaining such a condition of Western paralysis or admission of defeat is actually the goal of all of the bad behavior displayed by Moscow in the hope that foreigners will assume nothing can be done. Therefore, the Russian media is all too happy to report frequently that the West "accepts" the nature of Russia's "special democracy."[228] Indeed, at one point Lavrov even asserted that after a Putin-Bush summit meeting in 2004 "no concern was sounded" about the lack of democracy in Russia by the American side.[229]

But when uttered in the West, this observation represents a bizarre failure of applied political intelligence. We need not argue that American or Western power is unlimited or that its authority, legitimacy, and virtue are absolute—neither of which proposition is true—to realize that the strongest power in the world and the strongest alliance in the world do not lack the resources with which to influence Russian policy and that Russia has frequently adjusted to meet firm American policies. After all, George Kennan's containment strategy was just such a strategy that sought to compel an eventual "mellowing" of Soviet domestic and foreign behavior by applying political and other external pressures abroad. Similarly, the judicious application of the total weight of the instruments of power available to the West in world politics would surely frustrate or at least blunt the imperial drive and the restoration of autocracy that underlies so much of today's Russian foreign policy and force domestic changes as a result. As Vogel writes,

> This logic of "mutually assured dependency" (the po litical dimension of interdependence) implies a world of rational choices. In this world, the structural deficiencies of the Russian economy and its integration and interdependence with the international community restrict Moscow's ability to be uncooperative or engage in spoilsport behavior in international crisis management.[230]

Arguing that we have no leverage is not only bizarrely misguided but also reduces the Western pursuit of a viable Russian policy to incoherence.

But beyond realizing that we have leverage and the right, if not the duty, to use it, both on our own and in tandem with our allies, to advance our interests, we need to overcome the second obstacle to a sound Russia policy. Namely, we must devise and implement a coherent strategy, first of all within our own government, and then together with our allies in order to deploy that leverage to its most efficacious use. This strategy must be implemented in regard to key issues: Iran; the Middle East; the Western presence in the CIS; the sanctity of treaties signed by Russia; energy; arms control; and Korea; to name only a few. Doing so requires, first, that we overcome the fact that on numerous key issues, including apparently policies toward Russia, and in regard to at least some of these aforementioned issues, our policy process has been and is still broken. Any attentive reader of the newspapers can quickly discern that there exist major divisions among the players in Washington that inhibit unified and coherent policy formulation and implementation.[231] Until and unless we can overcome those problems, any approaches to our European and other allies regarding these issues will be compromised from the start. Of course, the EU has to overcome its own incoherence and internal divisions, but lectures from Washington on that particular subject can only go so far. The EU's members themselves have to come to a consensus on what they see as their future demands upon Russia and Russia's role in Eurasia for their own sake, not just ours. And it is now very clear to the EU that it must achieve its own internal consensus vis-à-vis its Russian agenda.[232]

There is no doubt that divisions within the topmost echelons of the U.S. policy process exist on whether or not to press Russia systematically on the issues of dispute in our common agenda, not least democratization.[233] Second, U.S. policy toward Russia as it is now carried out suffers from several shortcomings that obstruct realization either of strategic or democratic aims. The first problem is the false dichotomy that has existed among many commentators and in many administrations, including this one, that in order to achieve strategic goals, e.g., Iranian or North Korean nonproliferation, we have to soft pedal or even sacrifice democracy promotion, or vice versa. It is very clear that the current administration has opted for a relationship with Moscow that emphasizes strategic goals over democratization, for all its ringing invocation of universal democratic values.[234] And the results are hardly worth the neglect of Russian democratic issues or the effort invested in achieving coordination with Russia at the expense of those democratic issues. In fact, Michael McFaul's assessment of U.S. democracy promotion policy towards Russia even calls it "anemic."[235]

But aligned to that false dichotomy between promoting security objectives and democracy are procedural errors that impede realizing both strategic and democratic goals. As Dov Lynch of the European Union's Institute for Security Studies observes,

> U.S. policy toward Russia has been heavily presidential. This has meant that only decisions agreed at the highest level were recognized as being important by Moscow. This did allow the White House to "use" Secretary Powell—in the words of one U.S. official—as a "bad cop" on a number of occasions in 2004, but it did not always provide for the best result. As developments inside Russia and in Russian foreign policy became more worrying, the U.S. administration faced the difficulty of seeking to revise the policy in some areas while maintaining others, all the while avoiding the image of a radical shift in relations. The appointment of Condoleezza Rice as Secretary of State in 2005 led to a discreet reassessment of U.S. policy. The priorities remain firm on counterproliferation and nonproliferation. However, the spread of democracy in Russia's neighborhood has risen to the forefront, and the Administration has become more vocal in expressing its concerns about democracy and the rule of law inside Russia. Still, U.S. policy remains largely strategically-driven and its thrust is still minimalist in terms of seeking Russia's transformation. Russia matters for the United States less for itself and more in terms of how it can affect U.S. interests in other policy areas. [236]

Lynch's assessment subsumes within it as well the unwarranted emphasis on a personal relationship with Putin. As a result of the policy described by Lynch on both sides, there is little governmental implementation of agreements or progress on issues while the relationship stays focused on personalities rather than programs. This fact, unfortunately extends a well-established tradition, but also makes it harder for the Russian government to reform itself or ensure policy coordination and fulfillment when it does concur with the United States.

Therefore it is essential that the Bush administration, or failing that, its successor, undertake policy actions that will compel both our government and the Russian government to interact with each other on the basis of ongoing and constant mutual dialogue. Specifically, the administration or its successor should propose the recreation of a contemporary analogue of the Gore-Chernomyrdin commission that operated under President Clinton. As former Ambassador to Russia James Collins observes, doing so would obligate senior officials across a wide range of bureaucracies (not just the Pentagon and State Departments) to carry out serious projects that needed to be done. Second, this commission did and could again empower different ministry-department relationships that would force both the Russian and American bureaucracies to deal with each other on an intimate and permanent basis with a view to achieving real and constructive results.[237] By having such a permanent structure in place, both governments would have to talk to each other more often, more frankly, across many venues, and at a lower level that could actually achieve positive actions. Otherwise we will have the same kind of bureaucratic drift that has characterized both sides' policies for too long and in the American case helped contribute to the flaws in our policy that are outlined above.

A third case in which our policy toward Russia is in error is the absence of any sign of a truly coherent energy policy designed to reduce our or our allies' dependence upon Russian supplies and potential blackmail. As Putin has gone on one successful offensive after another in 2006-07 to lock up Eurasian energy reserves and access, the EU has been divided, timorous, and incoherent, and Washington has always been too late in replying or in fashioning attractive counteroptions for interested parties. And while the EU wants to negotiate a deal with Moscow formalizing the bilateral energy relationship with Russia while it simultaneously seeks other sources of energy, it is very unclear if not unlikely that Moscow can currently be forced to accept its own agreements or refrain from trying to penetrate European economies and thus governments as it has sought to do throughout Eastern Europe and the CIS.[238] Certainly Moscow has made it abundantly clear that it will not accept the EU's energy charter anytime soon.[239] Since energy is Moscow's main weapon in its current foreign policy, this absence of a strategy or of a policy puts us and our allies at a grievous political disadvantage and also makes it more difficult to help CIS members who are being blackmailed in various ways by Russia on this point or being threatened by Russia with unrelieved economic warfare and even Cold War.

This point is particularly urgent when we realize that due to the collapse of the Orange Revolution, Ukraine is approaching either a state of ungovernability or of enduring political stalemate which could allow Moscow to manipulate both the energy card and all the other resources of which its disposes in the Ukraine to destabilize that region or obstruct its democratization and Westernization. This also means that Ukraine's energy situation is one that at present makes it perpetually vulnerable.[240] Belarus too succumbed in early 2007 to Russian pressure and is now frantically seeking to diversify its sources. Other CIS states escaped this threat only because Iran or Azerbaijan provided them with energy.

Energy security is not just a question of supplying Europe or Asia, or from Russia's standpoint of ensuring its ability to meet foreign and domestic demand at a fair market price. Rather, it entails the basic security and opportunity for progress of the former Soviet states whether in Ukraine or in Central Asia.[241] While it is in these states' interests, and Russia's, that their energy relationships be marketized rather than subsidized, there is little doubt that Moscow's policies have been aimed at political results first, and Russia still charges differential prices to its customers in line with its political prerogatives.

Fourth, there are major divisions within the administration on how to deal with major proliferation issues like Korea which have led us to outsource our Northeast Asian policy to Beijing, which, in turn, allied increasingly with Moscow, aims to supplant American influence there, if not elsewhere.[242] Fifth, on Iran, it is unclear how far we are prepared to go to stop Iranian proliferation, and it certainly is even more unclear how far our European allies will go toward the same objective. Indeed, numerous commentators and the former Foreign Minister of Great Britain Jack Straw have said that European participation in a war with Iran over its nuclear threat is "inconceivable." But it is quite likely that without the threat of robust action, Iran will not acceded to demands to stop enrichment or its overall military nuclear program. Nor does the European response to the Lebanon crisis suggest any interest in playing a truly robust role in bringing peace to the Middle East either in part or in whole by disarming Hezbollah which is using Russian weapons supplied by Iran and Syria who bought them from Moscow.[243]

Certainly it is clear from the crisis generated by Hezbollah's unprovoked attacks on Israel in July 2006 that Moscow is not prepared to restrain Iran or its proxies. Indeed, even though the Foreign Ministers negotiating with Iran were finally driven by Tehran's dilatory tactics to agree to bring its nuclear program to the Security Council with a threat of sanctions, Lavrov has firmly and consistently opposed any effort to impose sanctions on Russia's arms trade with Iran.[244] In addition, there have been leaks suggesting that despite tough rhetoric our officials inwardly accept the fact that at the end of the day, Iran will have a usable nuclear weapon.[245] While much of this is due to the consequences of the U.S. invasion of Iraq, it also is the case that both Moscow and Beijing resolutely oppose doing anything that will injure Iranian interests or apparently impel Tehran (or Pyongyang, too) to stop building nuclear weapons even if they now recognize that Iran's nuclear program has military purposes that can threaten them.[246] If anything, they have aided Iran's, Pakistan's, and North Korea's quest for nuclear energy and for conventional weapons, including missiles, and deterrence capabilities against the United States.[247]

Finally, there are major divisions within the administration even now on how to proceed to deal with the challenges facing us in Central Asia which are posed by both domestic conditions favoring dictatorship and foreign threats, not the least of which is the Russo-Chinese alliance against reform, and to suppress the foreign policy independence of those states.[248] Furthermore, due to our own dilatoriness and overextension, Russia is gaining the upper hand in its efforts to marginalize American influence there, too.[249]

Until and unless those and other such differences among policymakers are overcome, no coherent Rus- sian policy is possible, let alone imaginable. But overcoming our own internal divisions on these issues is only the beginning of wisdom. For any approach to Russia to succeed, it must not be merely a unilateral one, but rather one shared by and with our European allies on the basis of genuine consultation and consensus. And it must be attuned to both Russia's domestic and its foreign policy behavior which are mutually reinforcing.

Despite unity with the EU on Iran to date, it is by no means clear if the Transatlantic Alliance has achieved a truly significant recovery since the invasion of Iraq in 2003 which shattered both the Transatlantic Alliance and any hope of a unified European common foreign and security policy. Thus after having edited another volume in the seemingly endless series of publications examining the troubled Transatlantic Alliance, Marcin Zaborowski concludes that,

> It is clear that the greater congruence of policies between both sides of the Atlantic was not followed by the convergence of principles and ideologies. Most importantly, the EU and the United States continue to have fundamentally different views on the role and importance of international institutions and agreements. The legacy of this disagreement is not just ideological, but it affects transatlantic cooperation in some specific policy fields, most prominent in the Middle East.[250]

These same observations may be invoked concerning Western policy toward Russia for even where assessments of Russian developments converge, policy recommendations and outcomes currently diverge. Even if there is a unified American position, if it is not coordinated with and implemented by our European allies and Japan in the Far East, it will fail to register with full force in Moscow whether it is about human rights, the frozen conflicts in the CIS, Central Asia, or energy. So beyond the reestablishment of our own internal policy coherence, there must be close coordination and a united course of action with our allies regarding an agenda of East-West negotiation. As Lynch writes,

> Transatlantic coordination is crucial for ensuring that Russia remains a positive player on the world stage, an inclusive player in its neighborhood, and a state led by the rule of law. Whether the agenda is thick or thin, internal developments cannot be divorced for long from external behavior. What happens inside Russia impacts on the nature of Russia as a partner for the EU and the US. At a time when Europe and America have less leverage over Russia's domestic development than they had, transatlantic cooperation becomes all the more vital. In this the EU and US should build on areas of overlap in their agendas, such as regional security questions in the Balkans and the Middle East, ensuring positive momentum in the former Soviet Union, and raising concerns with domestic developments in Russia.[251]

This also means that on occasion Washington will have to defer to the collective wisdom of its partners and even to China and Russia's arguments. But it also means that the United States needs to stimulate NATO and the EU to do better than they have in coming up with coherent policies towards Russia as regards Ukraine, Moldova, the Caucasus, energy issues, Central Asia, and democratization; for today the prevailing trend is towards incoherence and disunity within both organizations on these agenda issues.[252]

Strengthening Nonproliferation

It should now be clear that we cannot achieve our basic and primary strategic aim of strengthening the nonproliferation regime by tying Iranian and North Korean nonproliferation to externally imposed regime change or the threat of it by unilateral American military action. Our power and understanding of what needs to be done over both the short and long term in such cases are both limited thanks to our experience in Iraq. Moreover any such efforts, in the absence of forceful provocation by those or other states, will enjoy no support anywhere, further overtaxing the resource base for American power and limiting our capacity to preside over any kind of security order in the relevant region.

If our fundamental objective is nonproliferation, our resources should be focused on achieving that goal since the effort to link it to coerced regime change in Northeast Asia or the Gulf enjoys no support by the other negotiators and cannot be reached by any means available to the United States now or anytime soon. Objectionable as these regimes are, we have neither the means nor the legitimate international authority to change them by force, nor the wisdom to know how to achieve a legitimate order in these areas afterward by unilateral action.

Furthermore, by decoupling this demand from our demands for nonproliferation, we actually gain more flexibility to send a robust message to Iran, Syria, and North Korea should they then proliferate because they no longer have even the semblance of a justification for their position. Even if the invasion of Iraq may have given them a supposed justification for proliferation and sponsorship of terrorism, the fact that they will subsequently be held to account on the basis of existing international agreements to which they are parties to desist from proliferation and sponsorship of terrorism creates a sufficient justification for the use of pressure or the threat of force and releases us from the position of making threats that cannot currently be carried out. If we can change the international behavior of these regimes, by political means preferably but by force if absolutely necessary, then their current foreign and domestic policy behavior will gradually be rendered increasingly dysfunctional, forcing change upon them from within, not from outside. To the extent that they cannot then mobilize domestic or foreign support against the Bush administration, they will be compelled by force of circumstances and superior Western power to adjust their behavior over time. Admittedly, this is a slow process, but Iraq shows what happens when we seek instant , forceful, and externally imposed regime change. That lesson should induce behavior change in Washington first before we seek to persuade other key interlocutors of the soundness of our position.

Therefore, to effectuate change within Russia and other challenging states, we must change the external environment within which they operate by engaging them politically. This engagement also includes holding Russia to account for treaties and conventions that it has violated. Indeed, careful examination will show that there is no other realistic alternative. Despite all the inherent traps and snares in a dialogue between Pyongyang and Washington or between Tehran and Washington, we cannot compel their denuclearization by our refusal to talk to them; quite the opposite. Here we cannot hide behind multilateralism because all our partners except possibly Japan have urged Washington to engage in precisely such a dialogue with North Korea. Avoiding such dialogues and clinging to ringing but empty rhetorical positions only deepens our internal divisions and disputes with our negotiating partners and allies while failing to achieve denuclearization. If anything, the threat of coerced regime change powerfully accelerates these countries' nuclear programs which enjoy tacit or covert support from Moscow and Beijing precisely because they are joined in rejecting any further unilateralism by Washington, a position in which they are joined by both South Korea and our European allies.[253] While it would be satisfying to punish these states, e.g., Iran for its actions in provoking a war in Lebanon, our capabilities are circumscribed and limited.

Consequently we need a strategy that will force these proliferators to change their behavior over time by mitigating their and our security dilemmas and rendering their current behavior even more dysfunctional than is presently the case until it is no longer feasible to carry it out. Furthermore, such an engagement will work over time to dissolve the bonds linking China, Russia, and in the Korean case, South Korea because neither Moscow, nor Pyongyang, nor Seoul wants China to be the deciding voice in Northeast Asia, whatever their criticisms of Washington. But that is where our obstinacy is driving us with regard to the Korean peninsula where Beijing rather than Washington will become the arbiter of that peninsula's destiny. Endless statements from Beijing and Moscow reiterate the identity of these states' views about Korea and much else because we have done everything possible to drive them together. For example, with regard to Korea, we see the Russian and Chinese governments' oft proclaimed identity of interests and proposals.[254]

Indeed, Russian scholars now state that Russia works with China to coordinate their proposals in the Korean nuclear negotiations and numerous communiqués cite an "identity" of views on this topic.[255] Removing many of the reasons for their shared positions regarding either North Korea or Iran helps erode their unified position in these and other issues. As experts have argued that a working Russo-Chinese alliance is the greatest security threat we could face, a negotiating strategy designed to uncouple these two potential rivals against us but also against each other, makes perfect sense.[256]

This policy's wisdom would also be underscored by the fact that an examination of the historical record strongly suggests that a precondition for effective nonproliferation is mutual cooperation between Moscow and Washington as happened in 1986-96 and which has since evaporated due to Russian domestic regression to autocratic rule, American unilateralism, and the perception thereof abroad. [257] Once proliferation is uncoupled from regime change, it becomes much easier to fashion both a strong negotiating coalition against the former, which is the main threat, and to do so strictly on the grounds of international security and international treaties that must be observed. This allows us and the other treaty signatories to create a different security environment around proliferators, complete with binding accords, supervision, and inspections— an environment that safeguards their internal security but which contributes to rendering their form of rule even more dysfunctional than is now the case. But most importantly, it facilitates the reaching of verifiable agreements on these states' nuclear program which is the key point.[258]

Without the ability or rationale to justify threat- based programs, in the absence of a threat these states must then deal much more urgently with economic and political questions at home for which they have no answer and for which their structures are woefully inadequate, if not illegitimate. And since contemporary scholarly research suggests that proliferation policies are the product of various coalitions of domestic interest groups in these states, a policy that transforms the playing field on which these coalitions maneuver has a much greater chance of success than does unilateral rhetoric which in reality cannot be implemented except at ruinous cost.[259] That process, as was the case with Moscow in 1986-91, will generate a process of change that will be all the more powerful for being domestically generated rather than externally coerced.

ARMS CONTROL

The foundation stones of European and Eurasian security are the series of treaties beginning with the Helsinki treaty of 1975, its extension at Moscow in

1991, the 1987 Washington Treaty on Intermediate Nuclear forces in Europe (INF), the 1990 Paris Treaty on Conventional Forces in Europe (CFE), extended in 1999, the Paris and Rome treaties between NATO and Russia in 1997 and 2002, and the START and SORT treaties from 1991-2002. However, some, if not all, of these treaties are apparently at risk. And that risk has grown with Putin's announcement that Russia is suspending its participation in the CFE Treaty for 150 days (even though there is no legal basis for doing so in the treaty) in July, 2007. It also should be noted that there were numerous Russian warnings to this effect, e.g., Sergei Ivanov and his subordinates' warnings that Russia might withdraw from the CFE Treaty or that it might die a natural death.[260]

Recently, thanks partly to Western pressure, Russia agreed with Georgia that it would leave its bases there by 2008. But meanwhile it refuses to leave Moldova. Indeed, it seeks a 20-year lease on a base there to perpetuate its intervention on behalf of a separatist and visibly criminalized Russian faction across the Dniester River.[261] Russian officials also talk of launching political gambits to formalize Russia's incorporation of Georgia's breakaway province South Ossetia into Russia.

These actions not only violate Russia's 1999 agreement, putting the lie to claims that Russia has no juridical obligation to leave Moldova and Georgia, they also would shatter the basis of European security as outlined in the aforementioned treaties. Incorporation of South Ossetia or Abkhazia or Transnistria by force not only invokes Soviet and tsarist precedents, those actions violate the Helsinki and Moscow treaties, the Istanbul accords, and shatter the post-Cold War accords with NATO. Like Moscow's 2004 and 2006 intervention in Ukrainian elections, such actions betray Russia's continuing inability to accept the end of empire in Eurasia even though a Russian empire there inherently threatens Eurasian and even Russian security. Russia also claims that the Baltic States' failure to ratify the CFE treaty makes the Baltic a "gray zone" from which potential threats to Russian security could come even though they also admit that NATO's token forces there hardly represent a current threat.[262]

The INF treaty, too, is at risk. Clearly the efforts to withdraw from the INF and CFE treaties are also connected to Russian fears that Western military- political pressure will be used to consolidate post- Soviet states' membership in NATO and/or the EU, or to compel democratizing reforms in Russia or elsewhere in the CIS where Moscow supports the reigning authoritarians. Since Russia cannot compete militarily with the United States, let alone NATO, it has openly discussed using its strategic and/or tactical (or so-called nonstrategic) nuclear weapons in a first strike mode in the event of a threat by either of those parties against it or its interests in the CIS.[263] More recently, Sergei Ivanov has threatened once again to put missiles into Kaliningrad if NATO does not take up Russian complaints about these treaties.[264] Moscow already did this in 2001 and created a scandal thereby, indicating a continuing inclination in at least certain circles to conduct unilateral and even menacing political and strategic actions using Russian nuclear weapons.[265] For instance, Moscow long ago gratuitously extended its nuclear umbrella to the CIS even though none of those states invited it to do so. But such contingency planning could only truly be taken to its logical culmination if Moscow frees itself from these two treaties that are pillars of arms control and security in Europe and renounces its interest in the continuing stabilization of European security.

However, such an outcome reignites an arms race in Europe that, as Putin and Company knows, Russia cannot afford and which is in nobody's interest. Ironically, Russia actually depends for its security on the restraints imposed by those treaties upon NATO's members including Washington. Moreover, it depends on them for subsidies through the Nunn- Lugar Act or Comprehensive Threat Reduction program to gain control over its nuclear, biological, and chemical weapons arsenals. Without that funding, it is quite likely that the recent visible regeneration of the Russian armed forces would have been greatly impeded because at least some of those funds would have had to go to maintain or destroy decaying nuclear, biological, and chemical weapons. Russia also needs Western, and especially American help against terrorism emanating from Afghanistan, or Iranian and North Korean nuclearization and is still interested, as recent agreements show, in curtailing those states or terrorists' access to these materials.[266] Furthermore, it is no less at risk from Iranian missiles than anyone else (except possibly Israel), given the two states' hidden rivalry in the Caspian basin. Thus it needs to cooperate with the West on proliferation concerns, too. Therefore these efforts to withdraw from the relevant treaties are quite misguided insofar as Russia's real interests are concerned even though Moscow's legal right to withdraw from a treaty is obvious. But if Moscow persists in these gambits to weaken, eviscerate, or even leave these treaties, what does that signify concerning its goals and what then is the future of European and Eurasian security?

Therefore, an appropriate American response should be to maintain the validity of both the CFE and INF treaties, insist upon fulfillment of the former, and state U.S. willingness to reaffirm or extend the latter which is supposed to expire in 2008. Nobody benefits from a new arms race in Europe which should be a model of security practices, not a case of a model gone bad. And Russia's announced desire to renegotiate the START I Treaty that is to expire in 2009 should similarly provide an new opportunity for further reducing the likelihood and perceived value of nuclear weapons use or threats to use them among the two leading nuclear states.[267] Doing so would also reverse the trend toward greater reliance on nuclear weapons as warfighting instruments that has been in effect at least since 2000, and also possibly reduce the attractiveness of such weapons to would-be proliferators.

To say this, however, is not to abandon the need to put pressure on Russia to fulfill the treaties it has signed whether they deal with nuclear arms control or conventional weapons and Eurasian security. Indeed, such a strategy is all the more necessary for our policy toward Russia because just as we seek to achieve our immediate defense and security goals by invoking rhetorical abstractions of democratization vis-à-vis Iran and North Korea, so must we do so with regard to Russia where there is a legal justification, based on solemn international treaties, for doing so. Whatever our private beliefs might be about the justification for such pressure, in political terms it is only sustainable on the grounds that the treaties to which Russia is party explicitly invoke these values and processes and thus represent the constitutional foundation of our present world order.[268]

DEMOCRATIZATION

Putin and his clique, including Lavrov, regularly charge that demands for democratization are purely politically motivated and neo-colonialist in their rhetoric and an attack on Russia's system of governance, indeed an attempt to change it.[269] Actually they are partly right. Such attacks do represent an attack on Russian governance because that governance is increasingly at variance with solemn international accords that Russia freely signed and to which it must be held. Just as the United States resents attacks on conduct at Guantanamo or at Abu Ghraib but is nonetheless compelled to redress those situations through legal and democratic pressure and processes, so too is Russia subject to the same international constraints and standards that it freely accepted. However, it is clear that Moscow would prefer a relationship with the United States like that among realpolitikers in the 19th century, i.e., no discussions of democracy and rather a concentration on concrete bilateral interests.[270] For example, Lavrov protested the Euro-Atlantic Partnership Council complaints about democratic deficits in Russia. He charged that this was not part of the Council's remit and duplicated the work of organizations like the OSCE which Russia, not by accident, also seeks to deflect from making such complaints as part of its remit.[271] At the same time, the demand for an end to these attacks and this kind of defense by Putin et al. reflects both Moscow's demand for a free hand and its endless status insecurity or anxiety.

Indeed, the demand for an end to such attacks along with the assertion that America seeks to undermine all the other CIS governments as well as Russia had become a staple of Russian foreign policy argumentation even before Ukraine's Orange Revolution in late 2004.

Already in July 2004, Russian commentator M. Chernov wrote:

> The American Administration is beginning a campaign to topple the regime of Islam Karimov in Uzbekistan. . . . By all appearances Washington has decided to get rid of Karimov, relying on the successful experience of revolution in Georgia and using elements of the "Kosovo scenario," establishing control over the territory by creating "managed conflicts" in the Uzbek provinces [primarily in the Fergana valley] and bringing in peacekeeping force.[272]

The exact parallel of this so-called American strategy to Russian strategy in Georgia and Moldova is testimony, as psychologists have long observed, that the projection onto "the other" is a hallmark of paranoia, the latter being a long-established tradition in Russian politics, not least where foreign influence in the CIS is concerned. Not to be undone, two other commentators, Yevgeny Myachin and Aleksandr' Sobyanin, argued as well that Washington and European governments pursue a strategy of managed conflicts using terrorism to achieve their aims. Thus Sobyanin argued that the Islamic Movement of Uzbekistan (IMU) located in Afghanistan and Pakistan "works in close cooperation with Western intelligence services."[273]

The persistence of such neo-Soviet tactics and mentalities in Russian public discourse underscores the distance separating Russia from true democratization. By early 2005, Moscow's paranoia about the supposed democracy campaign orchestrated by Washington had merged with its anxieties about securing for itself an exclusive primacy in the CIS. The newspaper Kommersant reported on February 24, 2005, that,

> In response to the U.S. side's criticisms regarding Russian domestic and foreign policy, the Kremlin, according to Kommersant's information, has begun preparing counter-criticisms connected first and foremost with the growth of the West's planned activity aimed at replacing the ruling regimes in the CIS. In Moscow they are convinced that the velvet revolutions which have taken place or are being prepared are the result of the activity of Western nongovernmental organizations and the special services, which are nurturing and training opposition forces. In the Kremlin's opinion, such activity is particularly dangerous in regard to the countries of Central Asia where the export of revolution could lead to serious, long-term destabilization. Nor does Moscow like the military-political activity of the United States on CIS territory, in particular the intention to station military bases in Georgia [which has never been the case- author] and AWACS south of Kyrgyzstan, and also to assist in the creation of an association of Central Asian states (without the participation of Russia, China, and Iran). [There is no public record of such a proposal as of this time-author.] In the Kremlin they believe that all this could be perceived as the implementation of the strategic task of ousting Russia from the post-Soviet area, and they are suggesting that the United States cooperate in strengthening the "security zones" around Russia's borders so as to hinder the proliferation of international terrorism.[274]

But as long as it is not a democracy and an international law-breaker, Russia cannot expect to be acknowledged as a true member of the G-8 or any democratic club or as a great power, certainly not a great European power. Neither can it be exempted from what is now the common practice whereby all governments' internal policies are subjected to constant foreign scrutiny. And Russia, based on its record, certainly cannot be entrusted with an exclusive sphere of interest around its peripheries based on "security zones" when t is a prime fomenter of regional instability. Indeed, such policies only ensure the ultimate crash of the present Russian status quo.

Therefore that pressure for democratization must not only continue, it should grow and be regularly invoked by American leaders even as they seek to advance the grounds of human rights and adherence to democratic norms of conduct precisely because Russia and other Eurasian governments have signed all these treaties, going back to the Helsinki treaty of 1975. The cornerstone of our demand for this kind of policy is the basic building block of world order, namely the doctrine of Pacta Sunt Servanda (treaties must be obeyed). And the conditions that gave rise to those treaties with regard to democratization in Europe have not been fully overcome as Russian and even more Belarusian policy illustrate. Like it or not, Russia or its potential satellites cannot successfully pretend that they are being confronted with double standards, or talk about Russia being a sovereign democracy as it now does. The treaties now in effect clearly outline a diminution of unbridled sovereignty and arguably any recognized international treaty does so as well. That argument should be the cornerstone of our demands to treaty signatories coupled with meaningful sanctions, not just economic, for failure to uphold these treaties.

Of course, there are also equally good security or strategic reasons for upholding democratization at every turn even as we seek avenues for negotiation. It is not just because we believe, with considerable justification, that states which reach democracy are ultimately stronger, even if they have to cross through dangerous waters to get there, it also is that, as noted above, Russia shows no sign of wanting responsibility for its actions and their consequences, e.g., in the frozen conflicts in Moldova, Georgia, or in Ukraine, let alone its support for the repressive regimes of Central Asia or its arms sales abroad. To the extent that violence, crime, and authoritarian rule flourishes in these states, they are all at risk of upheaval, even sudden upheaval as we have seen in Georgia, Kyrgyzstan, Ukraine, and in the repeated manifestations of internal violence that shook Uzbekistan in 2004-05 and could easily do so again. Such violence and instability could easily spread to Russia as the example of Chechnya and the North Caucasus suggests.

Not pushing for reform even as we seek these states' security from attack by terrorists or from their incorporation in a Russian sphere of influence avails us little. For, as Tesmur Basilia, Special Assistant to former Georgian President Edvard Shevarnadze for economic issues, wrote, in many CIS countries, e.g., Georgia and Ukraine, "the acute issue of choosing between alignment with Russia and the West is associated with the choice between two models of social development."[275] Indeed, even some Russian analysts acknowledge the accuracy of this insight. Thus Dmitry Furman writes that, "The Russia-West struggle in the CIS is a struggle between two irreconcilable systems."[276] Indeed Furman even accepts the repressiveness of the current regime, saying that "Managed democracies are actually a soft variant of the Soviet system."[277]

The aptness of these observations transcends Georgia and Ukraine to embrace the entire post- Soviet region, since it is clear that Moscow opposes "exporting democracy" to it. Indeed, it regards the idea with contempt and thus attracts the local dictators who cleave to it for support against Western pressures for democratization.[278] Basilia also pointed to the local perception of Russia as security threat.

Nowadays there are many in the West who believe that Russia has changed—and, having reformed, seeks to interact with neighboring countries in conformity with international norms. Some Eurasian countries would disagree with this opinion, and believe instead that the Russian mentality has not changed much, and that Russia continues to deem the "near abroad" as its sphere of social influence. After the second war with Chechnya, many think that Russia regards violence as its major tool for resolving social and political problems, especially with regard to non-Russian peoples from the former empire. Thus integration into the international community should be viewed as a guarantee for security and further development.[279]

The current silence or relative silence on democratic issues facilities the exportation of Russia's sphere of influence and style of rule throughout the CIS, while strengthening Georgian, Ukrainian, and other democracies not only forestalls chances for internal upheaval in those states, it also rebuffs Russian imperialism and thus helps strengthen domestic Russian calls for reform. More urgently it reduces Russia's chances to engineer long-standing reversals of both Westernization and democratization in Ukraine and elsewhere, outcomes that only reduce security throughout the CIS.

The logic is the same as George Kennan's even if containment is not the policy choice here. By standing on the basis of international law and the democratic choice of those states' peoples, not our own unilateral and hegemonic power, and by working intensively with those states which wish the benefits of association with the West, we can create examples of progress that will resonate in Russia and elsewhere while checking the spread of deformations of governance that only add to Russia's and our own insecurity. NATO was and is correct in observing that its and the EU's expansions enlarge the domain of security in Europe and Eurasia to the benefit of Russia if not that of its elite which can only survive by imperialism and predation.

Ultimately then the tenacious, insistent, and unceasing proclamation by Russia of deviations from its own promised course of action are legally and strategically strongly founded and mutually invigorating. A strategy that engages not only Russia on its vital issues and agenda, but also the CIS on an equal basis with Russia and does so while unceasingly proclaiming that democratic values enshrined in treaties must be upheld, benefits everyone except Russia's rulers. But it certainly redounds to the benefit of the long- suffering Russian people.[280] Neither does it represent an effort to overthrow Russia unless one wants to accept at face value the self-serving pronunciamentos of the ruling group. What must be understood as a guiding strategic principle here is that Russian autocracy and its corollary, Russian imperialism, are the gravest security threats facing Eurasia (including Europe and Russia itself) and are ultimately incompatible with any progress of the Russian people, or Eurasia, to security, liberty, and prosperity.

Precisely because such a state constitutes a standing invitation to uncontrolled military adventurism — of which there has been much in Russia's brief history and not least due to the absence of democratic control over the power ministries—it has to be checked.[281] There is no contradiction between engaging Russia on the great issues of proliferation and arms control, and cooperating with it against the common enemy of terrorism, while at the same time insisting on its behaving according to European norms that it has accepted in the treaties it has signed, all with a view to integrating it with its European neighbors. While this is certainly difficult in practice, it is hardly less difficult than the policy we now are conducting which has left us attacked by unending crises with few if any governments willing to help us.

In fact, a policy that bases itself on treaties and laws rather than upon unilateral assertions of power is actually more effective than that alternative even if it means narrowing the scope of freedom of action for unilateral American ventures.[282] As Robert Wright's recent argument for reforming U.S. foreign policy in general towards what he calls progressive realism contends,

> There is principle here that goes beyond arms control: the national interest can be served by constraints on American behavior when they constrain other nations as well. This logic covers the spectrum of international governance, from global warming, (we'll cut carbon di-oxide emissions if you will) to war (we'll refrain from it if you will).[283]

Indeed, democratization is essential, first of all in regard to Russia's power agencies. The armed forces still regard NATO and the United States as their main enemies and their exercises confirm it, even to the point of often involving missile and nuclear strikes or large-scale conventional exercises against alleged terrorists. Second, although Putin and Ivanov have endeavored to restructure at least some of the armed forces to fight primarily against terrorist attacks, which are the current main threats to Russian security, this use of the military in a counterterrorist or counterintelligence force can have the most serious negative domestic outcomes as we have seen in Chechnya. Moreover, these forces could also easily be used, as Gorbachev and Yeltsin had sought to use them, i.e., against democratic reform at home.[284]

Third, the tendency to adventurism that led Moscow into its so called peacemaking operations in the Caucasus and Moldova have now embroiled it in situations where the threat of war, particularly with Georgia, is constant and where Russian policy seems mainly to consist of provocations of Tbilisi in order to get it to launch a violent conflict, or of responses to Tbilisi's own penchant for provocative acts.[285] So dangerous a policy inevitably has unforeseen consequences. The recent signs of military adventurism, buzzing Scotland, flights to Guam, the resumption of long-range air patrols, and submarine races to plant the flag of sovereignty in the Arctic, only serve the armed forces' myopic interest of "walking tall." They do nothing to enhance Russian security. And, finally, the lack of democratic control over the armed forces has been a constant and lethal aspect of Russian policy toward Chechnya which has resulted in frightful violations of human rights and which has generated in response a running series of low-intensity conflicts across the North Caucasus for which Moscow has no solution.

While democracy is not a panacea, it is safe to say that a democratically controlled military would have behaved differently as would its masters also. Indeed, it is arguable that what Russia's military fears most about NATO expansion is that it generates an external pressure that is supported by domestic reformers to democratize the entire range of Russian national security policy and subject it to civilian and democratic accountability under law, something that is anathema to that military-political elite.[286] Thus ultimately there are compelling geostrategic reasons why the vigorous and ongoing insistence on reforms as signed in international treaties is an essential and indispensable part of any sound Western policy toward Russia.

ENERGY POLICY

Every day Americans feel the lack of a sound energy policy. At the same time energy, in Putin's words, "is the heart of our economy." Thus, for Russia, its energy assets are the equivalent of a political Viagra making it seem that it is a great power and allowing the state and its servitors to amass fabulous wealth. Nonetheless, due to the organization of the Russian economy which follows the autocratic model of a rent seeking elite dealing with a rent-granting autocracy, it is very likely that by 2010, according to Russian analysts, Russia will be suffering from an energy shortage, in oil, gas, or electricity, if not all of these.[287] This also helps explain Putin's new nuclear power initiative.[288]

Neither the effort to blackmail Ukraine, the Baltic states, and Europe, nor Russia's need to dominate Central Asian and Caspian producers in order to retain its political-economic structure, is in America's interest. Neither are such policies in the interests of those states that would be victimized by such Russian policies, other key consumers like Europe and China, nor ultimately those of the Russian people who must bear the direct costs of an inefficient and autocratic petro economy, that is, in fact, growing more slowly than almost all the other post-Soviet states. Obviously, here we need to have a coherent and comprehensive domestic policy that reorients use of energy to more efficient systems, or other sources as they become affordable. But we should not delude ourselves that cheap oil or gas can return any time soon. This is due not only to our demand which is the greatest in the world, or to surging Asian demand, but also because approximately 80 percent, if not more, of world oil supplies are state-owned. These states are, except for Canada, Norway, and Great Britain, all too prone to use oil as a state weapon and turn into an economy dependent on energy rents. Cartels, in this environment, are the rule, not the exception.

Accordingly, Washington must fight fire with fire. It is already the case that numerous Asian and American scholars have called for an international energy association in the belief that such a system would not only alleviate North Korea's need for energy which it uses to justify its nuclear program, but also assist other Northeast Asian and Pacific states to satisfy their needs as well.[289] Such an organization also, or so they profess to believe, could lead to a stable structure or security discussions and peace in that region of the world.[290]

Whether or not that is the case remains to be seen. But it is quite important that China, Japan, South Korea, and India be integrated into global energy organizations and that the possibilities for energy rivalry with China, which fill policymakers here and in Beijing with anxiety be reduced.[291] Certainly one way to do so is to facilitate the integration of India and China into the International Energy Agency. Nevertheless, it clearly is in the geopolitical interests of Washington and its allies including the members of the International Energy Agency (IEA) to integrate the largest Asian consumers and do everything possible to persuade them of the benefits to them of such integration and of reliance on the global market compared to the wasteful and dangerous current practice of exclusive long-term supply deals.[292]

Another and possibly complementary tactic is to do everything possible to encourage national oil companies in other producer states and in consumer states to invest in increasing their productive capacity.[293] Indeed, the only way to do so is to demonstrate to Russia that its current method of oil and gas production cannot satisfy is own domestic needs, let alone the claims of importers who then remit to Russia valuable foreign currency. And without such investment at home and the accompanying transparency that it would generate, foreign direct investment in Russia's energy sector will not materialize, leaving it behind. If we cannot get the producers' attention in this fashion, it might be worthwhile to form the equivalent of a countercartel or at least a consumers' association through the IEA which would be made up of the EU, the United States, China, Japan, India, and South Korea, and which could influence the price of oil and/or gas by announcing that each member of the group a whole is prepared to buy its entire energy needs, or even a large percentage of them at a fair market price and auction, making sellers compete for those contracts. Obviously, to the extent that this is possible it forces prices downward.[294] Beyond forcing prices downward, this group should disseminate best technologies and practices among its members, allowing them to move toward ever greater efficiencies in energy use and to alternative sources of technology, particularly cleaner coal use which benefits the United States and China the most. Inasmuch as China has long been consciously seeking to reduce the energy intensity of its economy and per capita energy consumption, possesses enormous coal reserves, and is a large investor in alternative energy sources, such a policy would reduce demand and exercise downward pressures on prices.[295]

Third, such an organization would reduce the growing Sino-American tensions in the Gulf and Middle East which could contribute to an overall improvement in Sino-American relations and unite those governments around a compelling common interest.[296] Fourth, inasmuch as Russo-Chinese energy relations are tense and even rivalrous, if not a case of both sides seeking to exploit the other, such an organization would magnify those things that divide Russia and China while reducing those that divide China and America.[297] And since a new Russo-Chinese alliance is believed to be the greatest security threat we could face, this kind of outcome would represent no small achievement.[298]

Fifth, at the same time, such a solution would allow Russia to sell its oil and gas in Asia by creating a regularized forum at a fair market price and would help overcome the obstacles that have held back its ability to develop this market. If it stops trying to swindle its partners besides China, i.e., South Korea and Japan, as it has been doing for the last 3 years, it might actually get the investment it needs from them in return for a reasonable program of sales to them.[299] Then Russia would get a fair market price and could more easily participate in the regeneration of North Korea as part of any overall solution to its energy and security problems. Indeed, an energy association would answer Pyongyang's needs if it were to become serious about bargaining over its nuclear program. And facilitating such a settlement inviting Russia to become a major contributor to North Korea's future energy sources has long been a major objective of the Putin government.[300]

Russian participation under market conditions in such an arrangement would force reforms in its energy.industry, and thus its government. Such reforms might then allow for foreign investment, particularly in Siberia and its infrastructure, which is essential for the historical task of reviving Siberia, and rejuvenating Russia as a reliable Asian power. Russia would play a recognized role in a framework of security for Northeast Asia but it would not be able to blackmail its partners to the West and South because they would be able to build more pipelines to global markets and not be compelled to rely only on Russian pipelines. Finally, to the extent that the energy industry in Russia undergoes genuine reform and is unable to monopolize its customers, it will have to change. So, too, will the state; and hopefully other economic centers of excellence will arise in Russia, freeing it from its historic dependence upon a cash crop for export.

This strategy too depends upon transforming the external environment through creative U.S. statesmanship in order to effectuate change over time both in Russia and in the global order. In all cases of this strategy, whether it be proliferation or energy issues, the threat of force is existentially present as it always is, but it need not be invoked or called into play other than in cases of overwhelming threat. If carried through successfully, this strategy has the potential, in ways that force deployed unilaterally does not have, to bring about desirable changes over time in the world order on the basis of a shared consensus among America's partners operating under our leadership or in tandem with us.

CONCLUSIONS

We urgently need to rethink many of our policies, especially as they are linked to one another. To get Iran to renounce nuclear weapons, we must deal with Russia's plan for becoming a global center for nuclear power and spent fuel.[301] One could easily multiply such examples. But this very interconnectedness, plus the fact that the problems Russia poses are essentially nonmilitary and must not be allowed to reach that stage where they become military, call for a coordinated multidimensional strategy using all the instruments of power across a global backdrop. We cannot impose our favored form of regime upon Russia nor should we try, but we cannot passively allow it to flout international agreements and embark upon a course of autocracy, empire, and adventurism, that has repeatedly proven to be ruinous for its people and its neighbors.

Moreover, we cannot be either complacent or despairing. The oft-cited and even widely accepted ideas that we have little or no leverage, or its analogue that we need Moscow more than it needs us, are ridiculous.[302] Unfortunately those notions are tied to a belief that complex political issues can be solved in the blink of an eye, not by what Henry Kissinger called the "patient accumulation of nuance." Thus, some fallaciously argue that if we cannot fix the problem at once by Russia's capitulation to our pressure, it is supposedly hopeless to try. Yet it is clear that the agenda of issues with Russia goes far beyond strict bilateral U.S.-Russian relations in both geographical scope and complexity, and requires precisely a combination of patience and superior insight.

Neither can we yield to the opposing complacency that other issues are too urgent, or that we can wait for another time to tackle the Russian agenda, or that we can simply browbeat Russia because of our superior power and virtue. Conditions in Eurasia are already and rapidly becoming ever more crisis-prone. Russian analysts admit that Russia remains "a risk factor," not a reliable or autonomous pole of world politics.[303] The North Caucasus, as noted above, remains out of control, with some 250,000 Russian security personnel from the armed forces and Ministry of Interior, as well as the so-called multiple militaries being stationed there.[304] Russia's relations with Georgia could very easily spill over into active violent conflict over Georgia's breakaway province, Abkhazia, and South Ossetia, and its ties to Moldova are a permanent violation of the treaties it has signed with the West. In fact, at least some governments and militaries reject this complacency even if they defend against their anxieties sotto voce.

> Although never voiced publicly by elected European officials, there is concern about Russia. It is rarely announced as policy, but the force structure of the Bundeswehr — still, all these years after the end of the Cold War, organized to defend the homeland against tanks coming from the east—makes it obvious. In a way that frustrates and confounds its NATO partners, Germany still de facto prioritizes conventional territorial defense even if it pledges allegiance to the Petersberg tasks which presume force projection capabilities.[305]

Moreover, as former Secretary of State Colin Powell stated, in the current threat environment,

> This means we must do something statesmen have been reluctant to do since the birth of the modern state system. We have to understand and try to influence not just what states do outside their borders, but in some cases what goes on inside their borders. This marks a strategic rebalancing made necessary by circumstances.[306] (Italics in the original.)

Perhaps even more urgently, the current crisis in Ukraine which has brought the country to the brink of ungovernability, owes much to continuing Russian subversion and intervention there. If it is allowed to continue unchecked and the Ukrainian government is not strengthened to the point of being able to put its house in order, its democratization and Westernization processes will be set back for years. That not only means another quasi or virtual democracy as was the case before, but also a new satellite for Russia. Here we should always remember that Russia without Ukraine cannot threaten the peace of Europe because it is not an empire, just an aspirant to it. But with a Ukrainian satellite, Russia will be emboldened to carry further its efforts to destabilize neighboring regimes in Europe, only this time they will be NATO and EU members, Hungary, Romania, Slovakia, the Baltic states, and especially Poland. Finally, the condition of too many Central Asian states once their rulers depart the scene is too perilously close to violence or to failed state status to be complacent about trends in Central Asia. All these challenges, if not crises, are critical points in the East-West relationship because ultimately "The main reason why the West cannot remain complacent about Russia's actions is the fact that Russia's 'near abroad' is, in many cases, also democratic Europe's near abroad."[307]

In other words, time will not wait upon us. To quote David Ben-Gurion, "time works for us or against us depending on what we do with it." Neither will other states wait passively for us or let us off the hook of our responsibility, i.e., developing a coherent policy, the means to carry it out, and harmonizing it with our allies. Iraq cannot be the only issue in our foreign policy for it already bids fair to suck up all the oxygen needed to conduct a global security policy. In any case, neither Russia, its interlocutors, nor other states or issues will let us merely act in an ad hoc tactical fashion with no thought for long-term consequences or strategy. Like it or not America, for better or worse, is in Colin Gray's term "the sheriff" of world order.[308] We, as Lincoln said, "hold the responsibility and bear the burden." Therefore it is incumbent upon us to exercise this responsibility for and to the world judiciously, but we cannot let it evaporate due to inattention, fecklessness, or the lack of a strategic approach to our interests and those responsibilities.

REFERENCES

[1] "Russian Foreign Policy: A Chronology, April-June, 2007," Defence Academy of the United Kingdom, www.defac.ac.uk/colleges/ csrc/documen t-lis tin gs/russian-chronologies/a-russian-chronologyapril-june-2007/?searchterm=a%20russian %20chronology, p. 37.

[2] John Vinocur, "Politicus: America's Misplaced Hopes on Russia," International Herald Tribune, September 10, 2007, www.iht. com.

[3] Radio Free Europe Radio Liberty Newsline, September 10, 2007, September 11, 2007.

[4] Moscow, Agents tvo Voyennykh Novstey Internet Version, in English, May 16, 2007, Open Source Committee, Foreign Broadcast Information Service Central Eurasia (Henceforth FBIS SOV), May 16, 2007; Moscow, Ministry of Foreign Affairs Internet Version, Press Conference of Foreign Minister Sergei Lavrov with Secretary of State Condoleezza Rice, May 16, 2007, www.mid.ru.

[5] Tehran, Mehr News Agency Internet Version, in English, May 14, 2007, FBIS SOV, May 14, 2007.

[6] "Speech and the Following Discussion at the Munich Conference on Security, February 10, 2007," www.kremlin.ru/eng/ speeches/2007/02/10/0138; Poslanie Federal'nomu Sobraniiu Rossiiskoi Federatsii, April 26, 2007, www.kremlin.ru/speeches/2007/04/26. (Henceforth Poslanie).

[7] Vystuplenie na Voyennom Parade v Chest' 62-I Godovoshchiny Pobedy v Velikoi Otechestvennoi Voine, May 9, 2007, www.kremlin. ru/appears/2007/05/09/ 1127_type63374type82634type122381_12775 7.shtml.

[8] Poslanie.

[9] "CFE Treaty on Verge of Collapse, Iran Threat Overblown- Russian Gen," RIA Novosti, May 10, 2007.

[10] Viktor Litovkin, "In the Language of Ultimatums," Nezavisimaya Gazeta, June 25, 2007, retrieved from Johnson's Russia List, JRL #2007-140, June 25, 2007.

[11] Thom Shanker, " Russian Pullback on Arms Treaty Obscures Progress, Official Says," New York Times, July 16, 2007, www.nytimes.com.

[12] Moscow, Agentstvo Voyennykh Novostey, Internet Version, in English, July 2, 2007, FBIS SO V, July 2, 2007.

[13] Alex Rodriguez, "Rice Begins Russian Visit as Tensions Rise With U.S. Kremlin Growing Bolder With Criticism," Chicago Tribune, May 15, 2007.

[14] Moscow, Ekho Moskvy, in Russian, February 17, 2007, Open Source Committee, FBIS SOV, February 17, 2007.

[15] Yuri Ushakov, "From Russia With Like," Los Angeles Times, February 1, 2007, www.latimes.com.

[16] Vladimir Isachenkov, "Top Russian General Calls U.S. Expansion Top National Security Threat," Associated Press, February 9, 2007.

[17] Apart from works already cited, see Sergei M. Rogov, "A Strategic Partnership Is Still Possible," Moscow, Nezavisimaya Gazeta, in Russian, March 19, 2007, FBIS SOV, March 19, 2007.

[18] "Speech and the Following Discussion at the Munich Conference on Security," February 10, 2007

[19] Moscow, Vesti TV, in Russian, March 17, 2007, FBIS SOV, March 17, 2007; "Address by Russian Foreign Minister at Moscow University," Moscow, Ministry of Foreign Affairs Website (www.mil. ru), February 21, 2007.

[20] FBIS SOV, February 17, 2007.

[21] Moscow, Ministry of Foreign Affairs Internet Version, "Russian President Addresses Munich Forum, Answers Questions on Iran, February 12, 2007," FBIS SOV, February 12, 2007, the question and answer session from which these remarks are taken is not on the kremlin.ru website.

[22] "Interview with General Yuri Baluyevsky, First Deputy Defense Minister and Chief of the Russian Federation Armed Forces General Staff," Moscow, Rossiyskaya Gazeta, February 21, 2007, FBIS SO V, February 21, 2007.

[23] FBIS SOV, February 12, 2007; "Speech and the Following Discussion at the Munich Conference on Security," February 10, 2007.

[24] Vladimir Olegovich Rukavishnikov, "Values, Interests and Threats in U.S. and Russian Grand Strategies and Politics," Review of International Affairs, (Belgrade), No. 1118, April-June, 2005, p. 60.

[25] Steve Gutterman, "Russian Calls U.S. 'Difficult'," Associated Press, February 4, 2007.

[26] "U.S. Influence in World Affairs Weakening-Russian FM," RIA Novosti, March 17, 2007.

[27] "Russian Foreign Minister Acknowledges Growing Divergence with US," Mosnews, December 5, 2005, cited in Andrew Monaghan, "'Calmly Critical': Evolving Russian Views of US Hegemony," Journal of Strategic Studies, Vol. XXIX, No. 6, December, 2006, p. 988.

[28] Radio Free Europe Radio Liberty Newsline, March 6, 2007.

[29] Sergei Lavrov, "Global Politics Needs Openness and Democracy," Izvestiya, in Russian, April 24, 2007, FBIS SOV, April 24, 2007.

[30] John Lukacs, George Kennan: A Study in Character, New Haven, CT: Yale University Press, 2007, p. 58.

[31] Vice-Admiral John M. McConnell (RET), Director of National Intelligence, Annual Threat Assessment of the Director of National Intelligence for the Senate Armed Services Committee, Washington, DC, February 27, 2007.

[32] Prepared Statement of Secretary of Defense Robert Gates to the Senate Armed Services Committee, February 6, 2007, www. senate.gov.

[33] "Russia Starts Producing Topol-M Missile," AGENCE FRANCE-PRESSE, June 26, 2007.

[34] See, for example, Janusz Bugajski, Cold Peace: Russia's New Imperialism: Washington, DC: Center for Strategic and International Studies, Westport, CT: Praeger, 2004; Richard Krickus, Iron Troikas, Carlisle Barracks, PA: Strategic Studies Institute, U.S. Army War College, 2006; Keith C. Smith, Russian Energy Politics in the Baltics, Poland, and the Ukraine: A New Stealth Imperialism?, Washington, DC: Center for Strategic and International Studies, 2004; and Lincoln P. Bloomfield Jr., "Politics and Diplomacy of the Global Defense Posture Review," Carnes Lord, ed., Reposturing the Force: U. S. Overseas Presence in the Twenty-First Century, Newport, RI: Naval War College Press, 2006, pp. 57-58.

[35] Dmitri Trenin, "Russia Redefines Itself and Its Relations With the West," Washington Quarterly, Vol. XXX, No. 2, pp. 95- 105.

[36] Pavel Felgenhauer, "Russia's Imperial General Staff," Perspective, Vol. XVI, No. 1, October-November, 2005, www.bu.ed./ iscip/vol16/felgenhauer.

[37] Moscow, Agentstvo Voyennykh Novostey, Internet Version, in English, February 14, 2007, FBIS SO V, February 14, 2007.

[38] "Putin Interviewed by Journalists from G8 Countries- Text," www.kremlin.ru, June 4, 2007, retrieved from Nexis-Lexis.

[39] Moscow, Internet web Digest, in Russian, January 31, 2007, FBIS SOV, January 31, 2007; "Interview With Yuri Baluyevsky by Yuri Gavrilov," Moscow, Rossiyskaya Gazeta, in Russian, February 21, 2007, FBIS SOV, February 21, 2007.

[40] Viktor Litovkin, "V Yazyke Ultimatov," Nezavisimaya Gazeta, June 25, 2007; Viktor Yuzbashev, "Illusory Moratorium," Moscow, Nezavisimoye Voyennoye Obozreniye, in Russian, May 30, 2007, FBIS SOV, May 31, 2007; Remarks of Colonel Albert Zaccor to the Conference, "The Role of the Black Sea Region in the Transatlantic Security Agenda," Center for Strategic and International Studies, Washington, DC, June 21, 2007.

[41] Martin Walker, "NATO Means Business To Protect Pipelines," UPI, October 13, 2005; "US Missile Plans 'A Clear threat' to Moscow: Russian General," AFP, January 22, 2007; "NATO Should Play Greater Energy Security Role, Envoy," www. serbinna.com, June 29, 2007.

[42] Zaccor.

[43] Ibid.

[44] "Russia Says US Democracy Criticisms is Unfair," Reuters, June 29, 2007.

[45] "No final decision to quit INF treaty-FM Lavrov," RIA Novosti, February 16, 2007; "Russia Made a Mistake By Scrapping Its Mid-Range Missiles-Ivanov," Moscow, Interfax, in English, February 7, 2007, FBIS SOV, February 7, 2007.

[46] Moscow, ITAR-TASS in Englsih, February 26, 2007, FBIS SO V, February 26, 2007.

[47] Ibid.

[48] Ibid.

[49] Sergei Gavrov, "Is the Transition to Authoritarianism Irreversible?" Russian Social Science Review, Vol. XKVIII, No. 3, May-June, 2007, pp. 22-23.

[50] "Speech and the Following Discussion at the Munich Conference on Security, February 10, 2007"; Poslanie; Open Source Committee, OSC Analysis, "Russian Commentators Debate 'Besieged Fortress' Rhetoric," FBIS SOV, June 22, 2007.

[51] Philip Hanson, "The Turn to Statism in Russian Economic Policy," The International Spectator, Vol. XLII, No. 1, March, 2007, pp. 54-55.

[52] "Russian Commentators Debate 'Besieged Fortress' Rhetoric."

[53] Vladimir Dvorkin, The Russian Debate on the Nonproliferation of Weapons of Mass Destruction and Delivery Vehicles, No. 4, Cambridge, MA: Harvard University, Belfer Center for Science and International Affairs, 2004, p. 23.

[54] Bruce Jackson, "The Soft War for Europe's East," Policy Review, No. 137, June-July, 2006, www.hoover.org/publications/ policyreview/3202956.html.

[55] Robert Kagan, "End of Dreams, Return of History," Policy Review, No. 144, August-September, 2007, p. 31.

[56] See the remarks of Blair Ruble, Director of the Kennan Institute for Advanced Russian Studies, Moscow, Vremya Novostey, in Russian, July 2, 2007, FBIS SOV, July 2, 2007.

[57] Joseph Ferguson, "U.S.-Russia Relations: Energy and Strategy," Comparative Connections, July-September, 2006, p. 1, available from www.pacnet.org.

[58] 58Sergey Strokan, "No More Gushers and Summertime Summits," Moscow, Kommersant, in Russian, February 5, 2007, FBIS SOV, February 5, 2007; Fyodor Lukanov, "Where to Focus If Your Are Expecting Change," Moscow Times, February 7, 2007; Rodriguez.

[59] Audrius Baciulis, "Interview With Foreign Minister Antanas Valioinis," Vilnius, Veidas, in Lithuanian, December 29, 2005, FBIS SO V, December 29, 2005.

[60] Testimony of Walter Slocombe, The Future of the North Atlantic Treaty Organization (NATO): Subcommittee Hearing on Airland Forces, Armed Forces Committee, U.S. Senate, 104th Congress, First Session, April 5, 1995, Washington, DC: U.S. Government Printing Office, 1996, p. 5.

[61] Andrew A. Michta, The Limits of Alliance: The United States, NATO, and the EU in North and Central Europe, Lanham, MD: Rowman and Littlefield Publishers, 2006, p. 93.

[62] Kagan, p. 38.

[63] David Kerr, "The Sino-Russian Partnership and U.S. Policy Toward North Korea, "From Hegemony to Concert in Northeast Asia," International Studies Quarterly, Vol. XXXXIX, No. 3, September, 2005, pp. 411-437.

[64] Robert Jervis, "U.S. Grand Strategy: Mission Impossible," Naval War College Review, Summer 1998, pp. 22-36; Richard K. Betts, "Power, Prospects, and Priorities: Choices for Strategic Change," Naval War College Review, Winter 1997, pp. 9-22; John C.

Gannon, "Intelligence Challenges Through 2015," odci.gov/cia/ publicaffairs /speeches /gannon_speech_05022000.html.

[65] Constantine C. Menges, China: The Gathering Threat, Nashville, TN: Nelson Current Publishers, 2005.

[66] Ibid; Kerr, pp. 411-437; Minxin Pei, Assertive Pragmatism: China's Economic Rise and its Impact on Chinese Foreign Policy, Proliferation Papers, Institut Francais des Relations Internationales (IFRI), 2006, p. 17, www.ifri.org.

[67] Kim Yo'ng Hu'i, "The Relevance of Central Asia," Seoul JoongAng Ilbo Internet Version, in English, July 11, 2005, FBIS SOV, July 11, 2005.

[68] Lyle Goldstein and Vitaly Kozyrev, "China, Japan. and the Scramble for Siberia," Survival, Vol. XLVIII, No. 1, Spring, 2006, pp. 175-176.

[69] John J. Tkacik, Jr., "How the PLA Sees North Korea," Andrew Scobell and Larry M. Wortzel, eds., Shaping China's Security Environment: The Role of the People's Liberation Army, Carlisle Barracks, PA: Strategic Studies Institute, U.S. Army War College, 2006, pp. 160-163.

[70] James Brian McNabb, "The Unanticipated Utility of U.S. Security Structures: Avoiding Cold War II in Central Asia," Comparative Strategy, Vol. XXV, No. 4, October-December, 2006, pp. 307-327.

[71] Lukanov; Strokan, FBIS SO V, February 5, 2007; "Russia: U.S. Election Expected to Chill Relations Further," Radio Free Europe Radio Liberty, November 9, 2006; Sergei Rogov, "Washington's Attitude Toward Us Won't Change," Moscow, Izvestiya, in Russian, November 9, 2006, FBIS SOV, November 9, 2006. Rogov is the director of the Institute for the Study of the United States and Canada (ISKAN) in Moscow.

[72] Moscow, ITAR-TASS, in Russian, July 6, 2006, FBIS SOV, July 6, 2006; Andrei Zolotov, Jr., "Russia Experts Granted Ample Answers to Softball Questions," Russia Profile, September 10, 2006, quoted in Johnson's Russia List, No. 204-2006, September 10, 2006; Stephen Boykevich, "Putin Says Russia Doesn't Need Any Lectures," Moscow Times, July 17, 2006, retrieved from LexisNexis.

[73] John B. Dunlop, "Storm in Moscow: A Plan of the Yeltsin 'Family' to Destabilize Russia," Paper Presented to the Project on Systemic Change and International Security in Russia and the New States of Eurasia, Johns Hopkins University, Nitze School of Advanced International Studies, Washington, DC, 2004.

[74] Ibid; Stephen Blank, "The 18th Brumaire of Vladimir Putin," in Uri Ra'anan, ed., Flawed Succession: Russia's Power Transfer Crises, Foreword by Robert Conquest, Lanham, MD: Lexington Books for Rowman and Littlefield, 2006, pp. 133-170.

[75] Wojciech Kononczuk, "The 'Yukos Affair,' Its Motives and Implications," No. 24, Warsaw: Center for Eurasian Studies, 2006, www.osw.waw.pl.

[76] Gavrov, pp. 22-23; Lilia Shevtsova, Putin's Russia, Antonia Bouis, trans., Revised and Expanded Edition, Washington, DC: Carnegie Endowment for International Peace, 2005.

[77] Vitaly Shlykov, "The Economics of Defense in Russia and the Legacy of Structural Militarization," in Steven E. Miller and Dmitri Trenin, eds., The Russian Military: Power and Purpose, Cambridge, MA: MIT Press, 2004, pp. 160-182; Vitaly Shlykov, "The Anti-Oligarchy Campaign and its Implications for Russia's Security," European Security, Vol. XVII, No. 2, 2004, pp. 11-128; Leonid Kosals, "Criminal Influence/Criminal Control Over the Russian Military-Industrial Complex in the

Context of Global Security," NATO Defense College Research Paper, No. 1, March 2004, pp. 6-8; "Moscow," Ekho Moskvy in Russian, June 4, 2004, FBIS SOV, June 4, 2004; Moscow, ITAR-TASS, April 14, 2005, FBIS SOV April 14, 2005; Moscow Center TV in Russian, September 30, 2003; FBIS SO V, October 1, 2003; Moscow, Moskovskaya Pravda, in Russian, April 17, 2003, FBIS SOV, April 17, 2003; Moscow, "Interview With OAO Gipromez General Director Vitaly Rogozhin, "Rossiyskaya Gazeta, in Russian, July 13, 2005, FBIS SOV, July 13, 2005; Bugajski, Cold Peace; Krickus; Smith.

[78] Interview With Director General of the Political Technologies Center, Igor Bunin, Ezhednevnaya Gazeta, March 26, 2004, www.fednews.ru.

[79] Stephen E. Hanson, "The Uncertain Future of Russia's Weak State Authoritarianism," East European Politics and Societies, Vol. XXI, No. 1, January, 2007, p. 69.

[80] Timofei Bordachev, "Russia's Europe Dilemma: Democratic Partner vs. Authoritarian Satellite," Andrew Kuchins and Dmitri Trenin, eds., Russia: The Next Ten Years, A Collection of Essays to Mark Ten Years of the Carnegie Moscow Center, Moscow: Carnegie Center, 2004, p. 120.

[81] Jim Rutenberg, "Putin Offers to Expand Plan for Missile Defense," www.nytimes.com, July 2, 2007.

[82] Peter Finn, "In Russia A Secretive Force Widens: Putin Led Regrouping of Security Services," Washington Post, December 12, 2006, p. A25; Nicole Gallina, Law and Order in Russia: The Well-Arranged Police State, International Relations and Security Network, www.isn.ethz.ch, 2007, makes the explicit connection between the tsarist police state rooted in German cameralism of the XVII-XVIII centuries and Putin's Russia.

[83] Hanson, pp. 76-77.

[84] Lilya Shevtsova, "Anti-Westernism Is the New National Idea," The Moscow Times, August 7, 2007, p. 9.

[85] Vladimr Shlapentokh, "Are Today's Authoritarian Leaders Doomed to Be Indicted When They Leave Office? The Russian and Other Post-Soviet Cases," Communist and Post-Communist Studies, Vol. XXXIX, No. 2, Autumn, 2006, pp. 462-463.

[86] Minxin Pei, Assertive Pragmatism: China's Economic Rise and Its Impact on Chinese Foreign Policy, IFRI Proliferation Papers, No. 15, Paris, Institut Francais des Relations Internationales, 2006, p. 17, www.ifri.org.

[87] "Experts Say 'Main External Threat' to Russia Coming From US, Central Asia," RIA Novosti, October 2, 2005.

[88] Moscow, ITAR-TASS, in English, June 28, 2006, FBIS SO V, June 28, 2006; Jim Hoagland, "Don't Give Up on Russia," Washington Post, November 17, 2006, p. A25.

[89] "Press Conference Following Talks With German Chancellor Angela Merkel," Bocharov Ruchei, Sochi, January 21, 2007, www.kremlin.ru /eng /speeches /2007 /01/21/1910.

[90] Sergei Lavrov, "Russian Foreign Policy Going Strong," Moscow, Vesti TV, in Russian, September 1, 2006; FBIS SO V, September 1, 2006; FBIS SO V, April 24, 2007.

[91] Colonel A. A. Paderin, "Policy and Military Strategy: A Unity Lesson," Military Thought, in English, June 30, 2006, FBIS SOV, July 14, 2006.

[92] Alexei Pico, "Washington-Style Forecasting: Has a Chill Come to US-Russian Relations," Moscow, Krasnaya Zvezda, in Russian, June 10, 2006, FBIS SOV, June 10,

2006; Open Source Center, "Analysis: Anti-US Rhetoric Grows in Russia," FBIS SO V, July 11, 2006.

[93] Richard Weitz, Russian-American Security Cooperation After St. Petersburg: Challenges and Opportunities, Carlisle Barracks, PA: Strategic Studies Institute, U.S. Army War College, 2007; Gunnar Arbman and Charles Thornton, Russia's Tactical and Nuclear Weapons Part I: Background and Policy Issues, Stockholm, Swedish Defense Research Agency, 2003, Part II: Technical Issues and Policy Recommendations, Stockholm: Swedish Defense Research Agency, 2005.

[94] Weitz; "Russia Starts Producing Topol-M Missile."

[95] Ibid.

[96] Baluyevsky, "This Shield Is Aimed Against Russia," Warsaw, Dziennik, in Polish, September 6, 2006, FBIS SOV, September 8, 2006.

[97] Simon Saradzhyan, "Military to Get $189BN Overhaul," Moscow Times, February 8, 2007; "Russia to Put 50 Topol-M Millie Systems on Duty Before 2015, "RIA Novosti, February 7, 2007; Vladimir Isachenkov, "Weapons Plan Strives to Beat Soviet Readiness," Washington Times, February 8, 2007, p. 13; "Russian Defense Chief Unveils Army Spending Spree," defensenews.com, February 8, 2007.

[98] "Osnovnye Polozheniia Voennoi Doktriny Rossiiskoi Federatsii," Rossiiskie Vesti, November, 19, 1993.

[99] Pavel Felgenhauer, "Ivanov Comment Suggests Moscow Ignoring Nuclear Weapons Agreement with Washington," Eurasian Daily Monitor, September 13, 2006.

[100] "Russia Wants U.S. To Sign Deal Saying Militaries Don't Target Each Other," Associated Press, February 6, 2007.

[101] Ibid.

[102] "Analysis Russian Reactions to US Missile Defense Plan," OSC Analysis, FBIS SOV, February 8, 2007, Bloomfield, pp. 57-58.

[103] The treaty and accompanying documentation can be found at www.state.gov/t/ac/trt/18016.htm.

[104] "U.S. Air Shield Possible Only With Russia's Involvement, FM," RIA Novosti, March 23, 2007.

[105] Moscow, ITAR-TASS, in English, July 2, 2007, FBIS SOV, July 2, 2007.

[106] Baluyevsky Interview, FBIS SOV, February 21, 2007.

[107] "Interview with Foreign Minister Sergei Lavrov," Rossisyskaya Gazeta, February 21-28, 2007, www.mid.ru.

[108] Nuclear Posture Review www.globalsecurity.org/wmd/ library/policy/dod/npr.htm; Kerry M. Kartcher, "U.S. Nuclear Weapons and Nonproliferation: Dispelling the Myths," Presentation to the Carnegie Moscow Center, February 2, 2007, available at www.carnegie.ru/en/pubs/media/101192007.02.02.Presentation.ppt.

[109] Alexei Arbatov and General (Ret.) Vladimir Dvorkin, Beyond Nuclear Deterrence: Transforming the U.S.-Russian Equation, Washington, DC: Carnegie Endowment for International Peace, 2006, John F. Steinbruner, Foreword.

[110] FBIS SOV, February 26, 2007.

[111] "U.S. Air Shield Possible Only With Russia's Involvement, FM."

[112] David S. McDonough, "Nuclear Superiority: The 'New Triad' and the Evolution of Nuclear Strategy," Adelphi Paper, No. 383, 2006; Keir A. Lieber and Daryl G. Press, "The Rise of U.S. Nuclear Primacy," Foreign Affairs, Vol. LXXXV, No. 2, March-

April 2006, pp. 42-54; Keir A. Lieber and Daryl G. Press, "The End. of MAD?: The Nuclear Dimensions of U.S. Primacy," International Security, Vol. XX, No. 4, Spring 2006, pp. 7-44; George Bunn and Christopher F. Chyba, eds., U. S. Nuclear Policy: Confronting Today's Threats, Foreword, William J. Perry, Washington, DC: Brookings Institution Press, 2006.

[113] David McDonough, "The US Nuclear Shift to the Pacific," RUSI Journal, April, 2006, pp. 64-68.

[114] Report of the Defense Science Board Task Force on Nuclear Capabilities: Report Summary, Washington, DC: Office of the Under Secretary of Defense for Acquisition, Technology, and Logistic, December 2006, pp. 11-12.

[115] Ibid., pp. 12-13.

[116] Ibid.

[117] "US Report Warns of Russian Nuclear Threat," Jane's Intelligence Digest, January 26, 2007, jid.janes.com.

[118] Igor Plugtarev and Viktor Myasnikov, "Vice Prime Minister Sergey Ivanov, Governors, and Twenty Thousand Soldiers," Moscow, Nezavisimoye Voyennoye Obozreniye, in Russian, September 29, 2006, FBIS SOV, October 4, 2006.

[119] Aktual'nye Zadachi Razvitie Vooruzhennykh Sil' Rossiiskoi Federatsii, Moscow, 2003, www.mil.ru (Henceforth Aktual'nye Zadachi).

[120] Lieber and Press, "The Rise of U.S. Nuclear Primacy," pp. 42-54; Lieber and Press, "The End of MAD?: The Nuclear Dimensions of U.S. Primacy," pp. 7-44.

[121] Mcdonough, "The US Nuclear Shift to the Pacific," p. 68.

[122] Dvorkin, p. 9.

[123] Kartcher.

[124] For example, "US Missile Plans 'A Clear Threat' to Moscow: Russian General," AFP, January 22, 2007; "Russia Questions Target of US Anti-Missile Shield," Reuters, January 24, 2007; Sergei Blagov, "Iran threat Hovers Over US-Russia Missile Dispute," CNSNews.com www.crosswalk.comnew/1465996.html, January 29, 2006; Radio Free Europe Radio Liberty Newsline, January 25, 2007.

[125] "Interview With Russian Foreign Minister Sergey Lavrov: We Want to Be Heard," Der Spiegel, February 5, 2007, Johnson's Russia List, 2007-#30, February 7, 2007.

[126] "Threat to Russia May Come From Several Sides," ITARTass, February 9, 2007, retrieved from Lexis-Nexis; Baluyevsky, "The Shield Is Aimed Against Russia," FBIS SOV, September 8, 2006.

[127] Ibid; "Russia's Ivanov Slams U.S. Missile Shield Plans in Europe," RIA Novosti, February 9, 2007, "Press Conference with Political Analyst Alexei Arbatov and Vice President of the Academy of Geopolitical Problems Leonid Ivashov on Russian Foreign Policy," RIA Novosti, February 6, 2007, www.fednews. ru; Alexei Arbatov, "An Unnecessary and Dangerous Step," Nezavisimoye Voyennoye Obozreniye, No. 7, March, 2007, www. america-russia.net/eng/security/143683092.

[128] Ibid.; "Russia Wants U.S. To Sign Deal Saying Militaries Don't Target Each Other," Associated Press, February 6, 2007.

[129] Secretary of State Condoleeza Rice, "Interview on Fox News Sunday With Chris Wallace," February 25, 2007, www.state. gov/secretary/rm/2007/feb/81037.htm.

[130] Lieber and Press, "The Rise of U.S. Nuclear Primacy," pp. 42-54; Lieber and Press, "The End of MAD?: The Nuclear Dimensions of U.S. Primacy," pp. 7-44.

[131] Nikolai Sokov, "Second thoughts About a First Strike," Nonproliferation Review, Vol. XIV, No. 1, March, 2007, p. 141.
[132] Stephen Blank, The NATO-Russian Partnership: A Marriage of Convenience or a Troubled Partnership? Carlisle Barracks, PA: Strategic Studies Institute, U.S. Army War College, 2006.
[133] Moscow, Agentstvo Voyennykh Novostey Internet Version, in English, February 10, 2006, FBIS SOV, February 10, 2006.
[134] Felgenhauer.
[135] Nikolay Poroskov, "The Last Argument of the Generals: The Topic of Tactical Nuclear Weapons Will Continue to Be Raised Repeatedly," Voyenno-Promyshlennyi Kurier, in Russian, July 19, 2006, FBIS SOV, July 19, 2006.
[136] "Interview With Russian Foreign Minister Sergey Lavrov: We Want to Be Heard."
[137] Rukavishnikov, p. 60.
[138] "Bush Troop Redeployment Plan: A Threat to Russia?" pp. 1-4.
[139] Blank, The NATO-Russian Partnership: A Marriage of Convenience or a Troubled Partnership?
[140] For example, "Russian Defense Minister Calls START Treaty 'Cold War Relic'," Moscow, ITAR-TASS in Russian, February 11, 2007, FBIS SOV, February, 11, 2007.
[141] "Sergey Lavrov: CFE Treaty No Longer Relevant," The Moscow Times, February 19, 2007; Poslanie; "CFE Treaty on Verge of Collapse, Iran Threat Overblown-Russian Gen."
[142] Guy Dinmore, Demetri Sevatopulo, and Hubert Wetzel; "Russia Confronted Rumsfeld With Threat to Quit Key Nuclear Treaty," Financial Times, March 9, 2005, p. 1.
[143] "Scrapping Medium-Range Ballistic Missiles a MistakeIvanov-1," RIA Novosti, February 7, 2007.
[144] Demetri Sevastopoulo, Neil Buckley, and Daniel Dombey, "Russia Threatens to Quit Arms Treaty," Financial Times, February 15, 2007, www.ft.com.
[145] Martin Sieff, "Russia Rattles Missile Treaty," UPI, March 2, 2006.
[146] Interfax, February 27, 2006.
[147] Sokov, p. 141.
[148] Smith, p. 13.
[149] "US Defense Chief Sees Problems in Russian Withdrawal from INF," ITAR-TASS, February 16, 2007.
[150] "The ISCIP Analyst," Vol. XIII, No. 9, March 8, 2007, Boston, MA: Institute for the Study of Conflict, Ideology, and Policy, Boston University, www.bu.edu/iscip.
[151] "Cold War was 'Paradise' Compared to Modern Threats — Ivanov," RIA Novosti, January 16, 2007; Sergei Ivanov, "Russia Must Be Strong," Wall Street Journal, January 11, 2006, p. 14.
[152] "Russia's Angry New Military Doctrine," Jane's Intelligence Digest, August 2007.
[153] "Annual Address to the Federal Assembly of the Russian Federation," May 10, 2006, www.kremlin.ru/eng/ speeches/2006/05/10/1823_type70029type82912_105566.shtml.
[154] Ibid.
[155] Ibid.
[156] Ibid.
[157] China's National Defense in 2004, Beijing: State Council Information Office, December 27, 2004, pp. 2-4; China's National Defense in 2006, Beijing: State Council

Information Office, December 29, 2006, pp. 2-4, www.chinadaily.com.cn /china/2006-12/29/content_771191.htm.
[158] Moscow, Nezavisimoye Voyennoye Obozreniye, in Russian, December 5, 2003, FBIS SO V, December 5, 2003.
[159] Moscow, ITAR-TASS, in English, October 2, 2003, FBIS SO V, October 3, 2003.
[160] Moscow, Interfax in Russian, October 2, 2003, FBIS SOV, October 3, 2003.
[161] Conversations with Russian officials and analysts in Moscow and Helsinki, June 1999; Martin Nesirsky, "Russia Says Threshold Lower for Nuclear Weapons," Reuters, December 17, 1999.
[162] Aktual'nye Zadachi, pp. 16, 18.
[163] Viktor Myasnikov, "The Time of Nuclear Truncheons Has Passed," Moscow, Nezavisismoye Voyennoye Obozreniye, in Russian, July 7, 2006, FBIS SOV, July 7, 2006; Amy F. Woolf, "Nuclear Arms Control: The Strategic Offensive Reductions Treaty," Congressional Research Service, Report to Congress, January 3, 2007, RL31448, pp. 21-22; Peter Baker and Robin Wright, "U.S. and Russia Vow Further Cuts in Nuclear Arms," Washington Post, July 4, 2007, p. 12.
[164] Vladimir Putin, Speech at Meeting with the Ambassadors and Permanent Representatives of the Russian Federation, Ministry of Foreign Affairs, Moscow, June 27, 2006, www.president. ru.
[165] FBIS SOV, September 1, 2006.
[166] Ibid.; Viktor Yasmann and Liz Fuller, "Russia Threatens to Withdraw from the CFE Treaty," Radio Free Europe Radio Liberty Russian Political Weekly, Vol. VI, No. 2, January 26, 2006.
[167] Sergei Ivanov, "Maturing Partnership," NATO Review, Winter, 2005, www.nato.int/docu/review/2005/issue4/english/special. htm; Baluyevsky, "NATO Expansion Will Strike a Fatal Blow to the Treaty on Conventional Arms in Europe," Izvestiya, March 3, 2004, retrieved from Lexis-Nexis.
[168] Todd W. Fields, "Eastward Bound: The Strategy and Politics of Repositioning U.S. Military Bases in Europe," Journal of Public and International Affairs, Vol. XV, Spring 2004, p. 88.
[169] Ibid.; see also Zaccor's remarks.
[170] "Moscow's Plan To Build Military Base in Moldova Rejected-Voronin," Interfax, October 30, 2005.
[171] Gunnar Arbman and Charles Thornton, Russia's Tactical and Nuclear Weapons Part I: Background and Policy Issues, Stockholm, Swedish Defense Research Agency, 2003; Part II: Technical Issues and Policy Recommendations, Stockholm: Swedish Defense Research Agency, 2005.
[172] Sergei Ivanov, "Russia Must Be Strong," Wall Street Journal, January 11, 2006, p. 14.
[173] Vitaly Moroz, "Konstantin Sivkov of the Center of Military Strategic Studies of the General Staff is Worried by the Threat Posed by NATO," Krasnaya Zvezda, July 13, 2005, p. 1.
[174] Ibid.
[175] Ivanov, "Russia Must Be Strong," p. 14.
[176] "Minister Wants Full Transparency in Russian-NATO Relations," Baltic News Service, December 27, 2005, retrieved from Lexis-Nexis; Ivanov, "Maturing Partnership."
[177] Arbatov, "An Unnecessary and Dangerous Step."

[178] Peter Baker, "U.S. and Russia to Enter Civilian Nuclear Pact," Washington Post, July 8, 2006, p. A1.

[179] "RF President Putin's Speech to the Federal Assembly, May 10, 2006"; Baker and Wright, p. 12.

[180] Nicholas Kralev, "Russia, U.S. to Discuss START," Washington Times, March 6, 2007.

[181] "Confronting Today's Threats," George Bunn and Christopher H. Chyba, eds., U.S. Nuclear Weapons Policy, Washington, DC: Brookings Institution Press, 2006.

[182] Stephen Blank, "Undeterred: The Return of Nuclear War," Georgetown Journal of International Affairs, Vol. I, No. 2, Summer/ Fall, 2000, pp. 55-63.

[183] Phillip Bobbitt, The Shield of Achilles: War, Peace, and the Course of History, New York: Alfred A. Knopf, 2002, pp. 634-638; Caroline Kennedy-Pipe and Stephen Welch, "Russia and the United States After 9/11," Terrorism and Political Violence, Vol. XVII, No. 2, 2005, pp. 282-288.

[184] Remarks of Coit D. Blacker in "A World Remade: The United States and Rising Powers in the 21st Century," Leveraging US Strength in an Uncertain World, Washington, DC: Stanley Foundation Conference on National and Global Security, December 7, 2006, secure.stanleyfoundation.org/registration/securityconference/ panels/rising_powers, accessed on December 19, 2006.

[185] Trenin, "Russia Redefines Itself and Its Relations With the West," Washington Quarterly, Vol. XXX, No. 2, pp. 95-105.

[186] Lavrov, "Vneshnepoliticheskaya Samostoyaltel'nost' Rossii, Bezuslovyi Imperativ", ("Russia's Foreign Policy Autonomy is an Unconditional Imperative,") Moskovskiye Novosti, January 19, 2008, http://www.mn.ru/issue.php?2007-1-56.

[187] Francesca Mereu, "Putin's Campaign has Kiev on Edge," Moscow Times .com, October 28, 2004, www.moscowtimes.com/ stories/2004/10/28/001.html.

[188] Eugene Huskey "The State-Legal Administration and the Politics of Redundancy," Post-Soviet Studies, Vol. XI, No. 2, 1995, pp. 115-143; Peter Baker and Susan Glasser, Kremlin Rising: Vladimir Putin's Russia and the End of Revolution, New York: Scribner's, 2005, p. 417; Steven Rosefielde, Russia in the 21st Century: The Prodigal Superpower, Cambridge, MA: Cambridge University Press, 2004; Marshall T. Poe, The Russian Moment in World History, Princeton, NJ: Princeton University Press, 2003; Stefan Hedlund, Russian Path Dependence, London: Routledge, 2005; Emil Pain, "Will Russia Transform Into a Nationalist Empire," Russia in Global Affairs, Vol. III, No. 2, April-June, 2005, pp. 71-80; Stephen Kotkin, "It's Gogol Again," Paper presented as part of the project The Energy Dimension in Russian Global Strategy, James A. Baker III Institute for Public Policy, Rice University, Houston; and Richard Pipes, Russia Under the Old Regime, New York: Scribner's, 1975. These are only a few of the authors who now see the vitality of the Tsarist metaphor as a means of explaining Putin's Russia.

[189] Dmitri Trenin and Bobo Lo, The Landscape of Russian Foreign Policy Decision-Making, Moscow: Moscow Center of the Carnegie Endowment for International Peace, 2005, p. 9.

[190] U.S. Department of State, Briefing En Route to Moscow with Secretary Condoleeza Rice, April 19, 2005, www.state.gov.

[191] Janusz Bugajski, Cold Peace: Russia's New Imperialism: Washington, DC: Center for Strategic and International Studies, 2004; Richard Krickus, Iron Troikas.
[192] Francesca Mereu, "Putin's Campaign has Kiev on Edge," Moscow Times .com, October 28, 2004, www.moscowtimes.com/ stories/2004/10/28/001.html.
[193] Igor Torbakov, "Russia Plays up Kosovo Precedent for Potential Application in the Caucasus," Eurasia Insight, April 12, 2006.
[194] Henry Kissinger, Diplomacy, New York: Simon and Schuster, 1994, p. 152. More recently, we should take for example the 1999 agreement at the OSCE's Istanbul conference in 1999 to remove troops from Moldova and Georgia.
[195] Lilia Shevtsova, "Russia 2005: The Logic of Backsliding," New Europe Review, 2005, www.neweuropereview.com?English/ Shevtsova.cfm.
[196] Heinrich Vogel, "Europe and Russia—a Partnership Without a Vision," Johnson's Russia List, February 10, 2006, available from www.cdi.org.
[197] Ibid.
[198] Interfax, November 11, 2005.
[199] "Lavrov: West Needs to Acknowledge Russia's Interests," Interfax, November 11, 2005.
[200] Dmitry Furman, "A Cold War Without Words: Democratic Camouflage Keeps Russia from Properly Formulating Its Real Policy in the CIS," Moscow, Nezavisimaya Gazeta, in Russian, March 27, 2006, FBIS SOV, March 27, 2006.
[201] Trenin, "Russia Leaves the West," Foreign Affairs, Vol. LXXXV, No. 4, July-August, 2006, pp. 85-96.
[202] John Loewenhardt, "Russia and Europe: Growing Apart Together," Brown Journal of World Affairs, Vol. VII, No. 1, Winter- Spring 2000, p. 171.
[203] Shlapentokh, pp. 463-464.
[204] "Russia At Risk of Collapsing, Putin Says," Associated Press, April 18, 2005, retrieved from Lexis-Nexis; "Interview with Chief of the Presidential Staff Dmitri Medvedev," Ekspert Weekly, April 5, 2005, retrieved from Lexis-Nexis; "Vladislav Surkov's Secret Speech: How Russia Should Fight International Conspiracy," www.mosnews.com, July 12, 2005; "Interview with Vladislav Surkov," Moscow, Ekho Moskvy, FBIS SOV, September 29, 2004.
[205] Lieutenant General V. I. Ostankov, "Geopolitical Problems and Possible Solutions in the Context of RF Security," Voyennaya Mysl' (Military Thought), No. 1, 2005, p. 23.
[206] "Moscow, NTV in Russian, July 2, 2005, FBIS SO V, July 2, 2005; Charles Clover, "Ukraine Looks East," FT.com, January 21, 2001, p. 2; Charles Clover, "Kiev Warned on Neutral Policy," Financial Times, July 12, 2001, p. 1.
[207] Stephen Blank, "The Values Gap Between Moscow and the West: Sovereignty at Issue," The Diplo-Goat, No. 2, 2007, www. diplogo.at.
[208] Vladislav V. Froltsov, "The Post-Soviet Puzzle and Western Democracies," Connections: The Quarterly Journal, Winter 2005, pp. 99-101.
[209] Thomas Ambrosio, "The Political Success of RussiaBelarus Relations: Insulating Minsk from a Color Revolution," Demokratizatsiya, Vol. XIV, No. 3, Summer, 2006, pp. 407-434; Thomas Ambrosio, "Reacting to the Color Revolutions: Russia's Antagonistic Policy Toward Ukraine and Georgia," Paper presented at the Annual Meeting of the International Studies Association 48th Annual Convention, Chicago, IL, February 28, 2007.

[210] Radio Free Europe Radio Liberty Newsline, January 11, 2006.
[211] "Interview With Sergei Ivanov," Der Spiegel, November 28,2006,mil.ru/eng/1866/ 12078/details/index.shtml?id=18788;"Interview With Sergei Yastrzhembsky," Ekho Moskvy, May 22, 2004, retrieved from Lexis-Nexis.
[212] Natalia Ratiani, "The European Union Is Tired of Making Exceptions for Russia," Izvestiya, February 26, 2004, p. 2, retrieved from Lexis-Nexis.
[213] Vitaly Tretiakov, "Putin's Pragmatic Foreign Policy," International Affairs, No. 3, 2002, p. 19.
[214] Henk Houweling and Mehdi Parvizi Amineh, "Introduction," International Studies in Sociology and Social Anthropology, Mehdi Parvizi Amineh and Henk Houweling, eds., Central Eurasia in Global Politics: Conflict, Security, and Development, Leiden, The Netherlands: Brill, 2004, p. 15.
[215] Bugajski; Krickus; Keith C. Smith.
[216] Trenin, "Russia Leaves the West," pp. 85-96; Dmitri Trenin, "The Post-Imperial Project," Moscow, Nezavisimaya GazetaDipkurier, No. 2, January 31, 2006, retrieved from Lexis-Nexis.
[217] Stanislav Secrieriu, "Russia's Foreign Policy Under Putin: 'CIS Project' Renewed," UNISCI Discussion Papers, No. 10, January 2006, p. 291.
[218] Maura Reynolds, "Moscow Has Chechnya Back—Now What?" Los Angeles Times, June 19, 2000.
[219] Quoted in Boris Rumer, "Central Asia: At the End of the Transition," Boris Rumer, ed., Central Asia At the End of Transition, Armonk, NY: M. E. Sharpe and Co. Inc., 2005, p. 47.
[220] Quoted in Michael Emerson, "From an Awkward Partnership to a Greater Europe: A European Perspective," Dana Allin and Michael H. Emerson, eds., Readings in European Security, Vol. III, Brussels and London; Center for European Policy Studies and International Institute for Security Studies, 2005, p. 19.
[221] E.G., Alexei Pushkov, "Quo Vadis?: Scenarios for Russia," International Affairs, No. 3, 2002, p. 71.
[222] Julie Wilhelmsen and Geir Flikke, "Evidence of Russia's Bush Doctrine in the CIS," European Security, Vol. XIV, No. 3, September 2005, pp. 387-417.
[223] "Russian Political, Economic, and Security Issues and U.S. Interests," CRS Report for Congress, Updated January 18, 2007.
[224] "Testimony of Walter Slocombe; Michta, p. 93.
[225] Dimitri K. Simes, "End the Crusade," The National Interest, No. 87, January-February, 2007, p. 9.
[226] Dov Lynch, "Same View, Different Realities: EU and US Policy Toward Russia," Marcin Zaborowski, ed., Friends Again?: EU-US Relations After the Crisis, Paris: European Union Institute for Security Studies, 2006, p. 166.
[227] See, for example, Sergei Karaganov, "Dangerous Relapses," Russia in Global Affairs, Vol. IV, No. 2, April-June, 2006, pp. 82-85.
[228] "Closed-Type Democracy," www.gazeta.ru, October 6, 2005, cited in Johnson's Russia List, October 6, 2005, available at www.cdi.org; Natalya Gevorkyan, "The Bottom Line," Moscow, Kommersant, in Russian, October 17, 2005, FBIS SOV, October 17, 2005.

[229] Moscow, ITAR-TASS, in English, November 21, 2004, FBIS SOV, November 21, 2004.

[230] Heinrich Vogel, "Prospects for Coordination of Western Policies," Stiftung Wissenschaft und Politik: Berlin; and the Carnegie Endowment for International Peace, Hannes Adomeit and Anders Aslund, eds., Russia Versus the United States and Europe—or "Strategic Triangle," Berlin, 2005, p. 92.

[231] Ron Susskind, The One-Percent Solution: Deep Inside America's Pursuit of Its Enemies Since 9/11, New York: Simon and Schuster, 2006, pp. 224-228, 307-308; Peter Baker, "Russian Relations Under Scrutiny," Washington Post, February 26, 2006, p. 1; John Vinocur, "Putin's Brazen Moves Force Bush to Recalibrate," International Herald Tribune, February 27, 2006, p. 2, retrieved from Lexis-Nexis; "Russia: Friend or Foe of the USA?" prvda.ru, February 27, 2006, from Johnson's Russia List, February 27, 2006, available at www.cdi.org. On Korea, see C. Kenneth Quinones, "Dualism in the Bush Administration's North Korea Policy," Asian Perspective, Vol. XXVII, No. 1, 2003, pp. 197-224; David Ignatius, "A CEO's Weaknesses," Washington Post Weekly, September 12-18, 2005, p. 27; Karin Lee and Adam Miles, "North Korea on Capitol Hill," Asian Perspective, Vol. XXVIII, No. 4, 2004, pp. 185-207; Robert M. Hathaway and Jordan Tama, "The U.S. Congress and North Korea During the Clinton years," Asian Survey, Vol. XLIV, No. 5, September-October 2004, pp. 711-733; David E. Sanger, "Aftereffects: Nuclear Standoff, Administration Divided Over North Korea," New York Times, April 21, 2003, p. 15; David Rennie, "Rumsfeld Calls for Regime Change in North Korea," Daily Telegraph, April 22, 2003; Gordon Fairclough, "Talks Display U.S. Rift on Pyongyang," Wall Street Journal, June 28, 2004, p. 9; Bill Gertz, "USA Considers Reactor Deal With North Korea," Washington Times, May 19, 2004, cited by Aidan Foster-Carter, "Pyongyang Watch: Six-Party Glacier: Did the US Melt?" Asia Times Online, June 28, 2004, www.atimes.com. The author can attest to those policy divisions on Central Asia from his conversations with U.S. officials from the Department of State, Defense, and the National Security Council over the period May-2005 to the present. See also "The Pentagon's Mission Creep," Jane's Foreign Report, June 1, 2006, www.4janes.com/subscribe frp/doc_view.jsp?K2 DocKey= /content1/janesdat/mags.

[232] Jeffrey Donovan, "Energy: EU Throws Gauntlet Down to Russia's Gazprom," Radio Fee Europe Radio Liberty Features, September 19, 2007.

[233] Author's conversations with U.S. officials, 2005-06; Baker; Vinocur; "Russia Friend or Foe of the USA?"

[234] Lynch, pp. 168-169; Richard Wolffe and Eve Conant, "The Problem with Putin," Newsweek, May 9, 2005, p. 49; Fred Hyatt, "Silent on Putin's Slide," Washington Post, October 3, 2005, www.washingtonpost.com; Sergei Chirkin, "Washington Promotes Democracy More Cautiously," Rossiyskaya Gazeta, September 19, 2005, p. 2, retrieved from Lexis-Nexis.

[235] Michael McFaul, "American Efforts at Promoting Regime Change in the Soviet Union and Russia: Lessons Learned," Paper Presented to the Annual Convention of the American Political Science Association, Washington, DC, September 2-4, 2005.

[236] Lynch, pp. 168-169.

[237] James Collins, "To Keep a Broad Dialogue Going," International Affairs (Moscow), No. 4, 2007, p. 151.

[238] Bugajski; Krickus; Keith C. Smith.

[239] "Russia Will Not Ratify Energy Charter Soon," Alexander's Gas and Oil Connection, Vol. XI, No. 13, July 7, 2006, www.gasandoil. com/goc/news/ntr62775.htm; "Russia 'Will Not Ratify Charter'," Platt's Oilgram, accessed on August 1, 2006, www.platts.com/ Natural % 20Gas/Resources/News % 20Features/Ukrainega /charter.xml.

[240] James Sherr, "The School of Defeat," Camberley, Surrey, United Kingdom: Conflict Studies Research Centre, Defence Academy of the United kingdom, 2006.

[241] Statement of Steven R. Mann, Principal Deputy Assistant Secretary of State for South and Central Asian Affairs Before the House Committee on International Relations, Subcommittee on the Middle East and Central Asia, July 25, 2006 (henceforth Mann, Testimony); Zeyno Baran, "Assessing Energy and Security issues in Central Asia," Statement to the House Committee on International Relations, Subcommittee on the Middle East and Central Asia, July 25, 2006 (henceforth Baran, Testimony).

[242] Quinones, pp. 197-224; Ignatius, p. 27; Lee and Miles, pp. 185-207; Hathaway and Tama, pp. 711-733; Sanger, p. 15; Rennie; Fairclough, p. 9; David Kerr, "The Sino-Russian Partnership and U.S. Policy Toward North Korea, From Hegemony to Concert in Northeast Asia," International Studies Quarterly, Vol. XXXXIX, No. 3, September, 2005, pp. 411-437; Constantin C. Menges, China: The Gathering Threat, Nashville, TN: Nelson Current Publishers, 2005.

[243] Elaine Sciolino and Steven Erlanger, "U.S. and NATO Balk on Lebanon," New York Times, July 25, 2006, p. 1; Michael Abramowitz and Robin Wright, "Lebanon Buffer Force Proposed," Washington post, July 29, 2006, p. 1.

[244] "Russia-Iran Military Cooperation Cannot Be Target of Sanctions-Lavrov," Interfax, July 13, 2006; FBIS SOV, March 21, 2007.

[245] Author's Conversations with officials from the National Security Council, Department of State, and Department of Defense, May 2005 to July 2006.

[246] Jim Rutenberg and David Sanger, "Bush to Urge Putin to Aid in Pressuring Iran," New York Times, July 1, 2007, www. nytimes.com; M.K. Bhadrakumar, "Russia's Tango With Tehran," Asia Times Online, June 25, 2007, www.atimes.com; Moscow, Kommersant.com, in English, March 12, 2007; Moscow, Interfax, in English, March 12, 2007, FBIS SOV, March 12, 2007

[247] Stephen Blank,"Proliferation and Counterproliferation in Russian Strategy," Korean Journal of Defense Analysis, Vol. XII, No. 1, Winter-Spring 2000, pp. 149-191; Jason D. Ellis and Geoffrey D. Kiefer, Combating Proliferation: Strategic Intelligence and Security Policy, Baltimore, MD: Johns Hopkins University Press, 2004, pp. 36-54, 110-125, 197-199.

[248] Kerr, pp. 411-437; Conversations with U.S. officials, June 2005, December 2005, May 2006.

[249] Ilan Berman, "Russia Shows US The Central Asian Door," Jane's Defence Weekly, July 18, 2007, www4.janes.com/subscribe/ jdw/doc_view.jsp ?K2DocKey=/content1/janesdata/mags/jdw/history/ jdw2007/jdw33516.htm@currentandProd_Name=JDWandQueryText=.

[250] Marcin Zaborowski, "Friends Reunited? Recalibrating Transatlantic Relations in the 21st Century," Marcin Zaborowski, ed., Friends Again?: E U-US Relations After the Crisis, Paris: European Union Institute for Security Studies, 2006, p. 221.

[251] Lynch, p. 170.

[252] Jonathan Eyal, "NATO's Summit: A Disappointment to the Alliance's New Member States," RUSI Newsbrief, Vol. XXVII, No. 1, January, 2007, pp. 1-2; Angela Stent, "Berlin's Russia Challenge," The National Interest, No. 88, March-April 2007, pp. 46-51.

[253] Conversations with U.S. officials, June 2005; Kerr, pp. 411-437.

[254] Ibid., more recently, see the Russo-Chinese reporting on Chinese President Hu Jintao's visit to Moscow on March 26-27, 2007, which repeatedly stressed the identity of viewpoints of the two states on Korea and Asian-Pacific issues.

[255] Ibid.; Alexander Zhebin, "The Bush Doctrine, Russia, and Korea," in Mel Gurtov and Peter Van Ness, eds., Confronting the Bush Doctrine: Critical Views From Asia, Abingdon and New York: Routledge, 2005, p. 149.

[256] Robert Jervis, "U.S. Grand Strategy: Mission Impossible," Naval War College Review, Summer 1998, pp. 22-36; Richard K. Betts, "Power, Prospects, and Priorities: Choices for Strategic Change," Naval War College Review, Winter 1997, pp. 9-22; John C. Gannon, "Intelligence Challenges Through 2015," odci.gov/cia/ publicaffairs/speeches /gannon_speech_05022000.html.

[257] Christopher Jones, "The Axis of Nonproliferation," Problems of Post-Communism, Vol. LIII, No. 21, March-April 2006, pp. 3-16.

[258] Thomas Friedman, "A Choice for the Rogues," New York Times, August 2, 2006, www.nytimes.com.

[259] Etel Solingen, Regional Orders at Century's Dawn: Global and Domestic Influences on Grand Strategy, Princeton, NJ: Princeton University Press, 1998.

[260] Ibid.; Viktor Yasmann and Liz Fuller, "Russia Threatens to Withdraw from the CFE Treaty," Radio Free Europe Radio Liberty Russian Political Weekly, Vol. VI, No. 2, January 26, 2006.

[261] "Moscow's Plan To Build Military Base in Moldova Rejected-Voronin," Interfax, October 30, 2005.

[262] Sergei Ivanov, "Maturing Partnership," NATO Review, Winter 2005, www.nato.int/docu/review/2005/issue4/english/special. htm; Yuri Baluyevsky, First Deputy chief of the Russian General Staff, "NATO Expansion Will Strike a Fatal Blow to the Treaty on Conventional Arms in Europe," Izvestiya, March 3, 2004, retrieved from Lexis-Nexis.

[263] Gunnar Arbman and Charles Thornton, Russia's Tactical and Nuclear Weapons Part I: Background and Policy Issues, Stockholm, Swedish Defense Research Agency, 2003, Part II: Technical Issues and Policy Recommendations, Stockholm: Swedish Defense Research Agency, 2005.

[264] Sergei Blagov, "Missiles for Kaliningrad," ISN Security watch, July 16, 2007, www.isn.ethz.ch/news/sw/details. cfm ?id=1 7863.

[265] Nikolai Sokov, "'Tactical Nuclear Weapons' Scare of 2001," CNS Reports, January 4, 2001, cns.miis.edu/pubs/reports/tnw. htm.

[266] Peter Baker, "U.S. and Russia to Enter Civilian Nuclear Pact," Washington Post, July 8, 2006, p. A1.

[267] "RF President Putin's Speech to the Federal Assembly," May 10, 2006; Baker and Wright, p. 12.

[268] Phillip Bobbitt, The Shield of Achilles: War, Peace, and the Course of History, New York: Alfred A. Knopf, 2002, 634-638; Caroline Kennedy-Pipe and Stephen Welch, "Russia and the United States After 9/11," Terrorism and Political Violence, Vol. XVII, No. 2, 2005, pp. 282-288.

[269] Putin, Interviews; Radio Free Europe Radio Liberty Newsline, May 17, 2006; Moscow, Interfax, in English, September 1, 2005, FBIS SO V, September 1, 2005; Moscow, Interfax Russia and CIS Diplomatic Panorama, February 10, 2005, FBIS SOV, February 10, 2005.

[270] Moscow, Interfax Russia and CIS Diplomatic Panorama, February 14, 2005, FBIS SOV, February 14, 2005.

[271] Moscow, ITAR-TASS, December 8, 2005, FBIS SOV, December 8, 2005.

[272] Daniel Kimmage, "Analysis U.S. Aid to Uzbekistan; Carrots and Sticks," Radio Free Europe Radio Liberty Features, July 22, 2004.

[273] Ibid.

[274] Leonid Gankin, "Toward the Summit: Kowtowing Toward the East George Bush Finds Approach to Vladimir Putin," Moscow, Kommersant, February 24, 2005, FBIS SOV, February 24, 2005.

[275] Tesmur Basilia, "Eurasian Commentary," Jan H, Kalicki and Eugene K. Lawson, eds., Russian-Eurasian Renaissance?: U.S. Trade and Investment in Russia and Eurasia, Stanford, CA: Stanford University Press, 2003, p. 166.

[276] Dmitry Furman, "A Silent Cold War," Russia in Global Affairs, Vol. IV, No. 2, April-June, 2006, p. 72.

[277] Ibid., p. 73.

[278] "Putin Speaks Out Against "Exporting Capitalist Democracy," ITAR-TASS News Agency, April 11, 2003, retrieved from Lexis-Nexis; for an example from Turkmenistan, see Gennady Sysoev, "Saparmyrat Niyazov Seeks Protection," Moscow, Kommersant, in Russian, April 11, 2003, FBIS SOV, April 11, 2003.

[279] Basilia, p. 163.

[280] Garry Kasparov, "What's Bad for Putin Is Best for Russians," New York Times, July 10, 2006.

[281] One need only cite Russian interventions in the Caucasus, Moldova, an endless Chechen war that has now spread to the North Caucasus, and the bizarre intervention in Kosovo in 1999.

[282] Robert Wright, "An American Foreign Policy That Both Realists and Idealists Should Fall in Love With," New York Times, July 16, 2006, pp. E12-13.

[283] Ibid.

[284] Stephen Blank, "Russia's Project 2008: Reforming the Army and Preparing a Coup," Forthcoming, World Affairs, Fall 2006.

[285] Michael Mainville, "Armed Clash With Georgia Feared," Washington times, June 21, 2006, p. 14.

[286] Alexander Golts and Tonya Putnam, "State Militarism and Its Legacies: Why Military Reform Has Failed in Russia," International Security, Vol. XXIX, No. 2, Fall 2004, pp. 121-159; Aleksandr' Golts, Armiya Rossii: 11 Poteryannykh Let, Moscow, Zakharov, 2004.

[287] Moscow, ITAR-TASS, in English, December 8, 2005, FBIS SOV, December 8, 2005; "Russia Expects Oil Production Growth Rate to Fall in 2006," Alexander's Gas and Oil

Connections, October 11, 2005, www.gasandoil.com/goc/news/ntr54168htm; Rudiger Ahrend and William Tompson, "Unnatural Monopoly: The Endless Wait for Gas Sector Reform in Russia," Europe-Asia Studies, Vol. LVII, No. 6, September 2005, pp. 801-821; "Russian Economic Growth May Result in Electricity Shortages-Putin," Interfax, February 10, 2006; Vladimir Paramonov and Aleksey Strogov, New Russia's Strategic Choice: Regionalization Versus Globalization, Camberley, Surrey, United Kingdom: Conflict Studies Research Centre, 2004.

[288] "Putin Suggests Enrichment Centers in 'Nuclear Club' Countries," Interfax, January 31, 2006; "Russia Ready to Cooperate on International Nuclear Centers-Putin," Interfax, February 4, 2006; "Russia Draft Nuclear Energy Proposals for G8 Summit," Interfax, February 2, 2006.

[289] Ian Bremmer, Choi Sung-hong, and Yoriko Kawaguchi, "A New Forum for Peace," The National Interest, No. 82, Winter 2005-06, pp. 108-111; Shoichi Ito, Vladimir I. Ivanov, and Zha Daojiong, "China, Japan, and Russia: The Energy Security Nexus," Niklas Swanstrom, ed., Conflict Prevention and Conflict Management in Northeast Asia, Uppsala, Sweden: Uppsala University, 2005, pp. 121-142, available at www.silkroadstudies.org; Niklas Swanstrom, "An Asian Oil and Gas Union: Prospects and Problems," China Eurasia Forum, Vol. III, No. 3, 2005, pp. 81-97; Zha Daojiong, "An Opening for U.S.-China Cooperation," Far Eastern Economic Review, May 2006, pp. 42-45.

[290] Ibid.

[291] The White House, The National Security Strategy of the United States Washington, DC, 2006, www.whitehouse.gov; Robert B. Zoellick, "Whither China: From Membership to Responsibility," Remarks to the National Committee on U.S.-China Relations, September 21, 2005, www.state.gov/s/d/rem/53682.htm; Chad Kreikemeir, "Lights Out in China?: China's Energy Crisis and Opportunities for U.S. Engagement," International Affairs Review, Vol. XV, No. 1, 2006, pp. 13-30; Leverett and Noel, pp. 62-70.

[292] Leverett and Noel, pp. 69-70; Kreikemeier, pp. 113-130.

[293] Leverett and Noel, pp. 62-70.

[294] Kenneth Lieberthal and Mikal Herberg, China's Search for Energy Security: Implications for U. S. Policy, NBR Analysis, Vol. XVII, No. 1, Seattle, WA: National Bureau of Research Asia, 2006, pp. 24-41; Kreikemeier, pp. 113-130.

[295] "China Consumes Less Energy With Faster Economic Growth Rate," Alexander's Oil and Gas Connection, Vol. XI, No. 14, July 19, 2006, www.gasandoil.com/goc/new/nts62904.htm; Jonathan E. Sinton et al., Evaluation of China's Energy Strategy Options, China Sustainable Energy Program, 2005.

[296] Lieberthal and Herberg, pp. 24-41; Leverett and Noel, pp. 62-70; Flynt Leverett and Jeffrey Bader, "Managing China-U.S. Energy Competition in the Middle East," Washington Quarterly, Vol. XXIX, No. 1, Winter 2005-06, pp. 187-201, and the sources cited therein; Toshi Yoshihara and Richard Sokolski, "The United States and China in the Persian Gulf: Challenges and Opportunities," The Fletcher Forum of World Affairs, Vol. XXVI, No. 1, Winter-Spring 2002, pp. 63-78.

[297] Stephen Blank, Politics in Command: Russo-Chinese Energy Relations, London: Global Markets Briefing, 2006.

[298] Jervis, pp. 22-36; Betts, pp. 9-22; Gannon, "Intelligence Challenges Through 2015."

[299] Blank, "Politics in Command."

[300] Stephen Blank, "Economics and Security in Northeast Asia: The Iron Silk Road, Its Context and Implications," Global Economic Review, Vol. XXXI, No. 3, 2002, pp. 3-24.

[301] Baker, "U.S. and Russia to Enter Civilian Nuclear Pact."

[302] See, for example, Lynch, p. 166.

[303] Timofei Bordachev, "Russia's Europe Dilemma: Democratic Partner vs. Authoritarian Satellite," Andrew Kuchins and Dmitri Trenin, eds., Russia: The Next Ten Years, A Collection of Essays to Mark Ten Years of the Carnegie Moscow Center, Moscow: Carnegie Center, 2004, p. 120.

[304] John B. Dunlop and Rajan Menon, "Chaos in the North Caucasus and Russia's Future, Survival, Vol. XLVIII, No. 2, Summer 2006, p. 110.

[305] Mary Elise Sarotte, "Transatlantic Tension and Threat Perception," Naval War College Review, Vol. LVIII, No. 4, Autumn 2005, p. 32.

[306] Colin L. Powell, "Understanding and Strategy," SAIS Review, Vol. XXV, No. 1, Winter-Spring 2005, p. 170.

[307] John Roper and Peter Van Ham, "Redefining Russia's Role in Europe," Vladimir Baranovsky, ed., Russia and Europe: The Emerging Security Agenda, Oxford, UK: Oxford University press for SIPRI, 1997, p. 517.

[308] Colin S. Gray, The Sheriff: America's Defense of the New World Order, Lexington, KY: University Press of Kentucky, 2004.

In: Russian Political, Economic and Security Issues
Editor: Harold J. Kowen
ISBN 978-1-60692-407-5

Chapter 3

RUSSIA'S ECONOMIC PERFORMANCE AND POLICIES AND THEIR IMPLICATIONS FOR THE UNITED STATES*

William H. Cooper
Foreign Affairs, Defense, and Trade Division

ABSTRACT

The Russian economy has grown impressively since 1999 and, by some measures, has been one of the fastest growing economies in the world. The growth has brought an improvement in the standard of living of the average Russian citizen and has brought economic stability that Russia had not experienced in at least a decade. This strong performance is a major factor in the popular support that former President (now Prime Minister) Putin enjoys– some 70%-80% of the population view him favorably. The improvement in the Russian economy is also arguably a factor in the boldness with which the Putin leadership has reasserted Russia's status as a world power, challenging the United States, Europe, the other former Soviet states in economic and national security areas.

The Russian economy is highly dependent on the production and export of oil, gas, and other natural resources. Its success has largely been the result of record- breaking world energy prices, although prudent fiscal policies have also helped to promote economic stability. However, oil dependence could prove to be a double- edged sword. The Putin regime's failure to complete important economic reforms and its penchant for re-asserting government control over key economic sectors also loom among the possible roadblocks down the road. How Putin' s successor, President Dmitriy Medvedev, will proceed is still a matter of speculation.

Although its influence has been greatly diminished since the Soviet period, Russia remains a formidable force on the global stage, and its influence seems to be growing. Russia's economy is large enough to influence global economic conditions. Many European countries and former Soviet states are highly dependent on Russian natural gas. Russia is a significant player on a number of issues critical to the United States, for example, nuclear proliferation by Iran and North Korea. Russia's perceived national

* Excerpted from CRS Report RL34512, dated May 30, 2008.

interests do not always match those of the United States, creating an environment for disagreement if not conflict.

While U.S. exports to Russia are still relatively small, for some producers, such as poultry, energy equipment, and technology, Russia is an important market. Russia is also an important supplier of a number of raw materials that are critical to U.S. manufacturers. These links have drawn the attention of some Members of Congress. Hearings have recently been held on Russian economic performance and policies. Congress may consider in the near future whether to extend permanent normal trade relations (PNTR) status to Russia as Russia pursues accession to the World Trade Organization (WTO). This report on Russian economic conditions and policies will be updated as events warrant.

The Russian economy has grown impressively since 1999 and, by some measures, is one of the fastest growing economies in the world. The growth has brought an improvement in the standard of living of the average Russian citizen and has brought economic stability that Russia had not experienced in at least a decade. This success is a major factor in the popular support that former President (now Prime Minister) Putin enjoys–some 70%-80% of the population view him favorably. The improvement in the Russian economy is also arguably a factor in the boldness with which the Putin leadership has reasserted Russia's status as a world power, challenging the United States, Europe, the other former Soviet states in economic and national security areas. Putin himself acknowledged the potency of Russia's enhanced economic power:

...Russia's growing economic and military potential does allow us to be firmer in standing up for our national interests, both political and economic. We will never seek confrontation, but we do think it is our right to defend our interests, just as our partners do, and, indeed, we can learn from them.[1]

Some experts assert that the Russian economy will continue to strengthen and categorize Russia with Brazil, India, and China as among the fastest growing economies. Others argue that Russia's economic prospects face risks.

Russia has some of the world's largest reserves of oil, natural gas and other raw materials, many of which are critical to industrialized countries. Many European countries and former Soviet states are highly dependent on Russian natural gas. Russia is a significant player on a number of issues critical to the United States, such as, nuclear proliferation by Iran and North Korea. Russia's perceived national interests do not always match those if the United States, creating an environment for disagreement if not conflict.[2]

While U.S. exports to Russia are still relatively small, for some producers, such as poultry, energy equipment, and technology, Russia is an important market. Russia is also an important supplier of a number of raw materials that are critical to U.S. manufacturers. These links have drawn the attention of some Members of Congress.

Hearings have been held on Russian economic performance and policies recently.[3] Congress may consider in the near future whether to extend permanent normal trade relations (PNTR) status to Russia as Russia pursues accession to the World Trade Organization (WTO).[4]

Russian economic policies and performance raise important policy questions for the United States and the U.S.-Russian relationship which this report addresses, especially as a new president, Dmitriy Medvedev assumes power: Is Russia's current economic growth sustainable? Is an economically strong Russia a threat or benefit to the United States? Is Russia following economic strategies that promote a market economy that underlies the international trade system manifested in the WTO?

Table 1. The Russian Economy at a Comparative Glance (Key Economic Indicators)

	Russia	China	United States
GDP (2007) -Nominal (billions of $U.S.) -PPP (billions of $U.S.)a	 $1,290 2,087	 $3,242 7,238	 $13,841 13,841
Per Capita GDP (2007) -Nominal -PPP (U.S. Dollars)	 $9,060 14,660	 $2,450 5,480	 $45,820 45,820
Real GDP Growth Rates (2007)	8.1%	11.9%	2.2%
Average Annual Real GDP Growth Rate (1997-2007)	5.3%	9.5%	3.1%

Source: CRS with data from the Economist Intelligence Unit.

a. PPP stands for purchasing-power parity. PPP measures the cost of a basket of goods in the local economy in dollars. A number of experts consider PPP to be a more accurate estimate than nomianl measurements.

The Immediate Post-Soviet Period

The first years of Russia's transition from the Soviet central planned economy (1991-1998) were not easy. The seven years of the transition that coincided with most of the regime of President Boris Yeltsin were, by most accounts, a period of economic chaos, if not collapse and failure.

During the period, Russia lost close to 30% of its real gross domestic product (GDP), a decline reminiscent of the Great Depression of the 1930s in the United States.[5] Russia also suffered very high rates of inflation– over 2000% in 1992 and over 800% in 1993– before it declined to more tolerable, but still high, levels of around 20% by the end of the 1990s. The inflation robbed Russian citizens of their savings as the value of the ruble collapsed, eventually forcing the Russian government to issue new currency on January 1, 1998, with 1 new ruble equaling 1,000 old rubles. As a hedge against inflation, some residents, who were in a position to do so, invested in hard assets such as art works, foreign currencies, and real estate. But the greater portion of the population saw their savings evaporate. The disposable income (income available after taxes) of the average Russian declined 25% in real terms between 1993 and 1999.[6]

The quality of life of the average Russian deteriorated in other terms. In 1991, the life expectancy of the average Russian male was 64 years and for the average Russian woman it was 74 years. By 1999, the life expectancy had declined to 59 years for males and 72 for females.

Russia did not perform much better in the foreign sector. Foreign direct investments were meager given the size and needs of the Russian economy. Furthermore, Russia was incurring serious capital flight– some $150 billion between 1992 and 1999 by one estimate.[7] Russian foreign debt soared in part because Russia had taken on the foreign debts of the entire former Soviet Union in an arrangement made with the other former Soviet states. However, Russia had also incurred its own foreign obligations since the collapse of the Soviet Union.

The economic problems were in part a continuation of economic collapse that was a factor in the demise of the Soviet government. The problems were also in part the result of the rapid disintegration of an economic system in which the state, guided by the communist party, maintained complete control and market forces were an anathema. It was a system in which the government emphasized heavy industry production regardless of cost and to the detriment of other sectors including agriculture, services, and consumer industries. The central planned economy also operated huge production facilities that proved to be inefficient, not very adaptable to change, often producing products of poor quality, and not competitive in world markets.

However, the problems were also the product of poorly executed, if not poorly conceived, economic policies of the Yeltsin regime. The regime failed to rein in government spending as it tried to deal with the Soviet legacy of massive subsidies for industry and the population. During the period, the Russian government ran up large budget deficits that reached as high as 9.8% of GDP, forcing the government to finance debt at very high interest rates. The Yeltsin regime was also criticized for employing "shock therapy," or radical macroeconomic measures, as part of its economic reform program, largely attributed to Prime Minister Yegor Gaidar. Critics claimed that the measures unnecessarily created inflation and destabilized the economy because market prices were introduced too early in the reform process.

The most controversial aspect of the early post-Soviet economic transition was the effort to privatize state-owned and operated production facilities, in particular, the so-called loans for shares program. In 1995, the government auctioned off to local banks shares in 29 of the most potentially lucrative firms, including major oil companies and mineral producers (Yukos, Lukoil, Sufgutneftegas, and Novolietsk Iron and Steel).[8] The banks would hold the shares as collateral against which they issued loans to the government to finance its ballooning deficits. The auctions were controlled by individuals with close ties to the Yeltsin regime and whose banks won the bids. They obtained the shares at a fraction of their market value and were able to keep them when the government failed to pay back the loans. The government did not challenge their control of these assets because their owners, who became known as "oligarchs," financed Yeltsin's reelection as president in 1996. They used their new wealth to gain control over other interests such as the media. The privatization program also resulted in small and medium-sized firms owned by those who managed them during the Soviet period–the "red directors."[9]

Russia's economic problems came to a head in the financial crisis of August 1998. The crisis proved to be a pivotal event in Russia's transition to a market economy. It exposed many of the weaknesses of Russian economic policies and the need for economic reform.[10]

The crisis culminated in August 1998, when the government abandoned its defense of a strong ruble. It also defaulted on official domestic debt forcing its restructuring and imposed a 90-day moratorium on commercial external debt payments. The crisis led to the demise of many Russian banks, owned by "oligarchs," which had held government debt.

Symptoms of the crisis developed months before August: Russian interest rates soared; prices on the Russian stock market plummeted; and the value of the Russian ruble sank–between the end of July 1998 and the end of September 1998, the ruble lost 60% of its (nominal) value in terms of the dollar.[11] In addition, foreign reserves declined sharply–between the end of July 1998 and August 1998. The reserves, including gold, dropped from $18.4 billion to $12.5 billion,[12] and real GDP declined 4.9% in 1998.[13]

The immediate cause of the crisis was the accumulation of Russian government short-term debt in the form of Treasury bills (the GKOs) and bonds (OFZs), to finance burgeoning budget deficits. As long as the Russian government could service the debt, it managed to maintain large budget deficits without incurring inflation and was able to keep the ruble stable. But beginning in 1997 and into 1998, a number of forces came into play that placed Russia in a financially vulnerable position:

- World prices for oil and other commodities, on which Russia depends for much of its foreign currency earnings, plummeted, putting downward pressure on foreign currency reserves and making it more difficult to service the debt and defend the ruble.
- The Asian financial crisis made investors much more wary of holding risky short-term securities such as GKOs.

Foreign economic shocks that hit a financially vulnerable Russia largely explain the suddenness of the 1998 financial crisis. But Russia became vulnerable because of more fundamental problems associated with its economic policy and economic structure. These included the failure to institute tax reform, property rights, and bankruptcy laws and procedures.

Despite the setbacks, Russia made some strides toward economic reform during this period. It jettisoned the centrally planned economic system and introduced market prices for most goods and services, it made the Russian ruble convertible for trade transactions, and the economy was opened to foreign trade and investment. The downturn in the Russian economy was inevitable in a transition from an economy that was 100% controlled by the state at the direction of ubiquitous communist party officials. At the same time, the downturn was exacerbated by bad policies.

The turmoil of the economic crisis and Yeltsin's poor personal health and very low popular support led him to relinquish the Presidency to his Prime Minister, Vladimir Putin, whom Yeltsin had appointed in July 1999. Putin became acting President on December 31, 1999, which set him up to win election as president in his own right in March 2000.[14]

RECENT ECONOMIC TRENDS

Since 2000 and roughly contemporaneous with the Putin regime, Russia's economic fortunes reversed on many accounts. The radical improvement is arguably a factor in the wide popularity that Putin enjoyed during his term. At the same time, improved economic conditions have brought a significant degree of economic stability to Russia.

The economic trends during the last nine years raise several important questions: Why has Russia achieved economic growth and is it sustainable? What have been the economic policies of the Putin regime and do they help or hinder Russia's longterm economic success?

Internal Economic Conditions and Trends

As figure 1 and table 2 show, Russia has experienced strong economic growth over the last nine years (1999-2007), during which time its GDP has increased 6.9% on average per year in contrast to an average annual decline in GDP of 6.8% during the previous seven years (1992-1998). The positive GDP trends are reflected in other measurements that point to an improved Russian standard of living throughout the period. Average real wages in Russia increased 10.5% per year from 1999-2007. (Real wages actually increased 14.7% from 2000-2007, having declined by 23.2% in 1999 because of spike in inflation that year.) In addition, real disposable income (the income that the average Russian resident has available from all sources after taxes) increased 10.7% from 2000 to 2007 (8.5% from 1999 to 2007). The Russian unemployment rate has also declined during the 1999-2007 period, from 12.6% to 6.2%.

During the first years after the collapse of the Soviet Union, the Russian population was plagued by increasing rates of poverty. In 2000, 29% of the Russian population was living below the officially calculated poverty line. By 2006, the rate had dropped to 15%.[15] In addition, household consumption has increased–another sign of improved living standards--from 42.8% of Russian GDP in 1992 and to 57.3% of Russian GDP in 2006.[16]

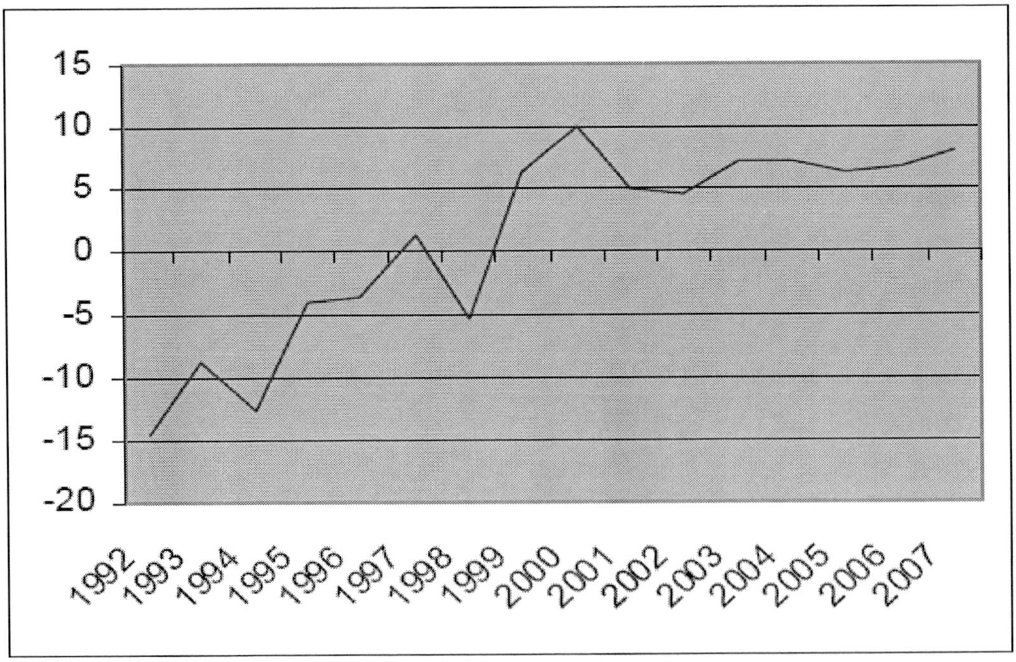

Source: CRS constructed from data collected by the Economist Intelligence Unit.

Figure 1. Growth of Real Russian GDP, 1992-2007.

Table 2. Major Russian Internal Economic Indicators, 1999-2007

(percentage growth from previous year)

Year	Real GDP Growth	Consumer Price Index	Average real wages	Real personal disposable income	Unemployment rate
1999	6.4	85.7	-23.2	-8.8	12.6
2000	10.0	20.8	18.0	11.3	10.5
2001	5.1	21.5	19.9	8.7	9.0
2002	4.7	15.8	16.2	9.7	8.1
2003	7.3	13.7	9.8	13.5	8.6
2004	7.2	10.9	10.3	8.6	8.2
2005	6.4	12.7	12.6	11.5	7.6
2006	6.7	9.7	14.4	10.2	7.2
2007	8.1	9.0	16.2	12.0	6.2

Source: Economist Intelligence Unit.

This favorable picture is somewhat tainted by continuing problems. While the Russian economy has been able to greatly temper inflation from the sky-high rates of the 1990s, inflation rates remain high. In 2006, the consumer price index rose 9.7%, and is estimated to have risen 9.0% in 2007, a rate that was above the government target. The life expectancy of the average Russian citizen, particularly males, remains low for an advanced country. In 2006, it was 72.4 years for a Russian woman and 58.9 years for a Russian male.[17] Increases in alcoholism and other diseases, some of which like tuberculosis have been nearly eradicated in developed countries, have contributed to the decline. It is also explained by the poor and deteriorating health system which has been slow to adjust to the transition from central planning. The high mortality rate is contributing to shrinkage of the Russian population of an average of 0.5% during 2002-2006 period. That means that the average age of the Russian population will increase, leading to a decline in the pool of working age individuals– a trend that does not bode well for economic growth in the future.

Economic data indicate also that, as the Russian economy has grown, the distribution of income within Russia has become increasingly unequal during the post-Soviet period. A standard measure of income distribution is the Gini coefficient (or index) which is on a 0.00 to 1.00 scale. The lower the number the more equal the income distribution. Thus, 0.00 is perfectly equal income distribution, while 1.00 is totally unequal. In 1992, Russia's Gini-coefficient was 0.289.[18] By 2007, it had increased to 0.422.[19]

Before the collapse of the Soviet Union, the richest 20% of the Russian population accounted for 30.7% of Russian income while the poorest 20% accounted for 11.9%. In 2006, the richest 20% held 46.8% of the income while the poorest 20%'s share had declined to 5.4%. The middle 60% of the population's share had declined from 57.4% in 1992 to 47.8% in 2006.[20] The two sets of income distribution measurements mean that while the Russian standard of living has improved, a small segment of the population is enjoying close to half of the benefits. Inflation might explain at least part of the skewered distribution as those who hold hard assets can protect themselves from inflation more easily than the less wealthy. The income distribution trends might also be explained by the large role played by exports, especially oil and natural gas, in Russian GDP growth as owners of energy- related assets reap the benefits of the surge in world energy prices.[21]

Foreign Trade and Investment Trends

The roots of Russia's robust economic growth during the last eight years are reflected in the surge in Russian trade and capital flows. (See Table 3)

Table 3. Select External Economic Indicators, 1999-2007

(billions of U.S. Dollars Unless Otherwise Noted)

Year	Exports	Imports	Merchandise Trade Balance	(CA)Trade Balance (mil$)	Foreign Reserves	Foreign Direct Investments into Russia
1999	75.5	39.5	36.0	24.6	12.5	3.3
2000	105.0	44.9	60.1	46.8	28.0	2.7
2001	101.9	53.8	48.1	33.9	36.6	2.7
2002	107.3	61.0	46.3	29.1	47.5	3.4
2003	135.9	76.1	59.9	35.4	76.9	8.0
2004	183.2	97.4	85.8	59.0	124.5	15.4
2005	243.6	125.3	118.3	83.3	182.2	12.9
2006	304.5	163.9	139.3	94.4	303.7	30.8
2007	355.5	223.4	132.0	78.3	476.4	55.0

Source: Central Bank of Russia.

Russia foreign trade has increased sharply in the last nine years (1999-2007). During that period Russian exports grew close to 400%, from $75.5 billion to $355.5 billion and Russian imports rose over 450%, from $39.5 billion in 1999 to $223.4 billion in 2007. As a result, Russia has experienced rapidly increasing trade surpluses. Its merchandise trade surplus rose from $36.0 billion in 1999 to $132.0 billion in 2007. Russia's current account balance (which includes balances on merchandise trade, trade in services, investment income and unilateral transfers) increased substantially, from $24.6 billion in 1999 to $78.3 billion in 2007. As a result, Russia has accumulated one of the world's largest foreign reserve holdings that have skyrocketed from $12.5 billion in 1999 to $476.4 billion in 2007.

Oil and petroleum-related products have dominated Russia's exports for some time, even during the Soviet period. However, they have become even more significant. In 2006, oil, natural gas, and other fuels accounted for 64.6% of Russian exports. If metals are included, the share of raw materials was 78.6% in 2006.[22] More than half (51.7%) of Russian imports consisted of machinery and equipment and another 16.9% consisted of food and other agricultural products.[23]

The 27-member European Union (EU) is by far Russia's most significant trading partner. In 2007, the EU accounted for 53% of Russian exports, mostly energy, and for 43% of Russian imports. China has emerged as the second most important trading partner, accounting for 5% of Russian exports and for 13% of Russian imports in 2007. If the EU members are considered separately, the Netherlands is the leading market for Russian exports, accounting for 15% in 2007, while Germany is the leading source of Russian imports, accounting for 13% in 2007.[24]

Russia's investment climate has improved significantly during the last few years a byproduct of Russia's robust growth. Between 1999 and 2007, annual foreign direct investment flows into Russia rose from $3.3 billion to an estimated $55.0 billion, or 4.5% of GDP, nearly double the FDI flows in 2006, and close to the flows recorded by China.[25] However, the Russian government recently passed a law which will restrict foreign investment in key sectors, which could hamper foreign investment in the future.

Russian Economic Policies

The 1998 financial crisis proved to be a blessing in disguise, albeit one that exacted a huge price in terms of Russian financial credibility. The economic growth that Russia has experienced since 1999 has been largely driven by favorable trends in the Russia's international economic interactions. The sharp depreciation of the ruble in 1998 cut demand for imports and encouraged domestic production of goods. But by definition, such factors are ephemeral. When Putin took the reins of authority in 1999-2000, first as acting President, then in March 2000 as President, his task was to avoid the economic chaos that had plagued Russia earlier and to put Russia on track toward long-term economic growth. To do so required the Putin leadership to take advantage of the window of opportunity of the post-1998 crisis economic surge and undertake some major economic reforms.

By the end of 1999, the Russian government had achieved a degree of financial stabilization as former Prime Minister Primakov had instituted measures to cut government spending and increase tax revenues. The Russian economy had begun to grow because of the severe depreciation of the ruble as a result of the 1998 financial crisis which boosted exports.[26] A key objective of the Putin regime would be to make sure to maintain stability especially after the effects of the depreciated ruble had disappeared.

Rationalize Government Expenditures and Revenues

The high inflation and general economic chaos of the 1990s contributed to political and social instability. The instability undermined the government's ability to build a market economy. In order to attain economic stability, the government would have to rein in profligate government spending to keep inflation under control.

Russian government national accounts data show that the government has improved budget balances and maintained tight control over fiscal policy. At the end of 1998, the Russian federal government had a budget deficit equal to 6.0% of Russian GDP with revenues equal to 11.4% of GDP and expenditures equal to 17.4%. In 1999, the budget deficit declined slightly to 4.2% GDP. During the ensuing years, Russian government revenues soared from 12.6% of GDP in 2000 to 23.6% of GDP in 2006, largely because of tax revenues generated by the surge in oil revenues. At the same time, the government managed to resist expanding expenditures, keeping them far below revenues with expenditures equal to 16.1% GDP in 2006. As a result, the Russian government has consistently earned budget surpluses and had a surplus of 7.5% of GDP in 2006.[27]

The Russian government's ability to maintain prudent fiscal balances is due in part to the establishment in January 2004 of a stabilization fund. The Ministry of Finance deposits in the fund government tax revenues obtained from oil production at oil prices (Urals crude) above $27/barrel. (When the fund was established in 2004, the threshold price was $20). The funds are to be used to finance government deficits that result when the oil price falls below $27. On February 15, 2008, the price of Urals crude was $90.75/barrel.[28] In addition, by law the government is to use funds in excess of a balance of 500 billion rubles for purposes approved by the Federal Assembly, the legislature. On January 30, 2008, the fund held an aggregate amount of 3.9 trillion rubles. The Russian government has used these funds to pay off partially its IMF and Paris Club debts and also to finance a deficit in the government-operated pension fund.[29]

The Putin government attempted to reduce government social and industrial subsidies as a another step in rationalizing government spending. In January 2005, the government replaced free access to transportation and health care with cash payments to vulnerable groups and also reduced energy subsidies for residents. The monetization program proved unpopular and protests erupted, a rarity during an otherwise very popular regime. While having to slide back on some of the measures, though, the government has maintained most of the reforms, thereby helping to keep expenditures in check.[30]

Implement Structural Economic Reforms

During Putin's first term (2000-2004), his government initiated some critical economic reforms that helped Russia emerge from the post-1998 financial crisis period more stable and stronger. During this period, reformers seemed to play the dominant role in economic policymaking.

One of the factors that had harmed business environment in Russia for both foreign and domestic investors was a plethora of high and overlapping taxes. They reflected the decentralized structure of the Russia government at the time where local, regional and federal government authorities were not clearly delineated. At times, competing levels of government placed a claim on the same revenues. As a result, businesses found it more advantageous to not pay taxes and risk getting caught. The tax regime encouraged under-reporting of economic activity and hiding income abroad. Tax delinquencies encouraged corruption. As a result, collected revenues were a fraction of potential revenues. At one point, Russian residents and businesses were subject to around 200 separate taxes, 30 of which were federal and 170 were regional and local.[31]

By 2004, the government had reduced the number of taxes to 16, 10 of which were federal and the remainder regional and local. Among the changes was an introduction of a 13% flat tax to replace a graduated personal income tax that peaked at 30%.[32] Four social taxes were compressed into one. Tax collection was centralized into the tax ministry which eliminated tax collection competition among several collection agencies that bred corruption and abuse.[33] Another important reform was the elimination of various turnover taxes that were legacies of the Soviet period.

During the early post-Soviet period, the business climate was also hampered by a large number of licensing requirements, inspections, and other regulations often promulgated and implemented by different local, regional, and federal government entities in conflict with one another. The burden and the capricious manner that the regulations were implemented made the system ripe for corruption and avoidance and also impeded the development of new business. The Putin government introduced regulatory reform by cutting the number of mandatory licenses and inspections to encourage the development of new small and medium sized enterprises.[34] These reforms have largely improved the business climate, although some authorities still conduct inspections contrary to the new regulations.[35]

The Russian government has also addressed the issue of corporate governance, particularly the protection of the rights of minority shareholders that were notoriously subjected to abuse in the 1990s. For example, the government established regulations on the times and venues for shareholders' meetings to ensure that a majority bloc of shareholders do not try to impair minority rights by holding meetings in secret and or at times and at places inaccessible to those shareholders.[36]

Agriculture has been one of the slowest sectors of the Russian economy to shed the legacies of collectivism rooted in Soviet central planning and even in earlier Russian history. Russian policymakers have had trouble dealing with the issue of land and agricultural reform, particularly converting land that been held collectively during the Soviet period to individual holdings and private ownership. Russian agriculture had been hard hit during the early transition period as demand for local production fell when it faced foreign competition from the United States and Europe.

The Russian government kept agriculture afloat with subsidies and low-interest loans that were eventually written off by the government. The sector rebounded, along with much of the rest of the Russian economy, as a result of the sharp depreciation of the ruble in the wake of the 1998 financial crisis and the resultant increase in import prices. But, the temporary drop in foreign competition reduced the incentives for reform and restructuring.

The agriculture sector once again faces problems as foreign competition has strengthened. Agriculture and land reform have remained challenges. In 2003, the Duma, the lower house of the Russian legislature, enacted a framework law on the sale and purchase of agricultural land , but its implementation had been dependent on regional governments passing and implementing laws, which they have been reluctant to do. The issue still remains a challenge for the government.[37]

Integrate Russia with the Global Economy

Russia first applied to accede to the General Agreement on Tariffs and Trade (GATT) in 1993. The application was converted to one for the World Trade Organization (WTO) in 1995 when that organization was formed and became the administrative body for the GATT and other multilateral trade agreements. The process slowed down during the Yeltsin period as the leadership was pre-occupied with other political and economic issues. Putin adopted WTO membership as part of Russian economic reform and a way to integrate Russia into the world economy:

> "It is our duty to... speed up the work on Russia's accession to the WTO on conditions that are acceptable to us and generally work to make Russia competitive in all senses of the word."[38]

Russia is the largest country not yet a member of the WTO. WTO members' concerns about weak protection of intellectual property rights (IPR) protection and Russian agriculture subsidies have been among the issues impeding Russia's accession.

Putin also called for total convertibility of the ruble, completing a process begun under Yeltsin, to ease the flow of capital between Russia and developed countries in order to facilitate trade and investment.

Despite the declared policies, the results in integrating with the world economy have been mixed. From 1994 to 2000, Russian exports as a percentage of GDP increased from 27.7% to 44.1% but declined to 30.3% in 2007. Russian imports as a percentage of GDP have declined from 22.9% in 1994 to 21.9% in 2007. On the other hand, trends in Russian foreign investment show clearer signs of economic integration. The stock of foreign direct investment in Russia as a percent of GDP rose from 0.1% in 1993 to 11.4% in 2007 and Russian foreign direct investment abroad has increased from 1.3% of GDP in 1993 to 9.7% of GDP 2007.[39]

Implement other Reforms

In 2002, the Putin government instituted pension reform to increase the level of retirement funds and reduce poverty among retirees. In addition, the reform was to move the responsibility for pensions from the government to employers. Implementation of pension reform has been slow.[40]

The Russian banking system has been notoriously inefficient. For much of the 1990s, the industry was dominated by state-owned banks, especially, the Sberbank, which held more than 70% of household savings deposits, and the Vneshtorgbank. The private-sector banking industry was dominated by many small banks that were owned by one investor or a financial group and acted as a financial conduit for the owners. Many of those banks failed during the 1998 financial crisis. In 2003, the Russian government implemented a government deposit insurance program, to partially level the playing field for private sector banks that had no such insurance, and the state banks that were backed by state funds. The deposit insurance program also was a way to introduce tighter supervision over the private sector banks that were required to meet financial health criteria by the Russian central bank before being eligible for the insurance.[41] Beginning in 2004, the Russian government also began phasing in the use of International Financial Reporting Standards (IFRS) to improve the transparency of Russian bank operations.[42]

In 2005, the regime launched "national projects" to strengthen education, health care, and housing. Critics have maintained that implementation of these projects, which has been under then-First Deputy Prime Minister and now President Dmitriy Medvedev, has been inadequate and a sign that the Putin regime "dropped the ball" on reform during his second administration and that the reforms have been stalled by those with vested interests in the status quo.[43] The Russian government also undertook reform of its judiciary– to establish clear lines of responsibility for the levels of courts and to root out corruption by increasing the salaries of judges.[44]

REASSERT STATE CONTROL OF "STRATEGIC" SECTORS

If President Putin's first term of office was marked by achieving economic stability and launching some critical reforms, the second term was largely characterized by the government's re-establishing control over critical sectors of the Russian economy. It has done so by acquiring the assets of companies that had been privatized during the Yeltsin regime and taken over by so-called oligarchs via questionable transactions. The Putin Administration has been re-nationalizing companies directly by taking control of assets or indirectly through ostensibly private sector companies in which the Russian government has substantial ownership.

The first major step in this direction was the government's attack on the Yukos oil company and its president, Mikhail Khodorkovsky. On October 25, 2003, Khodorkovsky was arrested and charged with tax evasion. Other Yukos executives were also arrested. Eventually Khodorkovsky was sentence to eight and a half year in an East Siberian prison. Khodorkovsky had acquired Yukos and several other companies in the loans for shares auctions in the mid-1990s. While his ostensible violation was tax fraud, many experts contend that Khodorkovsky' s real "crime" was to have crossed a "red line" in challenging Putin politically by financing several opposition political parties. Khodorkovsky also challenged the government's monopoly on oil transport by proposing the construction of privately owned oil pipelines. In the end, the government seized Yukos's assets to pay tax penalties and sold them at below market value prices to Rosneft, a state-owned oil company. Yukos was left bankrupt.[45] The case is noteworthy not only for the government's reassertion of control of the oil sector but also for the apparent weakness of the judicial system which allowed the government to skirt legal procedures that might have ensured impartiality.[46]

From 2005-2007, the government increased its stake in the oil industry through Gazprom, the state-controlled company that has a monopoly on Russian gas exploration and production. It bought controlling shares in Sibneft, a once private company. It also bought Sakhalin Energy company, which had been led by Shell Oil and in TNK-BP, a joint venture between BP and a group of private Russian companies. The latter two acquisitions occurred after the Russian government cited projects by these companies for environmental regulation infringements and licensing issues. As a result of these acquisitions, state control of the oil industry increased from around 18% to over 50% between 2004 and 2007, according to one estimate.[47]

From 2004 to 2006, the government took control of formally privatized companies in certain "strategic" sectors. oil, aviation, power generation equipment, machine-building and finance. For example, the state-owned defense equipment company Rosoboronexport took control of Avtovaz, the primary producer of Russian cars. In June 2006, it took 60% control of VSMPO-Avisma, a company that accounts for two-thirds of the world's titanium production. In 2007, United Aircraft Building Corporation (UABC), a company that is 51% government controlled, combined all of the Russian companies producing aircraft .[48] The OECD estimates that the government's share of Russia's equity market capitalization increased from 20% in mid-2003, to 30% in early 2006. In the oil sector alone, state-owned companies controlled 16.0% of crude oil production in 2003 and 33.5% in 2005, a figure that the OECD estimates to have risen eventually to over 40% after all of Yukos' s assets had been distributed.[49]

According to the European Bank for Reconstruction and Development (EBRD), in 1991, just prior to the collapse of the Soviet Union, 5% of Russian GDP was accounted for by the private sector. By 1997, that share had grown to 70%, but decreased to 65% in 2005 where it has remained. In comparison, in the Ukrainian economy, the share of GDP accounted for by the private sector increased from 10% in 1991 to 65% in 2002 where it has remained. In contrast, the share of the private sector in Poland's GDP rose from 40% in 1991 to 75% in 2001 where it has remained.[50]

The EBRD monitors the progress of former communist states' transition to market economies. One of the elements the bank examines is the degree to which the country has privatized state-enterprises. It does so using a scale of 1.00-4.00 with 1.00 indicating little private ownership and 4.00 indicating more than 50% private ownership. According to the EBRD, the status of Russia's privatization of large- scale enterprises fell from 3.33 in 2004 to 3.00 in 2007. At 3.00, Russia ranked ahead of Turkmenistan (1.00) and Tajikistan (2.33), is on par with Ukraine (3.00) and Moldova (3.00), and is behind Romania (3.67), Armenia (3.67) and Georgia (4.00). EBRD indices of small-enterprise privatization indicated that Russia has done better at 4.00 where it has been since 1995.[51]

The Role of Oil and other Natural Resources

Russia possesses the world's eighth largest reserves of oil and is the world's second largest oil exporter (next to Saudi Arabia). It also possesses the world's largest natural gas reserves and is the largest exporter of natural gas. In addition, Russia has the second largest coal reserves.[52] These natural resources, particularly oil, have been a major driving force of the Russian economy for a long time and a significant determinant of Russia's economic health. Therefore, the role of oil requires special attention in a discussion of Russia's economic conditions.

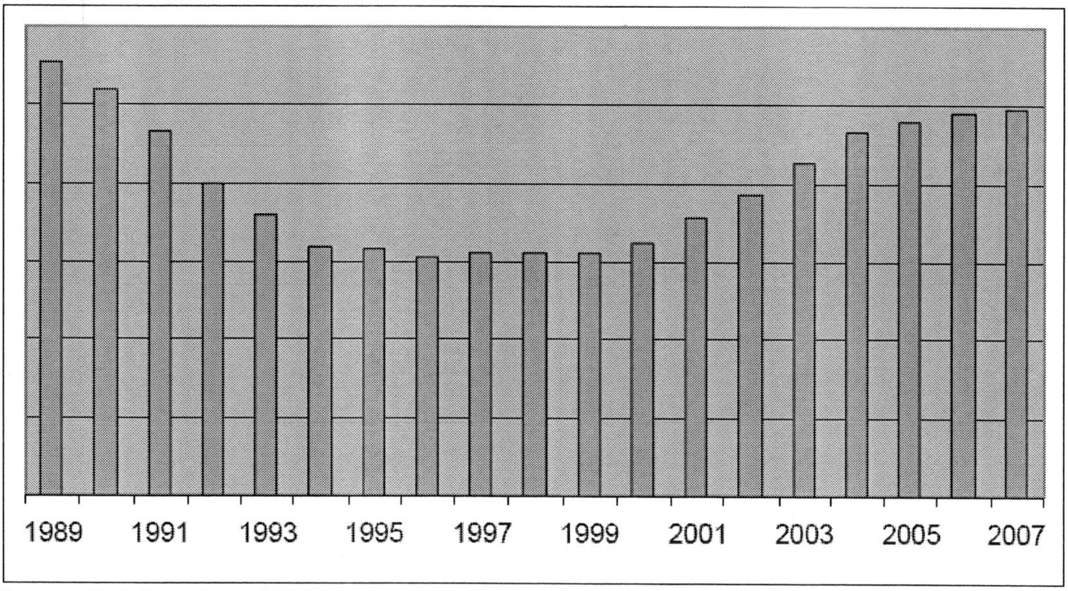

Source: CRS from data of U.S. Department of Energy. Energy Information Administration.

Figure 2. Russian Oil Production, 1989-2007 (Millions of Barrels/Day).

The levels of Russian oil production have varied over the years and have roughly mirrored overall conditions of the Russian economy. The graph in figure 2 above indicates that from 1989 to 1996, the volume of oil production decreased appreciably, from 11.1 million barrels/day to 6.1 million barrels/day or about 45%. This period is contemporaneous with the deep slide in Russian economic growth shortly before and immediately after the collapse of the Soviet Union. The decline was caused by a dramatic drop in world demand for oil, a decrease in world oil prices, the depletion of exploited Russian oil fields, and the lack of investment in discovering new ones. Production began to grow in 1997, at first gradually, then more rapidly reaching 9.9 million b/d in 2007, still below the 1989 level.[53] Oil production has continued to increase but at a decelerating rate, with possible implications for the future.[54] One report estimates that Russian oil production may have already peaked in early 2008 and could begin to decline.[55]

Among the factors which contributed to the deceleration of oil production was the Yukos case which led Russian oil companies to reduce investment in upstream activities. Also, the heavy taxation of oil revenues is another contributing factor. Most oil-sector investment in Russia is aimed at increasing current production rather than developing new fields; therefore, any slowdown in the growth of capital spending is soon reflected in slower growth of production and exports. Russia will be not be able to sustain oil production over the long term if the investment in the sector is not increased. [56]

While oil production activities represent a small direct part of Russian GDP, the income derived from oil production has contributed significantly through the multiplier effect to overall GDP growth. According to the International Monetary Fund (IMF), the Russian federal government budget enjoyed a fiscal surplus equivalent to 7.4% of GDP in 2006; however, if oil-related revenues are excluded, the budget would have been in a deficit equivalent to 3.8% of GDP.[57] Of course, the IMF calculation assumes that the Russian government would have maintained the level of expenditures. This analysis suggests that Russia is becoming more reliant on world oil prices increasing or at least remaining high.

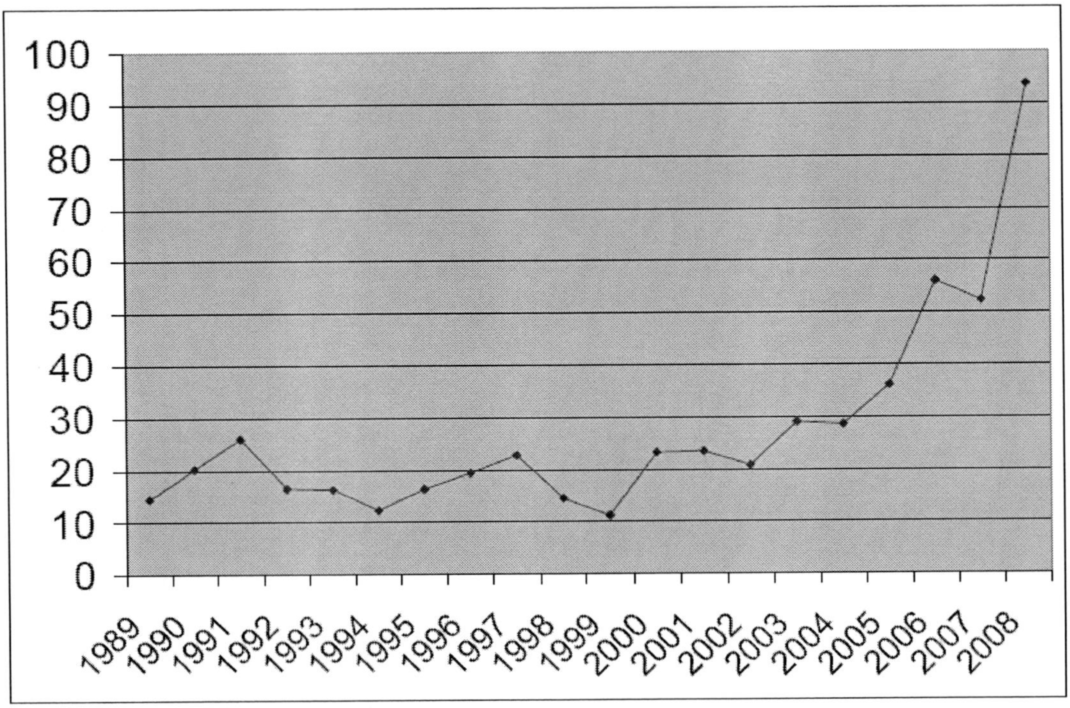

Figure 3. Oil Prices, 1989-2008 ($/barrel–U rals-32).

The significance of oil and other natural resources to the Russian economy is perhaps no more evident than in Russian foreign trade. Even during the Soviet period, oil and other natural resources were by far the primary source of hard currency revenues. They have maintained and, at times increased, their importance in post- Soviet era Russian foreign trade. In 2006, energy resources (oil, natural gas, and coal) accounted for 65% of total Russian export revenues. Exports of crude oil accounted for 34% of that share.[58]Russia's increasing reliance on exports oil and other energy resources makes Russian trade vulnerable to the volatility of international commodity prices. Exports of machinery and equipment accounted for only 6% of Russian exports outside the former Soviet Union.[59]

While the volume of Russian energy production and net exports (exports minus imports) have increased significantly since the mid-1990s, the rate of increase may have plateaued, suggesting that the growth and, perhaps, even the maintenance of surplus of oil-dependent revenues will depend on the world oil prices growing or at least remaining high. In 2005, the volume of net oil exports reached 6.8 million barrels/day and remained at that level in 2006. Nevertheless, the overall Russian trade surplus continued to expand in U.S. dollar terms, as the increase in oil prices offset both the weak export performance and the rise in imports. The trade surplus reached a record of $US 140 billion in 2006, up from US$118 billion the year before, owing to an increase of more than 20% in export prices.

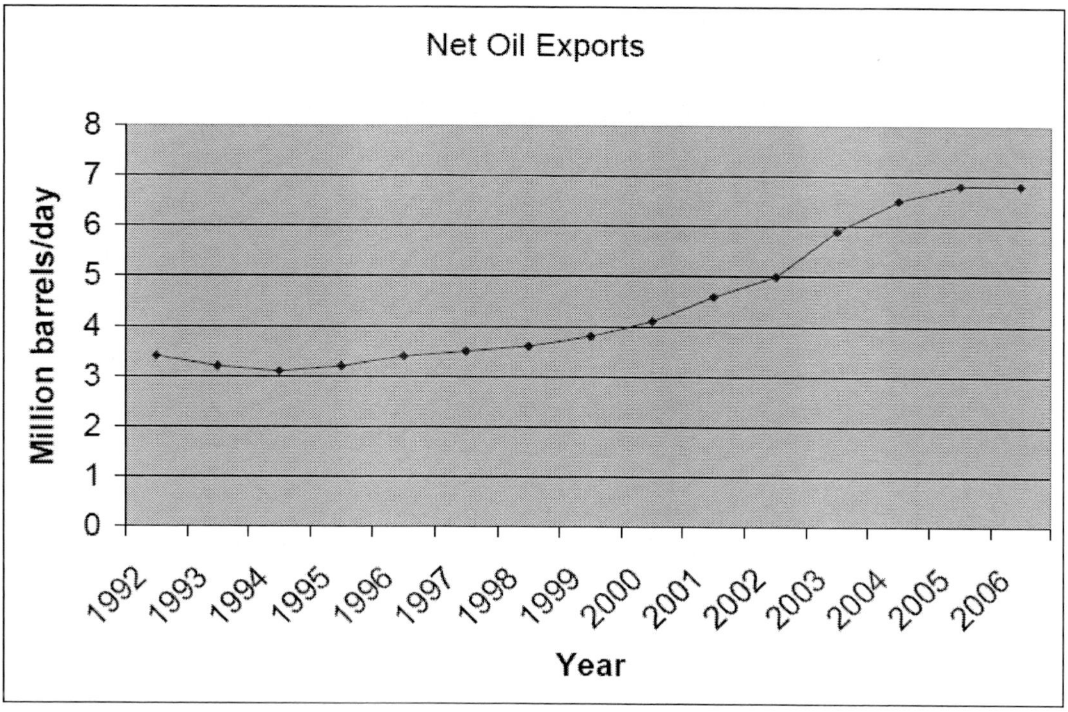

Figure 4. Net Russian Exports of Oil, 1992-2006(Million Barrels/Day).

Is Russia's Economic Growth Sustainable?

According to some economic forecasts, Russia's economic growth will continue for the next few years, albeit at lower rates. The IMF, for example, projects Russia's real GDP to average 6.1% between 2008 and 2013.[60] Global Insight, Inc. forecasts Russia's economic growth to average 5.9% between 2008 and 2012.[61]

The importance of Russia's economic growth leads to the question of how long can these trends continue, a question that itself requires an examination of some of the factors that will influence Russia's economic prospects. Some factors indicate good times ahead, others suggest trouble, and still others are ambiguous.

Is Russia's Economic Growth Sustainable?

According to some economic forecasts, Russia's economic growth will continue for the next few years, albeit at lower rates. The IMF, for example, projects Russia's real GDP to average 6.1% between 2008 and 2013.60 Global Insight, Inc. forecasts Russia's economic growth to average 5.9% between 2008 and 2012.61

The importance of Russia's economic growth leads to the question of how long can these trends continue, a question that itself requires an examination of some of the factors that will influence Russia's economic prospects. Some factors indicate good times ahead, others suggest trouble, and still others are ambiguous.

One favorable sign for continued growth is that the sources of GDP economic growth are becoming more balanced. For example, Russia has experienced double- digit growth in domestic consumption. In 2006, household consumption increased by 11.1% and by 12.9% in 2007, outpacing overall GDP growth.[62] Furthermore, the sources of growth have spread from the metropolitan areas, such as Moscow and St. Petersburg, to outlying industrial regions in the Ural mountains and in the Volga river basin.[63]

Russian fixed capital investment has increased 11.7% on average per year 1999- 2007. In 2007 alone, it increased 21.1% , the highest in recent Russian history.[64] Official Russian economic data show that investment is spread throughout the economy. About 14% of the fixed investments (in 2006) were in the energy sector, 16% were in manufacturing, 24% were in transportation and communication, and 16% were in real estate, renting, and business activities.[65] Growth in fixed investment indicates confidence in the future as firms replenish or add to production capacity.

The OECD indicates that despite the surge, Russia still lags far behind other emerging economies in terms of capital investment. The OECD calculated that from 2000-2005, Russia's average capital investment as a percent of GDP was around 18%, while that of China was close to 40%, South Korea's was 30%, and the Czech Republic's was 27%. These data would indicate that Russia still has much room to catch up with similar economies.[66] Philip Hanson, an expert on the Russian economy, has suggested that the excess industrial capacity that Russia inherited from the Soviet period has been used up or has become obsolete implying that Russia will need large amounts of new investments to ensure continuing economic growth.

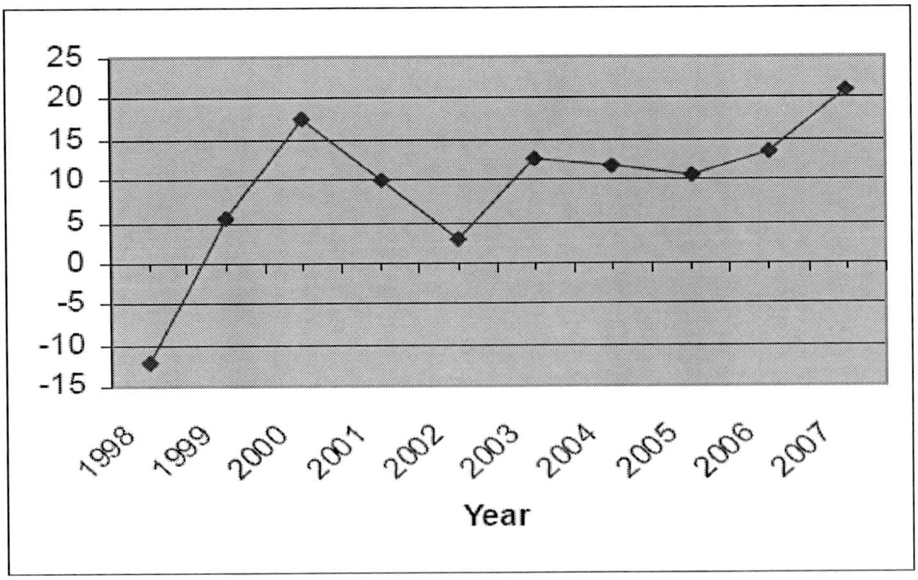

Source: CRS from data collected by the Economist Intelligence Unit.

Figure 5. Percentage Changes in Russian Annual Fixed Investment, 1998-2007.

Other factors could present problems for the Russian economy. One factor is ruble appreciation. Between 1998, the year of the financial crisis, and 1999 the ruble depreciated 25% in real effective terms.[67] The ruble appreciated in real terms from 1999 onward but only gradually, reaching its pre-financial crisis level not until 2002. During that period Russia's domestic producers benefitted from diminished competition from imports because they had become much more expensive. Since 2002, the ruble has appreciated much more rapidly, 43% by the end of 2007.[68] The rapid appreciation is causing concerns, particularly among Russia's manufacturing industries which are facing stronger import competition while they are still trying to develop.

The ruble appreciation has been caused in part by the strong demand for Russian energy exports, particularly oil. The trend has led some observers to surmise that Russia may have caught the "Dutch disease." This is a term that is applied when a country that is heavily dependent on one product, such as oil, in its exports, experiences a surge in export revenues. That country's currency will appreciate accordingly, forcing other industries to face stronger foreign competition and dampening exports of those other products. While ruble appreciation makes imports cheaper and help to dampen inflation, it also makes diversification of Russia's export base much more difficult.[69] Whether or not Russia has the "Dutch Disease," the strong ruble has put downward pressure on Russian non-energy exports. The OECD reported that the non-fuel trade balance has deteriorated beginning in 2005 even though the overall trade balance had remained strong because of rising oil prices.[70]

Inflation has been another factor of concern for Russia. Russia had been making considerable progress in controlling inflation, which had been a constant problem since the collapse of the Soviet Union. At the end of 2006, inflation was 9%, still high by U.S. standards but the first single-digit inflation since 1991. However, consumer prices in Russia began to rise more rapidly in 2007, 11.9% by the end of 2007. The rate of inflation has continued to increase, reaching 14.3% in April 2008 compared to April 2007.[71] A sharp rise in food prices has been the primary cause of the inflation spike, as well as increases in prices for raw materials and other industrial inputs.[72] Another contributing factor may be the increase in government spending. In 2007, Russian government expenditures rose to 18.1% of GDP from 16.0% GDP the year before, and are projected to increase to 21.2% GDP in 2008.[73] High inflation causes economic instability and political instability as it reduces consumer buying power and saps savings.

The Russian government's seizure of "strategic sectors" of the economy (discussed earlier) could be a factor that will impede Russian economic growth and development. The OECD cites the tendency of state-owned companies in Russia to be associated with corruption, lack of transparency, and rent-seeking. State representatives tend to interfere in day-to-day operations, which undermines the commercial effectiveness of the company.[74]

The increase in state control over the economy has also coincided with a sharp decline in the pace of economic restructuring and reforms that occurred during Putin' s first term. One indicator of the decline in economic reforms is the measure of the business environment in Russia. Each year the World Bank evaluates the ease of doing business in 178 countries by examining a range of criteria, such as ease of starting a business, closing a business, employing workers and, protecting workers. In April 2006, Russia ranked 96th.[75] In April 2008, it ranked 106th, although it had improved from 1 12th during the previous year. Nevertheless, Russia ranked behind such former Soviet republics as Azerbaijan (96th), Armenia (39th), Georgia (18th), and Kazakhstan (71st) . Singapore was ranked (1st) and the

United States was ranked (3rd) The Congo Democratic Republic was ranked 178th.[76] Another indicator is Russia's economic growth compared to those of other former Soviet states. In 2007, even though Russia's real GDP increased 8.1%, it was only 9th among the other former Soviet states.[77]

However, it is Russia's continue dependence on oil and the world price of oil that will be a dominant factor in Russia's economic prospects for the time being. As indicated earlier, this is a double-edged sword for Russia. On the one hand, Russia is clearly benefitting from record-high prices. On the other, its oil production capacity is limited and showing signs of strain.

Implications for the United States

Russia's economic prospects have direct and indirect implications for the United States. One way to measure the direct implications is by examining the status of U.S.- Russian economic ties.

U.S.-Russian trade and investment flows have increased in the post-Cold War period reflecting the changed U.S.-Russian relationship. Many experts have suggested that the relationship could expand even further. U.S. imports from Russia have increased substantially, rising from $0.5 billion in 1992 to a peak of $19.8 billion in 2006. A slight decline in 2007 to $19.4 billion was due to a sharp drop in imports of steel and aluminum products. The large increase in U.S. imports reflects not so much an increase in the volume of trade but the rise in world prices of raw materials, particularly oil, that comprise the bulk of those imports (57% in 2007).

Table 4. U.S. Merchandise Trade with Russia, 1992-2007 in billions of dollars

Year	U.S. Exports	U.S. Imports	U.S. Trade Balances	Year	U.S. Exports	U.S. Imports	U.S. Trade Balances
1992	2.1	0.5	1.6	2000	2.1	7.7	-5.6
1993	3.0	1.7	1.3	2001	2.7	6.3	-3.5
1994	2.6	3.2	-0.6	2002	2.4	6.8	-4.4
1995	2.8	4.0	-1.2	2003	2.4	8.6	-6.2
1996	3.3	3.6	-0.3	2004	3.0	11.9	-8.9
1997	3.4	4.3	-0.9	2005	3.9	15.3	-11.3
1998	3.6	5.7	-2.1	2006	4.7	19.8	-15.1
1999	2.1	5.9	-3.8	2007	7.4	19.4	-12.0
Major U.S. exports: machinery; vehicles; meat; aircraft.Major U.S. imports: mineral fuels; inorganic chemicals aluminum; steel.							

Source: Compiled by CRS from U.S. Department of Commerce Data. Bureau of the Census. FT900.

U.S. exports have increased from $2.1 billion in 1992 peaking at $7.4 billion in 2007. Major U.S. exports to Russia consist of machinery, vehicles, and meat (mostly chicken).[78]

Despite the increase in bilateral trade, the United States and Russia still account for small shares of each others' trade. In 2007, Russia accounted for about 0.6% of U.S. exports and 1.0% of U.S. imports. The United States accounted for 2.5% of Russian exports and 4.9% of Russian imports. On June 10, 2007, the Russian airline, Aeroflot, signed a contract to purchase 22 long-range Boeing 787 aircraft, a deal worth an estimated $3.5 billion.[79]

The United States accounted for $4.6 billion in foreign direct investment in Russia in 2006 most of which were in energy-related assets. The United States was technically the third largest source of foreign direct investment; however, the first two, Cyprus and Luxembourg, are considered to be largely sources of repatriated Russian capital rather than of original foreign capital.[80]

Russia and the United States have never been major economic partners, and it unlikely that the significance of bilateral trade will increase much in the near term. However, in some areas, such as agriculture, Russia has become an important market for U.S. exports. Russia is the largest foreign market for U.S. poultry. Furthermore, U.S. exports to Russia of energy exploration equipment and technology, as well as industrial and agricultural equipment, have increased as the dollar has declined in value. Russian demand for these products will likely grow as old equipment and technology need to be replaced and modernized. Russia's significance as a supplier of U.S. imports will also likely remain small given the lack of international competitiveness of Russian production outside of oil, gas, and other natural resources. U.S.-Russian investment relations could grow tighter if Russia's business climate improves; however, U.S. business concerns about the Russian government's seemingly capricious intervention in energy and other sectors could dampen the enthusiasm of all but adventuresome investors.

The greater importance of Russia's economic policies and prospects to the United States lie in their indirect effect on the overall economic and political environment in which the United States and Russia operate. From this perspective, Russia's continuing economic stability and growth can be considered positive for the United States. Because financial markets are interrelated, chaos in even some of the smaller economies can cause uncertainty throughout the rest of the world. Such was the case during Russia's financial meltdown in 1998. Promotion of economic stability in Russia has been a basis for U.S. support for Russia's membership in international economic organizations, including the International Monetary Fund (IMF), the World Bank, and the World Trade Organization (WTO). As a major oil producer and exporter, Russia influences world oil prices that affect U.S. consumers.

The impact of Russian economic policies and prospects also plays a role in U.S. national security interests. For example, Russia is a major supplier of natural gas to many U.S. European allies. In 2005, Russia accounted for 26% of France's, 30% of Italy's, and 43% of Germany's consumption of natural gas, making these allies possibly vulnerable to political pressure. On January 1, 2006, Russia temporarily shut-off gas supplies to Ukraine over a price dispute which affected supplies to Europe. [81] While Europe was not the target of the action, the disruption affected European views of Russia as a reliable supplier of gas. Russia is also a primary supplier of natural gas to other former Soviet republics, providing it with potential political leverage. The United States has been promoting the construction of pipelines that by-pass Russia, thus decreasing Moscow's monopoly control of Caspian and Central Asian energy flows.

REFERENCES

[1] Putin, Vladimir. Transcript of annual press conference. February 18, 2008. [http://www.kremlin.ru].
[2] For more information on U.S.-Russian relations, see CRS Report RL33407, Russian Political, Economic, and Security Issues and U.S. Interests, by Stuart D. Goldman.
[3] House of Representatives. Committee on Financial Services. Subcommittee on Domestic and International Monetary Policy, Trade, and Technology. Hearing. U.S.-Russia Economic Relationship: Implications of the Yukos Affairs. Serial No. 110-71. 2008. 65p.
[4] For more details on PNTR for Russia see CRS Report RS21123, Permanent Normal Trade Relations (PNTR) Status for Russia and U.S.-Russian Economic Ties, by William H. Cooper.
[5] CRS calculations based on official Russian data collected by the Economist Intelligence Unit (EIU).
[6] EIU.
[7] Capital flight is an abnormal flow of funds whose holders seek safe havens from financial uncertainty and taxation or to launder proceeds from illegal activities, It is a sign of lack of confidence in the local economy and deprives the local economy of the use of the capital and decreases tax revenues.
[8] OECD. The Investment Environment in the Russian Federation. 2001. p.148.
[9] Aslund, Anders. Russia's Capitalist Revolution: Why Market Reform Succeeded and Democracy Failed. Peterson Institute for International Economics. Washington. October 2007. p. 161-164.
[10] For a more detailed analysis of the financial crisis see (archived) CRS Report 98-57 8, The Russian Financial Crisis: An Analysis of Trends, Causes, and Implications, by William H. Cooper.
[11] Furthermore, the ruble continued to decline losing 71% of its value from April to the end of 1998. Measured on a real effective exchange rate basis (adjusted for inflation), the ruble depreciated 41% between April and December 1998. CRS calculations based on data in Central Bank of Russia data published in Russian Economic Trends. September 15, 2000. p. 29.
[12] Ibid.
[13] Ibid. p.22.
[14] Economist Intelligence Unit. Country Profile 2007: Russia. p.5.
[15] Official Russian government data from Goskomstat. [http://www.gks.ru].
[16] Ibid.
[17] Ibid.
[18] Goskomstat.
[19] Kommersant. February 27, 2008.
[20] Goskomstat.

[21] Economist Intelligence Unit. Country Profile 2007: Russia. p. 42.
[22] CRS calculations based on data from EIU. Country Profile–Russia. 2007. p.66.
[23] Ibid.
[24] Russian Customs Service data collected by Global Trade Systems, Inc in World Trade Atlas. October 27, 2007.
[25] EIU. Country Report: Russia. March 2008.
[26] Aslund. p. 190-197
[27] Data obtained from the Bank of Finland. BOFIT Russia Statistics. [http://www.bof.fi].
[28] U.S. Department of Energy. Energy Information Administration. Official Energy Statistics from the U.S. Government. [http://www.eia.doe.gov].
[29] Russian Ministry of Finance. [http://www.minfin.ru].
[30] EIU. Country Profile 2007: Russia. p.36.
[31] Åslund, Anders. Russia's Capitalist Revolution: Why Market Reform Succeeded and Democracy Failed. Petersen Institute for International Economics. November 2007. p.2 15.
[32] Ibid. p. 216.
[33] Ibid.
[34] Ibid., p. 217-218.
[35] EIU. 2007. p. 38.
[36] Organization for Economic Cooperation and Development. OECD Economic Survey of the Russian Federation.2004. p. 66.
[37] Aslund, p.219; OECD (2006), p.72-74.
[38] Office of the President of Russia. Annual Address to the Federal Assembly. April 3, 2001. [http://www.kremlin.ru].
[39] Data obtained from the Economist Intelligence Unit.
[40] EIU. Country Profile: Russia 2007. p. 38.
[41] OECD, 2004, p. 200.
[42] Ibid., p. 204
[43] Delany, Max. "Life Gets Better, But Only for Some." Moscow Times. February 27, 2007.
[44] OECD. 2004. p. 65.
[45] Aslund. p. 234-241. OECD 2006. p. 37-38.
[46] For more information, see (archived) CRS Report RS2 1673, Russia's Arrest of Mikhail Khodorkovsky: Background and Implications for U.S. Interests., by James Nichol.
[47] Hanson, Philip. The Russian Economic Puzzle: Going Forwards, Backwards, or Sideways? International Affairs. vol. 83. no. 5. p. 876-877.
[48] EIU. Country Profile 2007–Russia. p.38-39.
[49] OECD. 2006. p.38.
[50] EBRD. Economic Statistics and Forecasts. [http://www.ebrd.org].
[51] Ibid.
[52] EIA. Country Analysis Briefs: Russia. April 2007. [http://www.eia.doe.gov]
[53] Data were obtained from [http://www.bp.com].
[54] EIU. Country Profile Russia .2007. p. 45.
[55] Hoyos, Carola and Catherine Belton. Russia Braced for First Oil Production Fall in 10 Years. Financial Times. April 15, 2008. p. 2.
[56] OECD, 2006. p. 29-30.

[57] Ibid. p. 26.
[58] IMF. Russian Economic Report. November 2007. p. 29.
[59] EIU. Country Profile Russia. 2007. p. 52.
[60] IMF. World Economic Outlook database. [http://www.imf.org].
[61] Global Insight, Inc. database.
[62] EIU. Country Indicators.
[63] Sutela, Pekka. "The State of the Russian Economy. Economic Growth Remains Surprisingly High." Russian Analytical Digest. April 2, 2008. no. 38.p. 3.
[64] Ibid. p. 6.
[65] Russian Federal Statistics Service.
[66] OECD 2006. p. 27.
[67] Real effective terms means that it is calculated on trade-weighted basis with an emphasis on dollars and euros, Russia's primary trade currencies, and adjusted for relative prices changes.
[68] CRS calculations based on data collected by the Economist Intelligence Unit.
[69] "Dutch disease" is so-called because of the decline in the Netherlands's manufacturing sector as a result of surge in natural gas exports and the rapid real appreciation of the currency. OECD 2006. p. 82.
[70] OECD. 2006. p. 80
[71] Financial Times. May 7, 2008. p. 3.
[72] EIU. Country Report. Russia. April 2008. p. 16.
[73] Ibid. p. 17.
[74] OECD. 2006. p.39.
[75] Cited in Hanson, Philip. The Russian Economic Puzzle: Going Forwards, Backwards, or Sideways? in International Affairs. vol. 83. no. 5. p. 872.
[76] http://www.doingbusiness.org]. Accessed April 14, 2008.
[77] Azerbaijan's GDP increased 25.0%, Armenia 13.7%, Georgia 12.5%, Latvia 10.7%, Uzbekistan 9.5%, Lithuania 8.8%, Kazakhstan 8.5%, and Kyrgyz Republic 8.2%.
[78] Global Trade Information System.
[79] Financial Times. June 11, 2007. p. 16.
[80] Tendentsii I perspectiva (Trends and Outlook). 2007
[81] Department of Energy. Energy Information Administration. Country Analysis Briefs.Russia. April 2007. p. 10.

In: Russian Political, Economic and Security Issues
Editor: Harold J. Kowen
ISBN 978-1-60692-407-5

Chapter 4

RUSSIA'S ACCESSION TO THE WTO*

William H. Cooper
Foreign Affairs, Defense, and Trade Division

ABSTRACT

In 1993, Russia formally applied for accession to the General Agreement on Tariffs and Trade (GATT). Its application was taken up by the World Trade Organization (WTO), the successor organization of the GATT, in 1995. Russia's application has entered into its most significant phase as Russia negotiates with WTO members on the conditions for accession.

Accession to the WTO is critical to Russia and its political leadership. President Vladimir Putin has made it a top priority. He views accession as an important step in integrating the Russian economy with the rest of the world and in fostering economic growth and development by attracting foreign investment and by lowering trade barriers. For the United States, the European Union (EU) and other trading partners, Russia's accession to the WTO could increase stability and predictability in Russia's foreign trade and investment regime.

Differences over some critical issues remain, making the time for Russian accession to the WTO uncertain. The European Union and the United States have raised concerns about Russian energy pricing policies which allow natural gas, oil, and electricity to be sold domestically far below world prices providing, they argue, a subsidy to domestic producers of fertilizers, steel, and other energy-intensive goods. Russia counters that the subsidies are not illegal under the WTO. Concerns regarding Russian trade barriers in the services sector, high tariffs for civil aircraft and autos, intellectual property rights protection, and agriculture subsidies, have also slowed down the process. On November 19, 2006, U.S. and Russian officials signed a bilateral agreement on Russia's accession to the WTO, thus completing a major step in the accession process. Russia still needs to complete negotiations with working party members.

Congressional interest in Russia's accession to the WTO is multifaceted. Members of Congress are concerned that Russia enters the WTO under terms and conditions in line with U.S. economic interests, especially gaining access to Russian markets as well as safeguards to protect U.S. import-sensitive industries. Some Members also assert that

* Excerpted from CRS Report RL31 979, dated January 7, 2008.

Congress should have a formal role in approving the conditions under which Russia accedes to the WTO, a role it does not have at this time. A number of Members of Congress and members of the U.S. business community have advised the Bush Administration not to agree too quickly to Russia's accession to the WTO and to ensure that U.S. concerns are met. The Congress has a direct role in determining whether Russia receives permanent normal trade relations (NTR) status which has implications for Russia's membership in the WTO and U.S.-Russian trade relations. Without granting permanent NTR (PNTR) to Russia, the United States might not benefit from the concessions that Russia makes upon accession. Issues regarding Russia's accession to the WTO may arise during the second session of the 1 10th Congress. This report will be updated as events warrant.

In 1993, Russia formally applied for accession to the General Agreement on Tariffs and Trade (GATT). Its application was taken up by the World Trade Organization (WTO) in 1995, the successor organization of the GATT.[1] Russia's application has entered into its most significant phase as Russia negotiates with WTO members on the conditions for accession. The process is moving forward, but differences over some critical issues remain, making the time for Russian accession to the WTO uncertain.

Accession to the WTO is critical to Russia and its political leadership. President Vladimir Putin has made it a top priority. He views accession as an important step in integrating the Russian economy with the rest of the world and in fostering economic growth and development by attracting foreign investment and by lowering trade barriers. For the United States, the European Union (EU) and other trading partners, Russia's accession to the WTO could increase stability and predictability in Russia's foreign trade and investment regime as well as encourage economic reforms. Presidents Bush and Putin have discussed Russia's accession to the WTO at their various bilateral meetings.

Russian leaders have asserted that Russia is being forced to adhere to higher standards than current WTO members. At times they have publicly expressed reservations about the WTO and the accession process. On June 10, 2007, at a forum on the Russian economy in St. Petersburg, President called for the formation of new economic organizations. Putin claims that the WTO and the other multilateral organizations are "archaic, undemocratic, and unwieldy," and do not reflect the increasing economic power of Russia and other emerging markets.[2]

On November 19, 2006, U.S. and Russian officials signed a bilateral agreement on Russia's accession to the WTO, thus completing a major step in the accession process. Russia still needs to complete "multilateral" negotiations with the WTO working party, that consists of representatives from about 60 WTO member countries, including the United States.

Congressional interest in Russia's accession to the WTO is multifaceted. Members of Congress are concerned that Russia enters the WTO under terms and conditions in line with U.S. economic interests, especially gaining access to Russian markets as well as safeguards to protect U.S. import-sensitive industries. Some Members also assert that Congress should have a formal role in approving the conditions under which Russia accedes to the WTO, a role it does not have at this time. The Congress has a direct role in determining whether Russia receives permanent normal trade relations (NTR) status which has implications for Russia's membership in the WTO and U.S.-Russian trade relations. Without granting PNTR to Russia, the United States might not benefit from the concessions that Russia makes upon accession.

This report examines the issue of Russia's accession to the WTO, focusing on the implications for Russia, the United States, and the WTO. It begins with a short overview of the WTO accession process and reviews the history of the Soviet Union's relationship with the GATT/WTO. It provides a brief discussion of Russian economic conditions and the status of economic reforms as they are a major impetus for Russia's application to join the WTO. The focus of the report is the status of Russia's accession application and the outstanding issues. The report concludes with an analysis of the implications of Russia's accession to the WTO for Russia, the United States, the other WTO members and for the WTO itself and with an analysis of the outlook for the Russia's application. This report will be updated as events warrant.

THE WTO AND THE ACCESSION PROCESS

The WTO's membership of 151 countries and customs areas spans all levels of economic development, from the least developed to the most highly developed economies. The WTO came into existence in January 1995 as a part of the agreements reached by the signatories to the General Agreement on Tariffs and Trade (GATT) at the end of the Uruguay Round negotiations. The WTO's primary purpose is to administer the roughly 60 agreements and separate commitments made by its members as part of the GATT (for trade in goods), the General Agreement on Trade in Services (GATS — for trade in services), and the agreement on trade-related aspects of intellectual property rights (TRIPS).

The membership in the GATT/WTO has grown exponentially. The GATT was originally founded in 1947 by 23 countries, and the WTO now has 151 members. Vietnam and Tonga are the newest two members, having joined on January 11, 2007, and July 27, 2007, respectively. Membership in the WTO commits its members to fundamental principles in trade with other members, including:

- Most-favored nation treatment (MFN): The imports of goods and services originating from one member country will be treated no less favorably than imports of goods and services from any other member country. MFN is to be unconditional. In practical terms, this means that in most cases a country cannot apply a higher import tariff to a good from one member country than it applies to like goods from any other member country.
- National treatment: Imports of goods and services are treated no less favorably than like goods and services produced domestically. In practical terms this means that governments cannot discriminate against imports in the application of laws and regulations, such as regulations to protect consumer safety or the environment.
- Transparency: Government laws and regulations that affect foreign trade and investment are to be published and available for anyone to see. Procedures to implement the laws and regulations are to be open.
- Lowering Trade Barriers Through Negotiations: Since the GATT's creation, its members have conducted eights rounds of negotiations to lower trade barriers. At first these negotiations focused on lowering tariffs. But over time, the rounds have broadened GATT/WTO coverage to include nontariff barriers, such as discriminatory

government procurement practices, discriminatory standards, and trade-distorting government subsidies. The last completed round, the Uruguay Round (1986-94), resulted in the most ambitious expansion of rules to cover, for the first time, trade in agricultural products and services and government policies and practices pertaining to intellectual property rights protection and foreign investment regulations that affect trade.

- Reliance on tariffs: In order to promote predictability and openness in commerce, the WTO requires member countries to use tariffs and avoid using quotas or other nontariff measures when restricting imports for legitimate purposes, such as on injurious imports.

As part of its function to administer the rules established under the agreements, the WTO provides a mechanism for the settlement of disputes between members where the dispute involves alleged violations of WTO agreements. Moreover, each member's trade regime is reviewed by the WTO Secretariat from time-to-time to ensure that it conforms to WTO rules. Trade among WTO members accounts for about 90% of total world trade.[3]

The collapse of the Soviet Union and its East European Bloc and the movement of many developing countries toward liberal trade policies have spurred interest in joining the WTO. Article XII of the agreement that established the WTO sets out the requirements and procedures for countries to "accede." "Any state or customs territory having full autonomy in the conduct of its trade policies is eligible to accede to the WTO on terms agreed between it and WTO members."

The accession process begins with a letter from the applicant to the WTO requesting membership. The WTO General Council, the governing body of the WTO when the Ministerial Conference is not meeting, forms a Working Party (WP) to consider the application. Membership in the WP is open to any interested member-country. More than sixty member countries, including the United States, are part of the WP. The U.S. delegation is led by the Assistant U.S. Trade Representative for WTO and Multilateral Affairs and includes representatives from the U.S. Departments of Commerce and Agriculture.

The applicant submits a memorandum to the WP that describes in detail its current trade regime. The applicant and the WP then negotiate to determine what legislative and structural changes the applicant must make to meet WTO requirements and to establish the terms and conditions for entry of the applicant into the WTO. The WP' s findings are then included in a "Report of the Working Party" and are the basis for drawing up the "Protocol of Accession."

While it negotiates with the WP, the applicant must also conduct bilateral negotiations with each interested WTO member. During these negotiations the WTO member indicates what concessions and commitments on trade in goods and services it expects the applicant to make in order to gain entry, and the applicant indicates what concessions and commitments it is willing to make until the two agree and set down the terms. The terms of the bilateral agreements are combined into one document which will apply on an MFN basis to all WTO members once the applicant has joined the WTO. The accession package is conveyed to the General Council or Ministerial Conference for approval.

Article XII does not establish a deadline for the process. The length of the process depends on a number of factors: how many legislative and structural changes an applicant must make in its trade regime in order to meet the demands of the WP, how quickly its national and sub- national legislatures can make those changes, and the demands on the applicant made by members in bilateral negotiations and the willingness of the applicant to accept those demands. Because WTO accession is a political process as well as a legal process, its success depends on the political will of all sides — the WTO member countries and the applicant country. A formal vote is taken in the WTO that requires a 2/3 majority for accession, although in practice the WTO has sought to gain a consensus on each application. The process can take a long time: China's application took over 15 years.

THE SOVIET UNION AND THE GATT/WTO

The Soviet Union was not invited to become a contracting-party of the GATT in 1947 after it declined to join the International Monetary Fund (IMF) and the World Bank — the other two multilateral organizations that resulted from the Bretton Woods conference immediately following the end of World War II. In fact, Soviet trade and economic policy conflicted with the principles of the GATT. The GATT was based on removing barriers to trade and on developing economic interdependence among countries. Soviet foreign economic policy was largely based on the concept of self-sufficiency — the domestic economy would produce as much as possible for itself and import only those products which it could not produce. Exports were used merely to buy necessary imports, not to build markets. These economic policies helped to bring about the collapse of the Soviet Union. The Soviet Union modified the concept of self-sufficiency to include members of the Soviet Bloc-the East European countries, some Asian communist countries and Cuba, confining most of its trade with these countries in a system of limited international division of labor. Only a small amount of trade was conducted outside the Bloc. The Soviet Union spearheaded the formation of the Council for Mutual Economic Assistance (CMEA), what could be loosely described as the Soviet Bloc's version of the GATT.

In August 1986, the Soviet Union applied to take part in the Uruguay Round negotiations of the GATT as an observer with the intention of becoming a full member. The United States and other Western industrialized countries opposed the request because of the Soviet Union's central planning economic system.[4] In 1990, however, the Soviet Union received observer status to the Uruguay Round negotiations after GATT signatories, including the United States, concluded that the Soviet Union was moving toward becoming an open economy under President Mikhail Gorbachev.[5]

After the collapse of the Soviet Union in 1991, Russia retained the observer status held by the Soviet Union and, in June 1993, it formally applied to accede to the GATT. On June 16, 1993, the GATT established a working party on Russia's accession and, in January 1995, the application was converted to an application to become a member of the WTO.

RUSSIAN ECONOMIC CONDITIONS AND REFORM: AN IMPETUS FOR JOINING THE WTO

Russia's motivation for and progress toward accession to the WTO are directly related to efforts to dismantle the Soviet economic system of central planning and replace it with a more market-based economy. President Putin has made entry into the WTO a top priority, because he sees it as a mechanism for overcoming the political hurdles that have impeded economic restructuring. The possibility of accession to the WTO has been an opportunity for him to get some significant economic reform legislation through the Russian parliament. Many Russian and foreign experts have argued that these reforms and more are necessary if Russia is to achieve long-term economic growth and development. At the same time, a number of economic interest groups that favor the status-quo, such as agriculture, the auto industry, and raw material producers, have fought against economic reforms and oppose Russian accession to the WTO.

Domestic Economic Conditions

Russia has enjoyed economic growth (measured in annual changes in GDP) since 1999. Russian GDP increased 5.4%in 1999, 9.1% in 2000, and 5.1% in 2001, 4.7% in 2002, 7.3% in 2003, 7.2% in 2004, 6.4% in 2005, and 6.7% in 2006.[6] But the growth occurred after a long period of economic stagnation during the final years of the Soviet Union and a deep recession/depression during the 1990s. Many specialists have attributed the economic growth to the depreciation of the ruble at the end of the 1 990s and to the rise in world energy prices since 2001.

However, Russia has been plagued by economic problems including a high poverty rate and poor health conditions. In addition, economic growth has taken place unevenly throughout the country with the major cities of Moscow and St. Petersburg and regions well-endowed with marketable natural resources accounting for most of the economic growth, while less fortunate regions remained stagnant or have become poorer. Moreover, income distribution among the Russian population has become increasingly unequal as a small portion of the population acquires larger shares of wealth.

Russian Foreign Trade, Investment, and Debt

Since the collapse of the Soviet Union, the Russian economy has become more open to the rest of the world. The role of foreign trade in the Russian economy has grown. By 2006, Russian exports of goods and services were equivalent to 34.0% GDP and imports were equivalent to 21.3% of GDP.[7] Russian foreign trade has become more geographically diverse. In 2006, most of Russian foreign trade took place outside the former Soviet Union — only 14.3% of Russian exports and 15.4% of Russian imports were with former Soviet states.[8]

Russia has been experiencing increasing current account surpluses largely due to the rapid growth in the value of Russian exports of crude oil, natural gas, other fuels, and other natural resources. In 2006, Russia's current account surplus was $95.6 billion, an increase from $29.1 billion in 2002.[9] However, the surpluses could prove ephemeral. Russia exports primarily raw materials for which market prices tend to be highly volatile. In 2006, oil, natural, and fuel (such as coal) accounted for 65% of total Russian exports of goods. Metal and chemicals accounted for another 20%. [10] While Russia has clearly benefitted from current high prices for fuels, a more diversified trade structure could stabilize its trade situation. Russian imports, especially of machinery and equipment and of processed foods, have increased sharply recently.[11]

Foreign direct investment in Russia has surged in the last few years indicating some investor confidence in Russian economic prospects despite Putin government measures to re-nationalize the energy sector. In 2002, $3.5 billion in foreign direct investment (FDI) flowed into Russia; in contrast $28.7 billion in FDI flowed into Russia in 2006.[12] However, the level of foreign direct investment ($67.9 billion at the end of 2006) is still considered low given the size and needs of the Russian economy.

RUSSIAN ECONOMIC POLICY AND RESTRUCTURING

Russia's transition from central planning was bound to be more difficult and longer than that of the Central and East European states. The communist system was much more entrenched in the Soviet Union than it was in the rest of the Soviet Bloc. Furthermore, Russia does not have a legacy of a market economy to draw on as is the case with some of the Central and East European countries. Russia has had to deal with the legacy of a Soviet economy that was administered to meet the needs of the military while civilian production and investment were given low priority.

However, Russia's economic problems also were the result of policy failures during the transition. These failures included loose monetary and fiscal policies early in the transition period. They have also included structural problems such as poorly developed and executed privatization programs that have left many potentially productive assets in the control of enterprise mangers from the Soviet period or in the hands of a few politically-connected individuals ("oligarchs") who extracted the value from many of these assets rather than making them commercially viable for the long run. In addition, an inefficient banking system, the lack of private land ownership protection, the absence of adequate commercial laws, and an inefficient and corrupt government bureaucracy have inhibited economic growth and development.

Despite the setbacks, Russia has made some important strides:

- The government has eliminated price controls on most goods and services. This reform has been important because it allows the market forces of supply and demand to guide producers and consumers on purchasing, production and investment. Controls have remained on some important items, such as energy, housing, and transportation, but these, too, are to be removed eventually.
- The structure of Russian production more closely resembles that of an open economy than of a militarized economy. For example, the services sector, once a minor part of Soviet economy, has emerged in the post-Soviet Russian economy and now accounts for more than half of national output.
- The private sector has grown and accounts for roughly 3/4 of national output.

Since taking the reins of power, President Putin has forced Russia into a new phase of economic reform. Putin has enjoyed a high degree of popularity among the Russian people that has translated into overwhelming political clout in the Russian parliament. In addition, the continuing period of economic growth has provided a window of opportunity for Putin and his government to tackle economic restructuring. He has been able to push important economic legislation through the Russian parliament: tax reform; land reform; reform of government bureaucracy to make it more responsive to the needs of the economy rather than an impediment to development and growth; judicial reform; and improvement in corporate governance, especially the protection of minority shareholders' rights.

The fragile basis of Russia's economic growth strongly suggests that Russia has far to go in economic reform. Analysts point to Russia's weak and underdeveloped financial sector, poorly developed system of commercial laws, and confusion over federal vs. regional and local responsibilities in important economic policy areas. Furthermore, even though Russian laws have been passed to restructure the economy, the success of their implementation remains to be seen. Furthermore, since 2004, the Putin government has shown signs of braking, if not halting, reforms and has reestablished state control over critical sectors, particularly energy, generating some skepticism regarding Putin' s commitment to Russian economic reform.

Russia's Foreign Trade and Investment Regimes and Policies

In determining the terms and conditions for Russia's accession to the WTO, WP members scrutinize Russia's foreign trade and investment regimes and policies to ascertain to what degree they conform to WTO rules and where Russia needs to change. Russia has made significant strides in that regard. It eliminated two important pillars of Soviet central planning in November 1991, the state monopoly on foreign trade and the ban on foreign investment in the Russian economy.

In October 1992, another legacy of central planning was eliminated when the Russian ruble was made convertible into foreign currencies and multiple exchange rates were eliminated. A dual exchange rate was briefly introduced in January 1999 as a result of the August 1998 financial crisis but was eliminated in June 1999. In the early to mid-1990s, the Central Bank imposed fixed or pegged exchange rates in an attempt to control ruble depreciation. Since the August 1998 crisis, the ruble has been allowed to float but the Central Bank of Russia intervenes by buying or selling rubles. The ruble has remained relatively stable since 1999.

In 1992, the Russian government adopted the Harmonized Tariff System that is used by WTO members, and it maintains a system of two-column tariff rates — MFN and non-MFN tariff rates. Tariff rates on non-agricultural products range from 0 to 30%. Some countries receive tariff advantages under Russia's Generalized System of Preferences(GSP) program in the form of tariff rates that are 25% below the MFN rate. A tariff-rate quota is applied to imports of sugar from countries receiving Russian GSP treatment.[13] Of the more than 11,000 commodity categories in the Russian tariff tables, only fifty have tariff rates above 30%.

Over time, the Russian government has lowered tariff rates. In 1995, the trade- weighted average tariff rate was 16.0%; by 2001 it was 1 1.1%.[14] Most products can be traded without restrictions, but the government requires exports and imports of some products, for example, pharmaceuticals, alcoholic beverages, precious metals and stones, to be licensed.[15] Russia also applies export tariffs on oil to ensure that domestic oil supplies are adequate and to compensate for the large differential between domestic and export oil prices. In 1998, the Russian government passed laws to provide for antidumping, countervailing, and safeguards measures against imports.

THE STATUS OF THE ACCESSION PROCESS AND OUTSTANDING ISSUES

In early 1995, Russia submitted to the working party(WP) the "Memorandum on the Foreign Trade Regime" which describes the structure of its foreign trade regime and also the structure, policies, and practices of its economy that would likely affect its conduct of trade.[16] Subsequently, the WP members submitted questions based on the memorandum, to which the Russian delegation replied. The process of submitting the original description of the trade regime, followed by a series of questions and replies established a benchmark on which the negotiations to determine the terms and conditions of Russia's accession would be based. The initial series of questions, replies and follow-up responses indicated strong concerns by the WP members in a broad range of areas including privatization, property rights, price controls, government financial support for business, and the structure and implementation of the tax regime.[17]

The Russian accession process is now at a critical stage. As with most negotiations, however, the last stages are the most difficult because negotiators now face the most contentious issues.[18] The United States, the European Union, and other participants have had strong reservations about Russian policies and practices on intellectual property rights, energy pricing, agriculture, sanitary and phytosanitary regulations, trade in services, civil aircraft, and other issues. Russia's accession to the WTO will likely hinge on the resolution of these issues, which are examined below in more detail.

ENERGY PRICING

The energy sector dominates the Russian economy. Not only do oil, natural gas, and electricity drive industry and provide heat to residents, but energy is also the largest Russian export and hard currency earner. The current structure of Russia's energy sector is largely a legacy of the Soviet Union. The oil industry has been broken up into several privatized companies. Natural gas and electricity are largely monopolies run by Gazprom and United Energy Systems (UES), respectively, which are joint-stock companies with significant government ownership. The structures of these companies are now the subject of reform, but that process has proved politically controversial and therefore slow.

Domestic prices for Russian energy are regulated by the government while exports of energy products command world prices. Domestic prices are lower than world prices, in some cases significantly, although the Russian government has been raising domestic energy prices and reducing the subsidies. The EU and the United States have pointed out that the gap between the world price for natural gas and the Russian domestic price has been as large as six to one, for electricity — five to one, and for oil — four to one.[19] The "dual pricing" is partially a result of a policy of providing affordable heating and electricity to residential customers regardless of ability to pay and providing favorable fuels rates to enterprises and to government agencies, such as the military. [20]

Some WP members, particularly the EU, and to a lesser extent the United States, have raised concern that dual energy pricing gives Russian manufacturers an unfair competitive advantage and would be illegal under the WTO subsidy agreement.[21]

WTO disciplines regarding subsidies are contained in the "Agreement on Subsidies and Countervailing Measures." Under the agreement, a subsidy is actionable only if it is a "specific subsidy," that is, it is a subsidy that is available only to an enterprise, an industry, a group of enterprises or industries in the country that gives the subsidy. The agreement defines three kinds of subsidies:

- Prohibited subsidies are ones that distort international trade, for example, subsidies that require recipients to meet exports targets or to use domestic products. These subsidies must be eliminated; otherwise, the country that complains about them can take countermeasures.
- Actionable subsidies are not prohibited unless it is determined that the subsidy causes injury. If such a determination is made, then the complaining country can impose a countervailing duty.
- Non-actionable subsidies are non-specific, or are specific subsidies for industrial research or development activity, for assistance to disadvantaged regions, or for adapting existing facilities to new environmental laws or regulations. They cannot be challenged in the WTO.[22]

European and U.S. fertilizer producers have been strong opponents of Russia's energy pricing policies because natural gas is a significant input in fertilizer production, accounting for 3/4 of the final price, according to one estimate.[23] The Russian government and Russian delegates to the WTO negotiations have strongly argued that Russian energy prices are not an actionable subsidy under WTO rules because they are available to all industries. They assert furthermore, that Russia's domestic energy prices reflect its comparative advantage in energy production. The EU and Russia came to an agreement on the dual energy pricing issue where Russia agreed to gradually increase domestic energy prices. The agreement was a part of the EU's bilateral agreement on Russia's accession to the WTO.

INTELLECTUAL PROPERTY RIGHTS PROTECTION

WTO members are calling on Russia to be in full compliance with the WTO agreement on trade-related aspects of intellectual property rights (TRIPS) at the time of its accession, in terms of laws in place and enforcement. All WTO members are bound by the provisions of the TRIPS agreement, which was designed and ratified to introduce predictability and order to intellectual property rights (IPR) protection in all WTO members, because it has become an important factor in international trade. The TRIPS agreement requires WTO members to apply the fundamental principles of national treatment and most-favored-nation treatment in intellectual property rights protection. The agreement also requires WTO members to ensure protection of copyrights, trademarks, geographical indicators of products, and patents by imposing and enforcing appropriate laws.[24]

Russia has passed a number of laws to protect the holders of copyrights, patents, and trademarks and is a a member of the major multilateral intellectual property rights conventions. While acknowledging that Russia has taken steps to improve IPR protection, U.S. industry has complained that the Russian government does not adequately enforce its laws, allowing intellectual property piracy to continue and grow with impunity — culprits are either not caught, or if caught they are not adequately punished.[25] One concern of the United States and some other WTO members has been that in 2006 the Russian parliament (the Duma) passed a revision of Part IV of the Russian Federation Civil Code. This revision replaced Russia's IPR laws with one law. The United States and the EU want Russia's assurance that the revision does not signify a weakening of legal protection of intellectual property rights.

For the past 11 years, the United States Trade Representative (USTR) has placed Russia on the Special 301 Priority Watch List.[26] U.S. producers of copyrighted material have cited unauthorized Russian reproduction of American-made films, videos, sound recordings, books, and computer software as a source of lost revenues. Russian production of pirated DVDs has increased and has been a special source of concern. U.S. industry and government officials have complained about Russia- based websites that distribute unauthorized music recordings, films, and books. Losses due to copyright piracy of U.S. products in Russia in 2006 are estimated at $2.1 billion dollars.[27] The production of counterfeit American products has become so large that they now make up the vast majority of Russian purchases of these products.[28] Russia has argued that its enforcement of intellectual property rights is improving, and that it should not be singled out since intellectual piracy continues to take place in WTO member countries. IPR protection is of serious concern to the U.S. Congress.

Agriculture

Agriculture has been a sensitive part of the economy throughout Russian/Soviet history. Its political importance far outweighs its share of the Russian economy (7.2% of Russian GDP in 2001).[29] Agriculture has been severely affected by the transition to a market economy as much as, or more than, any other sector of the economy. According to one estimate, agricultural production declined around 40% in volume terms since 1991, much of the decline occurring in livestock production.[30]

Several factors have contributed to the downturn. One factor is Soviet agriculture policy. The Soviet government determined what and how much the economy should produce and directed resources accordingly. In the 1960s, the government decided that the Soviet people should eat more meat, and it subsidized animal feed production and imports of animal feed to fulfill this objective. The government set meat prices at a low level to make it affordable to consumers. However, after the collapse of the Soviet Union, market prices were instituted and state subsidies were dramatically cut, increasing the cost of meat production.[31] Furthermore, when the Russian government liberalized trade, Russian producers of poultry and other meats could not compete with foreign producers who could sell them more cheaply.

While the Russian federal government has cut support, local and regional governments have continued to provide assistance in the form of equipment, favorable credits, and export subsidies. They are concerned about food security and unemployment and about maintaining the supply of housing, education, and other services that state farms provided to the rural communities during the Soviet period and continue to provide.

A second factor contributing to the decline in agricultural production has been the slow pace of restructuring of Russian farms. Despite the introduction of privatization, the vast majority of former state and collective farms remain intact as joint stock operations or cooperatives and operate in virtually the same inefficient manner as they did under the Soviet government.

The Russian federal government is under pressure from regional and local governments and from factions within the Russian parliament to protect agriculture from further erosion and to provide time and resources to permit it to become competitive. This pressure has translated into a difference in positions in the accession negotiations between Russia and agricultural exporting countries including the United States, Canada, and Australia over the level and longevity of government support to agriculture. The Russian government has argued for higher levels and longer phase-out periods for supports than its negotiating partners are willing to accept. Russian negotiators have also asserted that it should not be required to bind itself to dramatically lower support levels during the accession process while other WTO members are currently in the process of negotiating the agriculture subsidies in the current round of WTO negotiations, Doha Development Agenda (DDA). The WTO members have argued that the subsidies that Russia wants to maintain distort trade and are concerned that they give Russian agriculture producers an unfair advantage. The Russian side has argued that without government support, Russian agriculture could not compete with EU and U.S. agriculture, both of which receive sizeable government subsidies.[32]

Another controversy in agriculture has emerged over Russia's decision to restrict meat imports. On January 23, 2003, the Russian government announced it would impose a three-year quota on poultry imports effective May 1, 2003. At the same time the government announced tariff-rate quotas (TRQs) on imports of beef and pork effective April 1, 2003, and to remain in effect until 2010.[33] Meat exporting WTO member- countries, including the United States, Canada, Argentina, Australia, and New Zealand, have expressed stiff opposition, claiming that the restrictions may retard the process of Russia's accession to the WTO. They specifically argued that Russia has violated the "standstill" principle under which countries applying for WTO membership are to refrain from imposing new trade restrictions during the accession process. Russia counters that it is imposing the restrictions to protect its domestic meat producers from import surges, a right that is enjoyed by WTO members.[34]

During the Uruguay Round, WTO members agreed to expand disciplines over trade in agricultural products, and agricultural trade is on the agenda of the current round, the DDA. Under the Agricultural Agreement all WTO members, except least developed countries, are committed to reduce tariffs and subsidies on the production and export of agricultural goods.[35]

SANITARY AND PHYTOSANITARY REGULATIONS

Some WP members have raised concerns over Russia's sanitary and phytosanitary (SPS) standards, that is standards and certification procedures that determine the safety of meats and other animal products, plants, and plant products. They argue that these procedures are not scientifically based and discriminate against imports thus violating WTO rules. Under the Agreement on Sanitary and Phytosanitary Measures (SPM), WTO members are permitted to apply controls on products in order to protect public health and safety, but those controls must be scientifically based and must not discriminate against imports.[36] Russia has argued that its SPS controls meet the requirements of the SPM agreement.

The United States has expressed particular concern about this issue. In March 2002, the Russian government imposed a ban on imports of U.S. poultry because of the possible presence of avian influenza. Russia had become the largest market for U.S. exports of chicken. After months of negotiations, the United States and Russia agreed in August 2002 on a new veterinary certificate for U.S. poultry that would include inspections by Russian veterinarians of U.S. processing and storage facilities, but technical issues remained that prevented the process from being implemented. On April 3, 2003, the two sides announced the resolution of the problems, allowing the inspection of the facilities to go forward and U.S. poultry exports to resume.[37] Nevertheless, the United States is concerned that Russia would impose similar restrictions in the future and has pressed Russia to adhere to the WTO requirements as part of the conditions of its accession.

SERVICES

Services, especially financial services (banking, insurance, and securities), are a relatively new phenomenon in the Russian economy. Under the Soviet Union, services were government owned and operated and were confined to personal services (for example, lodging, hair salons, restaurants). They were not well developed because they were not a government priority. Financial services were virtually non-existent in the Soviet Union because their function as intermediaries between savers and borrowers of capital had no role in the Soviet planned economy.

The services sector has grown rapidly during Russia's transition to a market economy but has not matured in most cases. The United States, the EU, and other advanced developed WTO members have argued that Russia needs an efficient financial services industry to promote economic growth and development and that opening the industry to foreign investment would introduce expertise and new capital.

Russian officials and business representatives claim that their service industries must have government protection as "infant industries," because they are too immature and would be wiped out if they had to face foreign competition too soon. An example is the fledgling Russian insurance industry. Private insurance companies have been developing since the government monopoly was removed after the collapse of the Soviet Union, but not sufficiently to meet demand. Foreign insurance companies that could help fill the gap and bring expertise and a wide range of products are restricted. For example, the government: limits total foreign capitalization to 15% of the domestic insurance industry; requires the general director and the chief accountant to be Russian citizens; restricts participation to foreign companies that have been in business no less than 15 years in their home country; and requires that foreign insurance companies operate as a minority shareholder in a Russian insurance company before they can be granted their own license. In addition, foreign providers are prohibited from underwriting and reinsuring mandatory insurance — auto and health insurance and insurance taken out by government entities — the fastest growing insurance market in Russia.[38] Russian negotiators assert that those restrictions should remain while U.S., EU, and other working party participants want them loosened or removed.

The Russian banking sector is similarly underdeveloped. About 30% of the volume of Russian banking activity is conducted by two banks — Sberbank and Vneshtorgbank, both of which are owned by the Central Bank of Russia. Sberbank holds roughly 70% of the Russian savings deposits. Foreign participation in the banking sector is restricted by government laws and regulations. Foreign banks may operate in Russia only as subsidiaries and not as branches of the parent bank. Foreign banks have cited the lack of an effective deposit insurance program as a disincentive for new, private banks to develop. The government in effect backs deposits of Sberbank 100%.[39] Russian negotiators claim that the government will establish a deposit insurance program for deposits in all banks but argues that the limit on foreign participation in Russian banking must be maintained to allow domestic banks to become competitive.[40] U.S. negotiators and negotiators from some of the other working party countries are requesting that Russia liberalize its banking sector to increase foreign participation, arguing that the foreign influence would increase, not undermine, the competitiveness of Russian banks by promoting stability and popular confidence. Furthermore, a liberalized banking sector would likely boost other sectors of the economy.

In telecommunications, Russia permits 100% foreign ownership of telecommunication services providers, but it has requested to be bound by a commitment of only 49% foreign ownership. U.S. and EU negotiators oppose such a ceiling because they view the Russian telecommunications market as potentially lucrative for its firms. The Russian government has also indicated it wants long distance and international telephone communications to remain in the control of a monopoly, Rostelcom, until 2010.[41]

WTO rules on trade in services, including financial services, are contained in the General Agreement on Trade in Services (GATS) which was agreed to during the Uruguay Round. In general, the GATS is designed to apply internationally accepted rules, such as most-favored-nation treatment, to trade in services that are similar to those applied to trade in goods. In important respects, however, the GATS is less comprehensive than the GATT. For example, WTO rules on goods trade contained in the GATT apply to all goods, but many of the rules, contained in the GATS, including, "national treatment," apply only to those services and the modes of delivery of those services on which that the member country has identified in its schedule of commitments.

CIVIL AIRCRAFT

Russian aircraft manufacturers, as the case with the Russian defense-related industries in general, have seen demand for their production plummet after the government dramatically cut defense expenditures and after airlines from former Communist countries in Central and

Eastern Europe and the former Soviet Union shifted to European and U.S. manufacturers for their aircraft. The Russian government wants to protect domestic aircraft manufacturers from further erosion of business. It imposes a 20% ad valorem tariff on imported aircraft. Russia argues that its aircraft industry is operating at only 0-15% of capacity and is in great need of modernization. For it to become competitive, it needs to be protected from foreign competition and therefore must apply high tariffs to imported aircraft. The United States and EU are pressing Russia to sign on to the plurilateral WTO Civil Aircraft Agreement (CAA) (only 26 members are currently signatories) which commits the signatories to eliminate tariffs on trade in civil aircraft and some related equipment. In an 1996 bilateral Memorandum of Understanding with the United States, Russia stated that it would sign the CAA but has backed off that commitment during the accession negotiations. Because its is a plurilateral agreement, a WTO member is not required to sign the CAA as part of its obligations.

Russia does grant some tariff waivers to allow domestic airlines to fulfill needs that cannot be accommodated by domestically manufactured aircraft. It has recently favored the European firm, Airbus Industries in granting those waivers. The United States has demanded that the waivers should be granted without favoring any particular company.[42]

Other Issues

In addition to the above issues, the United States, the EU, and other working party members have raised other issues about Russia's trade and foreign investment regime and want Russia to make changes as part of the conditions for its accession to the WTO. They include:

- Tariffs: The Russian government has lowered tariffs on most categories of products in the tariff schedule. Nevertheless, it maintains high tariffs on some items to protect fledgling industries from foreign competition. High tariffs on autos, for example, have been a concern of U.S. manufacturers. Tariffs and excise taxes (that vary depending on the engine displacement) can add over 70% to the delivery cost of an imported new car. The Russian government also recently increased tariffs on used vehicles that are 3-7 years of age because they compete with Russian domestically produced new cars.[43] U.S., Japanese, and Korean delegations want Russia to lower tariffs on autos.[44] The Russian government asserts that the fledgling domestic auto industry requires some temporary protection from more developed foreign producers in order to become competitive.
- Customs regulations: Some WP members have argued that the implementation of federal customs regulations is inconsistent, leading to confusion and inhibiting trade. Some also raised problems with the policy of restricting trade of certain goods to specific ports, making it difficult for imported products to be delivered to customers. Legislation establishing a new customs code is pending in the parliament.
- Import licensing: The Russian government requires import licenses on certain products: pharmaceuticals, sugar (to implement a tariff- rate quota on sugar imported under Russia's Generalized System of Preferences program), precious metals and stones, and alcoholic beverages. Some WP members have expressed concern that

Russia might impose additional licensing requirements that would further impede imports and are asking Russia to commit to removing import restrictions and not impose new ones that are not consistent with WTO requirements. Legislation to simplify the import licensing procedures is pending in the parliament.

- Government procurement: WP members have requested that Russia join the plurilateral Government Procurement Agreement which commits signatories to open contracts for government purchases to bids from other signatory countries.

THE BILATERAL AGREEMENT AND OTHER DEVELOPMENTS

On November 19, 2006, USTR Susan Schwab and Russian Minister of Economic Development and Trade German Gref, signed the bilateral agreement on Russia's accession to the WTO and accompanying sideletters while attending the APEC summit in Hanoi, Vietnam. The agreement symbolized Russia's reaching critical milestone in its WTO accession process, although other milestones remain The agreement allowed the United States to address sensitive issues in its economic relations with Russia, although the United States did not accomplish all of its original objectives. Any debate in Congress on PNTR for Russia will likely include an evaluation of the bilateral agreement. The agreement and the sideletters cover a broad range of issues.

Agriculture

The bilateral agreement addresses some sensitive issues regarding Russian imports of U.S.-origin beef, some of which arose well after Russia's WTO accession process began. Russia had banned imports of beef and beef by-products since a case of bovine spongiform encephalopathy (BSE), or "mad cow disease," was discovered on a farm in Washington State in 2003. Under the bilateral agreement, Russia agreed to permit the immediate resumption of imports of de-boned beef, bone-in beef, and beef by-products from cattle younger than 30 months and to allow imports of beef and beef by-products from cattle of all ages after the United States receives a positive evaluation as a beef producer from the World Organization for Animal Health.

Under the agreement, Russia accepts U.S. Department of Agriculture's Food and Safety and Safety Inspection Service (FSIS) certifications of pork and poultry producing facilities for producing products that can be exported to Russia and procedures to expedite the certification process. Russia also agreed to accept U.S. freezing as a adequate measure to prevent trichinae infestation in pork to be sold for further processing or for retail sale. Russia previously had only allowed frozen pork to be imported for further processing.

The bilateral agreement also covers various Russian government tariff-related measures. It commits Russia to continue to apply until 2009 the provisions of a U.S.- Russia bilateral agreement on meat that established tariff-rate quotas including in- and over-quota tariff rates and to conduct bilateral negotiations on the treatment of meat imports after the agreement expires. The agreement also commits Russia to bind its tariffs on some agricultural products at current levels and to lower tariffs on other agricultural products.

Market Access for Non-Agricultural Goods

Russia has agreed to accede to the WTO Information Technology and Telecommunications Agreement (ITA), which means that it will eliminate tariffs on information technology products. It has agreed to comply with 95% of the ITA commitments within its first three years of WTO membership. On the other hand, Russia did not agree to U.S. demands to accede to the WTO Civil Aircraft Agreement but did agree to reduce tariffs on wide- body aircraft, parts for civil aircraft, and on leased aircraft. It will also reduce tariffs on narrow-body aircraft. Russia has agreed to establish procedures to expedite imports of products of encryption technology and reduce duties on exports of scrap metal.

Services

Regarding insurance, Russia acceded to U.S. demands that foreign insurance companies be permitted to own 100% of insurance operations and to establish branches in Russia, but Russia retains the right to impose limits on foreign direct investment in banking and insurance if the share of foreign direct investment of total investments in those sectors exceeds 50%. After five years, Russia will consider whether to lift the discretionary restriction on foreign investment in banking and insurance. Russia still will not allow foreign bank branches to operate. Russia also agreed to increase market access of foreign providers to other service areas including telecommunications, audio-visual services, energy services, express delivery services, distribution services, business services, and environmental services.

IPR

The bilateral agreement and sideletters commit Russia to strengthen enforcement of intellectual property rights, including the elimination of plants that produce optical disks, closing down websites that distribute pirated products, and strengthening enforcement at its borders to ensure that pirated goods are not imported. Russia also made a commitment to accede to the provisions of the WTO agreement on trade-related aspects of intellectual property rights (TRIPs) and to protect proprietary information provided by pharmaceutical companies to obtain marketing approval.

Other Developments

Russia still needs to complete negotiations with the working party. The working party members, including the United States, have argued that Russia still needs to resolve issues regarding government support of the agriculture sector and that its fulfillment of its commitments on IPR protection and industrial goods trade will be closely watched by them before finalizing the accession process.[45]

U.S.-Russian Economic Ties and WTO Accession

The United States has strongly supported Russia's accession to the WTO since Russia first applied to join the GATT in 1993. The U.S. government has provided advice to the Russian government on how to make its trade and investment regime WTO compatible and to educate Russian firms on the implications of WTO accession. Because the United States is the world's largest economy, its support is critical to the success of Russia's application. However, the United States has also insisted that Russia enter the WTO on "commercial terms," that is, on terms that do not distort trade, and that Russia immediately adhere to WTO agreements upon accession.

U.S. support for Russian accession is just one part of post-Cold War U.S. trade and economic policy that has encouraged Russian endeavors to establish a market economy. And the trade and economic policy is itself part of a larger U.S. foreign policy strategy to anchor Russia in the world community and to reshape the U.S.- Russian relationship into one of cooperation.

U.S. support to Russia in the trade and investment areas has come in the form of technical assistance, trade preferences (including tariff preferences under the U.S. GSP program), and financial assistance to U.S. exporters to and investors in Russia through the U.S. Export-Import Bank and the Overseas Private Investment Corporation (OPIC). Since 1992, the United States has granted Russia conditional normal trade relations (NTR), or most-favored-nation (MFN), status, which means that lower tariffs are applied to imports from Russia than was the case when Russia did not have NTR status.

U.S.-Russian trade and investment flows have increased in the post-Cold War reflecting the changed U.S.-Russian relationship, although they remain lower than what many observers consider their potential. U.S. imports from Russia have increased substantially since the end of the Cold War from $0.5 billion in 1992 peaking at $19.8 billion in 2006. U.S. exports have increased but not as significantly, from $2.1 billion in 1992 peaking at $4.7 billion in 2006. Since 1994, the United States has incurred growing trade deficits with Russia, peaking at $15.1 billion in 2006. The large increase in U.S. imports may reflect not so much an increase in the volume of trade but the rise in world prices of raw materials, particularly oil, that comprise the bulk of those imports.

Table 1. U.S. Merchandise Trade with Russia, 1992-2006

in billions of dollars

Year	U.S. Exports	U.S. Imports	U.S. Trade Balances	Year	U.S. Exports	U.S. Imports	U.S. Trade Balances
1992	2.1	0.5	1.6	2000	2.1	7.7	-5.6
1993	3.0	1.7	1.3	2001	2.7	6.3	-3.5
1994	2.6	3.2	-0.6	2002	2.4	6.8	-4.4
1995	2.8	4.0	-1.2	2003	2.4	8.6	-6.2
1996	3.3	3.6	-0.3	2004	3.0	11.9	-8.9

Year	U.S. Exports	U.S. Imports	U.S. Trade Balances	Year	U.S. Exports	U.S. Imports	U.S. Trade Balances
1997	3.4	4.3	-0.9	2005	3.9	15.3	-11.3
1998	3.6	5.7	-2.1	2006	4.7	19.8	-15.1
1999	2.1	5.9	-3.8				

Source: Compiled by CRS from U.S. Department of Commerce Data. Bureau of the Census. FT900.

Despite the increase in bilateral trade, the United States and Russia still account for small shares of each others exports and imports. In 2006, Russia accounted for about 0.5% of U.S. exports and 1.1% of U.S. imports. The United States accounted for 3.1% of Russian exports and 4.4% of Russian imports. Major U.S. exports to Russia in 2006 consisted of machinery, vehicles, and meat (mostly chicken), and major U.S. imports from Russia consisted of oil, steel, and aluminum.[46] On June 10, 2007, the Russian airline, Aeroflot, signed a contract to purchase 22 long-range Boeing 787 aircraft, a deal worth an estimated $3.5 billion.[47]

The United States accounted for $4.6 billion in foreign direct investment in Russia in 2006. The United States was technically the third largest source of foreign direct investment; however, the first two, Cyprus and Luxembourg, are considered to be largely sources of repatriated Russian capital rather than of original foreign capital.[48]

U.S. exporters and investors claim that a number of factors make them cautious about entering the Russian market: the lack of adherence to international standards of accounting; weak enforcement of intellectual property rights; the lack of protection of share-holders rights; burdensome taxation; and poor legal protection of contract sanctity. These concerns are largely mirrored in the demands the United States has made on Russia during its negotiations in the WTO.

For their part, Russian policymakers have asserted that U.S. trade policy has also been slow to adjust to the post-Cold War era. For example, they point out that the United States only recently removed the "nonmarket economy status" that was applied in antidumping duty cases against Russian imports.[49] Under U.S. antidumping laws, "fair value" for imports from nonmarket economies is calculated differently than for imports from other economies. That methodology leads to higher dumping margins and antidumping duties and, therefore, placed imports from Russia at a competitive disadvantage vis-a-vis other imports or U.S. domestic production. In response to requests from Russian steel producers, the U.S. Department of Commerce examined the possibility of no longer treating Russia as a nonmarket economy and removed the designation on June 7, 2002.[50]

More critical for Russia has been the U.S. government's continued application of the Jackson-Vanik amendment to trade relations with Russia. Russia's current conditional NTR status from the United States is governed by Title IV of the Trade Act of 1974, as amended. Section 401 of Title IV requires the President to continue to deny NTR status to any country that was not receiving such treatment at the time of the law's enactment on January 3, 1975. In effect, this meant all communist countries, except Poland and Yugoslavia. Section 402 of Title IV, the Jackson-Vanik amendment, denies the countries eligibility for NTR status as well as access to U.S. government credit facilities, such as the Export-Import Bank, as long as the country denies its citizens the right of freedom-of-emigration. These restrictions can be removed if the President determines that the country is in full compliance with the freedom-of-emigration conditions set out under the Jackson-Vanik amendment. For a country to retain that status, the President must reconfirm his determination of full compliance in a semiannual report (by June 30 and December 31) to Congress. His determination can be overturned by Congress via the enactment of a joint resolution of disapproval at the time of the December 31 report.

The Jackson-Vanik amendment also permits the President to waive full compliance with the free emigration requirement, if he determines that such a waiver would promote the objectives of the amendment, that is, encourage freedom of emigration. This waiver authority is subject to an annual renewal by the President and to congressional disapproval via a joint resolution. Before a country can receive NTR treatment under either the presidential determination of full compliance or the presidential waiver, both the United States and the country in question must have concluded and enacted a bilateral agreement that provides for, among other things, reciprocal extension of NTR (or MFN) status. The agreement and a presidential proclamation extending NTR status cannot go into effect until a joint resolution approving the agreement is enacted. In 1990, the United States and the Soviet Union signed a bilateral trade agreement. The agreement was subsequently applied to each of the former Soviet states. The United States first granted NTR treatment to Russia under the presidential waiver authority beginning in June 1992 and, since September 1994, under the full compliance provision. Presidential extensions of NTR status to Russia have met with virtually no congressional opposition.

Russian political leaders have continually pressed the United States to "graduate" Russia from Jackson-Vanik coverage entirely. They see the amendment as a Cold War relic that does not reflect Russia's new stature as a fledgling democracy and market economy. Moreover, Russian leaders argue that Russia has implemented freedom-of-emigration policies since the fall of the communist government, making the Jackson-Vanik conditions inappropriate and unnecessary.

While Russia remains subject to the Jackson-Vanik amendment, some of the other former Soviet republics have been granted permanent and unconditional NTRKyrgyzstan on June 29, 2000, and Georgia on December 29, 2000. Perhaps, what has particularly irked Russian leaders is that on January 1, 2002, the United States granted permanent and unconditional NTR status to China, which is ostensibly still a communist country.

Granting Russia permanent and unconditional NTR status will have little direct impact on U.S.-Russian trade, since Russian imports have entered the United States on a NTR basis since 1992. The initiative would be a political symbol of Russia's treatment as a "normal" country in U.S. trade, further distancing U.S.-Russian relations from the Cold War. For investors and other business people, PNTR may mean a more stable climate for doing business. But many observers have concluded that U.S.-Russian economic ties will grow only when Russia has undertaken sufficient economic reforms to improve the climate for trade and investment.

It has a direct bearing on the WTO accession issue since the WTO requires its members to extend mutual unconditional MFN status to one another's exports. If the United States does not extend permanent NTR to Russia, the United States would not benefit from the concessions, except tariff reductions, that Russia makes upon acceding to the WTO.

Implications of Russia's Accession to the WTO

Because the major trade powers — the United States, the EU, and Japan — strongly support Russia's entry into the WTO, the pending question is not whether Russia will accede but when. The answer to that question depends on when Russia and the more than sixty members of the working party can finish hammering out the conditions of accession. Negotiators have reportedly reached agreement on most issues, but disagreements on difficult issues of energy pricing, agriculture, services, civil aircraft, and intellectual property rights, have slowed down the process and the original goal of accession by the September 2003 WTO Ministerial Meeting in Cancun, Mexico unattainable. Several other desired deadlines have passed.

Implications for Russia

The stakes for Russia in joining the WTO are high. Russia's political leadership, led by Putin, has made a commitment to join the WTO. In his April 18, 2002 address to the Federal Assembly, the bicameral Russian legislature, Putin underscored his administration's priority to get Russia into the WTO. In the speech, Putin emphasized the need for the Russian government to establish the conditions to improve the economic well-being of the Russian people and linked that effort with joining the WTO:

> Tight competition is a norm in the international community and in the modern world, competition for markets, investments, economic and political influence. Russia must be strong and competitive in this fight.
>
> The world market is already here and our market has become part of the system...
>
> The WTO is an instrument. He who knows how to use it grows stronger; he who prefers to sit behind a fence of protectionist quotas, and duties — he is doomed, absolutely doomed strategically.
>
> Our country is still excluded from the process of making world trade rules. We are already in the world trade but we have no say in shaping the rules of trade. This tends to stunt the Russian economy and make it less competitive.[51]

In acceding to the WTO, Russia is making a legally binding commitment to conform to WTO rules. In so doing, it agrees to make its foreign trade and investment regimes open to the scrutiny of the WTO and its members. At the same time, the WTO provides a multilateral forum for Russia to settle trade disputes with other WTO members. As a WTO member, Russia will have a voice in how those rules are made and implemented. It would be a major step in integrating Russia within the international trade system.

But before it can accede to the WTO, Russia must satisfy WTO members that it is ready to meet its obligations. The working party negotiations and the bilateral negotiations to date suggest that those countries are not satisfied and require that Russia make major adjustments in policies and regulations.

The adjustments include reviewing and possibly changing more than 100 Russian laws and reviewing more than 1,000 international agreements that Russia has with various countries.[52] However, the overall impact of WTO accession on Russia will depend on the terms and conditions of accession that Russian and its trading partners in the WTO finally agree on. In general, Russia will likely have to reduce tariffs and other protective measures for import-sensitive industries such as autos and aircraft and will have to open up key financial service industries — banking and insurance — to foreign competition. In the short run, such adjustments could lead to the loss of jobs in those areas and the need for the Russian government to provide unemployment insurance and other adjustment assistance.

However, globally competitive industries, such as the raw material producers, could see markets abroad opening up and an increase in foreign investment as accession forces Russia to restructure its economy. In the long run, mainstream economic theory and the record of economies that have gone through similar transitions suggest that trade liberalization will lead to a more efficient Russian economy and to raising the living standard of the average Russian citizen.[53] New industries will probably emerge over time helping to diversify the Russian economy.

The Russian business community is divided on the issue of accession. Some have expressed skepticism if not out right opposition to accession. Among this group is Oleg Deripaska, an influential and powerful aluminum and auto business magnate. He is concerned that WTO accession will force Russia to eliminate protection and that the domestic auto industry will face competition from U.S., European, and Japanese manufacturers. He is also concerned that Russia would have to charge higher prices for energy, a major input in aluminum production. Similarly, representatives of aviation, furniture, financial services, telecommunications, and agriculture have asserted that Russia stands to lose more than it will gain from accession because Russia has not matured sufficiently to meet the competition.[54]

Views on accession cut across regions with support coming from regional political leaders in the major business centers of Moscow and St. Petersburg and in regions where raw material production is located. Political leaders in regions where fledgling import-sensitive manufacturers are located have been skeptical or opposed to accession. For most Russians, accession has not attracted much interest.[55]

Putin and the current Russian political leadership have made economic growth and development their highest priority and they view Russia's admission into the WTO as an essential part of the strategy to fulfill those goals. Putin appears to view the accession process as a way of forcing the government bureaucracy, the Duma, and Russian industry to confront the changes that are required if Russia is to attain long-term sustainable economic growth and development. While Putin' s political future probably does not depend directly on whether Russia gets into the WTO, it will likely be evaluated on the basis to what degree economic life in Russia has improved.

WTO accession would be a further sign of Russia's acceptance and participation in the major multilateral economic institutions: the World Bank, the International Monetary Fund; and the G-8. In so doing, Russia would distance itself further from its Soviet past.

Implications for the United States

For U.S. exporters and investors, Russia's accession to the WTO may improve the business climate in Russia which has been unpredictable. The U.S. business community often cites poor intellectual property rights protection, inconsistent and opaque customs regulations, inconsistent enforcement of the regulations, and irrational SPS and technical trade barriers as among the impediments to trade and investment. Accession could bring more stability and openness in the business climate since Russia would have to adhere to WTO rules that promote these conditions.

The volume of U.S. imports from Russia has been low primarily because Russia's limited export-base. Nevertheless, some U.S. import-sensitive industries, for example steel, may face increased competition from Russian producers. These industries may press U.S. negotiators to include as part of the terms and conditions for Russia's accession, a special safeguard provision, beyond that provided in the WTO agreements, that would cushion the potentially adverse impact of a large increase in Russian imports upon accession. Such a provision was included in the conditions for China's accession to the WTO and was codified in U.S. law as Section 421 of the Trade Act of 1974.

Similar to Section 201 (escape clause) provision of the Trade Act of 1974, Section 421 allows the United States to temporarily restrict fairly traded imports that cause or threaten to cause injury to the domestic injury. Unlike Section 201, however, Section 421 permits the restrictions to be applied solely to imports of like products from China, rather than requiring them to be applied on an MFN basis on imports of like products from all countries. In addition, the required thresholds of cause and level of injury to the domestic industry for relief under Section 421 is lower than under Section 201. Section 201 requires that imports be a "substantial" cause of "serious injury," whereas Section 421 requires only that the imports be a "significant cause" of "material injury." For many in the U.S. business and agricultural community, the issue is not whether Russia should be allowed to join the WTO but one of assurance that Russia will enter under conditions that are commercially sound and will have minimal negative impact on U.S. industries.

Implications for Other Countries and the WTO

Russia is the largest and most populous country that is not a member of the WTO. If Russia accedes, it would significantly expand the geographical coverage of WTO rules to all major economies leading to a larger degree of stability and transparency to the international trading system.

At the same time, Russia's entry into the WTO would continue a trend in which as the membership of the WTO becomes larger and more diverse, it becomes more difficult for that membership to reach a consensus on important issues. In addition, trade disputes between Russia and its trading partners will be brought to the WTO for resolution rather than addressed bilaterally, adding to the ever growing caseload of the WTO.

As an economy still in transition, Russia would bring its own perspective to WTO negotiations. For example, Russia could be expected to challenge the positions the United States and other countries have taken in the WTO on the role of subsidies in trade and the degree to which trade in services should be liberalized.

References

[1] These agreements include the General Agreement on Trade in Services (GATS) and theagreement on Trade-Related Aspects of Intellectual Property Rights (TRIPS), among others.

[2] Financial Times. June 11, 2007. p.1

[3] Based on WTO background information located at [http://www.wto.org].

[4] It should be noted that other nonmarket economies had acceded to the GATT, albeit under special conditions: Poland (1967); Hungary (1973); and Romania (1971). The United States was also concerned that the Soviet Union intended to use GATT membership for political purposes. The Soviet Union sought observer status once before in 1982. Kennedy, Kevin C, The Accession of the Soviet Union to the GATT, Journal of World Trade Law, April 1987, p. 23-39.

[5] Naray, Peter. Russia and the World Trade Organization. Palgrave. New York. 2001. p.

[6] The World Bank. Russian Economic Report. November 2007. p. 2.

[7] Calculations based on data found in Economist Intelligence Unit, Country Profile: Russia, 2007.

[8] Customs Committee of Russia.

[9] Economist Intelligence Unit. Country Profile– Russia. 2007. p. 66.

[10] Ibid.

[11] Ibid., p. 52.

[12] Economist Intelligence Unit data base.

[13] GSP is a program under which a country gives preferential tariff treatment to imports from developing countries. Many industrialized countries have GSP programs to encourage economic growth and development in developing countries.

[14] WTO, Draft Report of the Working Party, WT/ACC/SPEC/RUS/25/Rev. 1 p. 124.

[15] Some working party members wanted to be assured that Russian traders were not favored over foreigner traders in license approval process. Ibid. p. 19-23.

[16] 16 WTO L/7410.

[17] World Trade Organization, Accession of the Russian Federation: Questions and Replies to the Memorandum on the Foreign Trade Regime, Geneva, June 2, 1995. WT/ACC/RUS/2

[18] World Trade Organization, Draft Report of the Working Party on the Accession of the Russian Federation to the World Trade Organization, WT/ACC/SPEC/RUS/25/Rev. 1.

[19] Ibid. p. 16.

[20] OECD, OECD Economic Surveys 2001-2002: Russian Federation, p. 125.

[21] Ibid. p. 17.

[22] The description of the agreement is taken from "What is the WTO?" located on the WTO website: [http://www.wto.org].

[23] International Trade Reporter, November 7, 2002, p. 1904.

[24] The description of the agreement is taken from "What is the WTO?" located on the WTO website: [http://www.wto.org]

[25] Office of the U.S. Trade Representative, National Trade Estimate Report on Foreign Trade Barriers, April 2007, p. 554.

[26] Special 301 refers to a statutory requirement under Section 182 of the Trade Act of 1974, as amended, that the USTR annually identify those countries that are the egregious offenders

of denying IPR protection and against which the United States could take action. In practice, the USTR has also identified countries which do not fit the category of most egregious offenders but bare serious monitoring on its annual "priority watch list."
[27] Office of the United States Trade Representative. 2007 Special 301 Report.
[28] Office of the U.S. Trade Representative, p. 335.
[29] Economist Intelligence Unit, Country Profile 2002: Russia, p. 58.
[30] Liefert, William, Agricultural Reform: Major Commodity Restructuring but Little Institutional Change, in Joint Economic Committee, p. 278.
[31] Ibid.
[32] Bush, Keith, Russian Economic Survey, April 2003, p. 25.
[33] USDA, Foreign Agricultural Service, Russian Federation Livestocks and Products, Gain Report # RS3006, February 20, 2003, p. 7; and USDA, Foreign Agricultural Service, Russian Federation Poultry and Products, Gain Report, #RS3001, February 10, 2003, p. 1. TRQs are restrictions in which a limited volume of a product can be imported at one tariff rate but imports above that limit can be imported only at another, usually much higher tariff rate.
[34] Inside U.S. Trade, March 14, 2003.
[35] WTO, op. cit.
[36] Ibid.
[37] Ibid., p. 332. Washington Trade Daily, April 7, 2003, p. 1.
[38] Vastine, Bob and Vladimir Gololobov, Moscow and the WTO: A Unique Chance to Modernize Russia, European Affairs, Winter 2003; and The Russian Ministry of Finance has proposed that the ban on foreign company issuance of compulsory insurance be lifted, EIU, Country Report: Russia, March 2003, p. 28.
[39] Coalition of Service Industries, CSI Background Paper on Russian Banking Services, May 22, 2002.
[40] Legislation to establish deposit insurance for other Russian banks is pending in the lower house of the Russian parliament, the Duma, but has not received action, Reuters, June 3, 2003.
[41] Washington Trade Daily, January 23, 2002.
[42] USTR, p. 340.
[43] USTR, p. 333.
[44] Moscow Times, March 4, 2002, p. 12
[45] Much Work Remains Before Russia Will be Able to Join the WTO, U.S. Official Says. International Trade Daily. November 24, 2006.
[46] Global Trade Information System.
[47] Financial Times. June 11, 2007. p. 16.
[48] Tendentsii I perspectiva (Trends and Outlook). 2007.
[49] Washington Trade Daily, June 7, 2002.
[50] Ibid.
[51] Annual Address by President of the Russian Federation Vladimir Putin to the Federal Assembly of the Russian Federation Moscow, April 18, 2002, [http://www. russiaeurope. mid.ru].
[52] Likhachev, Aleksei Evgenievich (State Duma Committee on Economic Policy and Enterprise), Presentation at Adam Smith Institute International Congress on Russia's Accession to the WTO, October 16-17, 2002, Moscow

[53] For an examination of the possible economic impact of accession see, Stern, Robert M., An Economic Perspective on Russia's Accession to the WTO, William Davidson Working Paper Number 472, June 2002, The William Davidson Institute at the University of Michigan Business School.

[54] Financial Times, April 15, 2002.

[55] EastWest Institute, Regional Report, vol 7, no. 22, July 10, 2002.

In: Russian Political, Economic and Security Issues
Editor: Harold J. Kowen
ISBN 978-1-60692-407-5

Chapter 5

NUCLEAR COOPERATION AGREEMENT WITH RUSSIA: STATUTORY PROCEDURES FOR CONGRESSIONAL CONSIDERATION*

Richard S. Beth
Government and Finance Division

ABSTRACT

On May 13, 2008, President Bush submitted to Congress a proposed agreement for nuclear cooperation with the Russian Federation. The Atomic Energy Act (AEA) prescribes that the text of such an agreement be submitted to the Senate Committee on Foreign Relations and the House Committee on Foreign Affairs for at least 30 days of consultation. Also, the agreement itself is to be submitted to Congress for 60 days, during which the committees consider it and report recommendations. The agreement goes into effect unless a joint resolution of disapproval is enacted by the end of the 60-day period. This report will be updated to reflect congressional action.

The President's letter of transmittal states that the May 13 action meets all requirements for both submissions, and stipulates that the 60-day period start immediately upon conclusion of the 30-day period. Both periods are measured in "days of continuous session," which the AEA defines to include all days except recesses of either house of more than three days, with "continuity" broken only by the sine die adjournment of a Congress. By this definition, the 60-day period may begin on June 24. If both houses take recesses as scheduled, the projected sine die adjournment on September 26 may be only the 78th day of continuous session. In this case, the statutory period for disapproval would have to start over again when Congress reconvenes in January, 2009. On the other hand, if both houses hold pro forma sessions during scheduled recesses, as they did in some recent instances, the disapproval period could end, and the agreement take effect, as early as August 11.

The AEA prescribes the text for a disapproval resolution and directs House committee leaders and Senate floor leaders (or designees) to introduce it when the 60-day period starts (in addition, a House Member introduced such a resolution at the start of the 30-day period). The AEA also requires the President to state his approval of the

---

* Excerpted from CRS Report RL34541, dated June 20, 2008.

agreement before the 60-day period begins, but he did so in his initial transmission letter, perhaps rendering moot the consultive purpose of the 30-day period. Yet both committees of referral met with State Department officials on the agreement during the 30-day period, which may constitute the consultations the AEA directs during that period, but might also be taken as the hearings mandated during the 60-day period.

The AEA prescribes an expedited procedure for Senate floor consideration of a disapproval resolution, including a non-debatable motion to take up the measure, a 10-hour limit on consideration, and a prohibition on amendments. For House consideration, the AEA invites the Committee on Rules to prescribe similar terms. Congress could also disapprove the agreement, or approve it with conditions, by enacting an alternative measure under its general rules. The President, however, might likely veto any disapproval or conditional approval, in which case the agreement would go into effect unless Congress overrides the veto before the end of the disapproval period. Inasmuch as the President may take 10 days for his action, the timely enactment of a disapproval resolution may be feasible only if Congress initially passes it with more than 10 days remaining in the disapproval period.

Introduction and Overview Nuclear Cooperation with Russia and the Atomic Energy Act

On May 13, 2008, President Bush submitted to Congress a proposed agreement for civil nuclear cooperation with the Russian Federation.[1] In accordance with the non-proliferation provisions of the Atomic Energy Act, as amended (AEA or "the act"),[2] agreements for nuclear cooperation may go into effect only following an opportunity for congressional consideration defined by section 123. of the act (42 U.S.C. 2153),[3] on account of which these agreements are sometimes known as "123 agreements." The effect of these provisions is that an agreement with terms like that of the proposed agreement with Russia will go into effect at the end of 90 "days of continuous session" of Congress after it is initially submitted to Congress, unless, during that time, a joint resolution disapproving the agreement is enacted through procedures defined in section 130. of the act (42 U.S.C. 2159).

This report first sketches the procedures prescribed by the AEA for congressional action in relation to agreements of this kind, then summarizes legislative proceedings occurring in relation to the proposed agreement with Russia, beginning with its recent submission. Thereafter, the report addresses several questions of the implementation and intent of these statutory requirements that are raised by their application to the proposed agreement with the Russian Federation. Special attention is given to the definition of "days of continuous session" and possible implications of this definition depending on whether or not the requisite period ends before the end of the 1 10th Congress.

Other questions addressed in this report about the effects of congressional action on the proposed agreement include

- What does the President submit, when, to whom, and with what effect?
- How and when are resolutions of disapproval introduced?
- How might the requirement for automatic discharge of the disapproval resolution come to bear'?

- How might congressional action on the disapproval resolution come about?
- What proceedings would have to occur for the nuclear cooperation agreement with Russia to be disapproved?
- What possibilities of disapproval (or approval) of the agreement exist other than pursuant to the statutory procedures?

Summary of Procedural Requirements

Section 123.a. of the AEA establishes nine requirements that a proposed agreement for nuclear cooperation must either meet or receive presidential exemption from meeting. The remainder of section 123. prescribes different regulations for congressional action depending on whether or not the agreement requires this exemption and on other features of its terms. As explained below, the procedural regulations applicable specifically to the proposed agreement with Russia depend principally on three features of the agreement: (1) it requires no exemption for failure to meet any of the nine requirements; (2) it includes provisions relating to "large reactors;" and (3) it covers only civil uses of atomic energy.

Section 123.a. provides that if a proposed agreement requires no exemption, it may go into effect at a prescribed point unless Congress has previously acted to disapprove it.

Section 123.b. specifies that unless an agreement involves military-related uses of nuclear energy, the President is to submit its text to the Senate Committee on Foreign Relations and the House Committee on Foreign Affairs for a period of "not less than 30 days of continuous session" for consultation.[4] This submission is to be accompanied (for agreements like that with Russia) by an unclassified Nuclear Proliferation Assessment Statement (NPAS) prepared by the Department of State.[5]

Section 123.d. directs that if the agreement involves large reactors,[6] the President is to submit it, along with additional supporting documents, to Congress for a period of 60 "days of continuous session." The supporting documents include (1) any classified annexes to the NPAS; and (2) a statement of the President's approval of the agreement and determination that it "will promote, and will not constitute an unreasonable risk to, the common defense and security." The measure is to be referred to the same two committees as specified under section 123.b., and these committees are to hold hearings on the proposal and report recommendations to their respective chambers. The agreement goes into effect unless, by the end of this 60-day period, a joint resolution of disapproval is enacted into law pursuant to procedures prescribed by section 1 30.i.

Section 1 30.i. specifies the text for this joint resolution of disapproval and provides that it be automatically introduced in each chamber, at the beginning of the 60-day period, in the House by the chairman and ranking minority member of the Committee on Foreign Affairs, and in the Senate by the two party floor leaders, or, in either case, by their designees. If a committee of referral does not report the measure within 45 days,[7] it is automatically discharged from further consideration. For the Senate, section 130.i. provides that the disapproval resolution may be called up on a non-debatable motion, time for consideration is limited to 10 hours, and amendments are prohibited. For the House, the statute invites the Committee on Rules to report a special rule incorporating comparable restrictions.

LEGISLATIVE ACTION

President Bush transmitted the proposed agreement for civil nuclear cooperation with the Russian Federation to Congress on May 13, 2008.[8] The President's letter of transmittal states that the agreement is accompanied by his "approval and determination,"[9] as well as by the requisite unclassified NPAS.[10] The transmittal letter also states that the classified annex would be submitted separately (and it appears, in fact, that the committees of jurisdiction had already received this annex on May 12).

The inclusion of the unclassified NPAS meets the requirements of the AEA to begin the 30-day period, and the inclusion of the President's "approval and determination," together with the separate submission of the classified annex to the NPAS, meet the requirements for the 60-day period to start. The President's transmittal letter, accordingly, states that this submission "shall constitute a submittal for purposes of both sections 123.b. and 123.d. of the Atomic Energy Act." The letter of transmittal, nevertheless, also expresses an understanding that the two periods will not both commence immediately, but instead will occur consecutively. It goes on to declare that the 60-day period shall commence "upon completion of the 30-day period." These stipulations, which appear to conform to recent past practice on agreements for nuclear cooperation, seem intended to enable the two periods to be treated, for practical purposes, as a single uninterrupted period of 90 days of continuous session.

In accordance with section 123. of the AEA, the President's message and the accompanying papers were referred to the House Committee on Foreign Affairs and the Senate Committee on Foreign Relations.[11] On May 14, 2008, a joint resolution of disapproval with the text required by section 130.i. was introduced in the House by a member of the Committee on Foreign Affairs.[12] On June 12, the House Committee held a hearing on "Russia, Iran, and Nuclear Weapons: Implications of the Proposed U.S.-Russia Agreement," at which John C. Rood, Acting Under Secretary of State for Arms Control and International Security, appeared as a witness. On June 17, the Senate Committee on Foreign Relations received a closed briefing from William J. Burns, Under Secretary of State for Political Affairs, on "Russia, Iran and U.S.-Russian Nuclear Cooperation," but by that date no resolution of disapproval had been introduced in that chamber.

PERIOD FOR CONGRESSIONAL DISAPPROVAL DEFINITION OF "CONTINUOUS SESSION"

Section 123. of the AEA specifies that the two time periods involved in the proceedings prescribed for the nuclear cooperation agreement with Russia are to be measured in days of continuous session, as defined by section 130.g. of the AEA. Section 1 30.g.(2) stipulates that

[F]or purposes of this section insofar as it applies to section 123 ... continuity of session is broken only by an adjournment of Congress sine die; and ... the days on which either House is not in session because of an adjournment of more than three days are excluded in the computation of any period of time in which Congress is in continuous session.[13]

Under this provision, (1) any period of continuous session ends with the final adjournment of the last session of a Congress; and (2) days on which either house has recessed its session are not counted toward the required time periods.[14]

The definition established by section 1 30.g.(2) is evidently meant to correspond to the constitutional requirement that neither house may adjourn for more than three days without the consent of the other. Congress may adjourn for more than three days either by ending its annual session (an adjournment sine die) or by taking a recess within its annual session. In either case, the two houses typically grant each other the required consent by adopting a concurrent resolution.[15] Under the statutory definition, accordingly, the continuity of session is broken just when Congress adjourns its last session pursuant to a concurrent resolution for a sine die adjournment, and the count of "days of continuous session" pauses on exactly those days on which both houses, or either one of them, is not in session pursuant to a concurrent resolution for a recess of more than three days.[16]

This arrangement is apparently intended to prevent a situation in which an agreement would go into effect only because Congress was not in session, or did not remain in session long enough to act on a disapproval resolution. At the same time, however, days on which either house, or both, is out of session for three consecutive days or fewer are not excluded from the count. If both houses adjourn from Friday to Tuesday, for example, not only the days of session in the preceding and following week, but also the intervening three days of the extended weekend, will count as days of continuous session.

Under the definition of section 130.g.(2), accordingly, until the final *sine die* adjournment of the 1 10th Congress, every calendar day will be counted as a day of continuous session except those on which at least one house is out of session pursuant to a concurrent resolution providing for a recess of more than three days. Under the Constitution, however, the term of the 1 10th Congress expires on January 3, 2009, and at some point before then, accordingly, the 1 10th Congress will presumably adjourn its last session *sine die*. As Under Secretary Rood affirmed in testimony before the House Committee on Foreign Affairs on June 12, this *sine die* adjournment will put an end to the existing period of continuous session.[17] If Congress adjourns sine die without acting on the proposed agreement, and before 90 days of continuous session are completed, the agreement will not take effect until a new period of continuous session, beginning ab initio when the 111th Congress convenes, has reached the requisite length.[18]

In colloquy with members of the Committee, Under Secretary Rood also gave it as his understanding that the 90-day period was measured separately in each house and, for each house, included all the days on which that house was in session. On this understanding, for example, if the House were out of session on Thursday while the Senate met, and the Senate were out of session on Friday while the House met, one day would be counted for each chamber.[19] This interpretation appears to overlook that days of continuous session of Congress may occur when either or both houses are out of session (as long as they are out of session for no more than three consecutive days). In addition, section 131.g. is not couched in terms of separate counts in each house, but explicitly refers to the continuous session of Congress as a whole. The language quoted at the outset of this section implies that a single count covers both houses, and states explicitly that when either house takes a recess (of more than three days), the count of days pauses until both houses are back in session. The estimates in the following sections follow this last interpretation of the quoted provision.

DAYS OF CONTINUOUS SESSION IN THE 110TH CONGRESS

After President Bush submitted the nuclear cooperation agreement with Russia on May 13, 2008, Congress remained in continuous session, as defined by the AEA, until May 22. It then entered a recess for Memorial Day,[20] from which it returned on June 3. The period from May 13 through May 22 amounted to nine days of continuous session, and the period from June 3 through June 17, when the House Committee on Foreign Affairs held its hearing, included another 15 days.[21] It accordingly appears that June 17 constituted the 24th day of continuous session since submission of the agreement.

Any future projection of days of continuous session is dependent on assumptions about the schedule the two houses will follow. The simplest assumption is that each house will take recesses, and will adjourn sine die, as projected in the schedules announced by its majority party leadership.[22] These schedules project the following recesses for the part of 2008 following submission of the proposed agreement:

- From Saturday, May 24, through Sunday, June 1, for Memorial Day;
- From Saturday, June 28, through Sunday, July 6, for Independence Day;
- From Saturday, August 2, through Sunday, September 8, for the summer recess of the House; and
- From Saturday, August 9, through Sunday, September 8, for the summer recess of the Senate.

The House schedule projects adjournment sine die on September 26, 2008; the Senate schedule includes no projection for this event.

Under this schedule, days of continuous session will continue to accrue from June 17 until the 30th day is reached on Monday, June 23. Pursuant to the declarations in President's letter of transmittal, June 23 would count as the last day of the 30-day period for consultation, and the following day, June 24 (the 31st day of continuous session after May 13), would become the first day of the 60-day period for congressional action (and the day on which the automatic introduction of disapproval resolutions would occur).

Thereafter, if each house of Congress takes recesses as listed above, so that the count of days of continuous session pauses during each recess, then it appears that September 26, 2008, will be the 78th day of continuous session. If Congress adjourns sine die on this date, as the House schedule projects, continuity of session will be broken before the 90th day is reached, and a new period of continuous session will have to begin when the 111th Congress convenes. Under these conditions, the nuclear cooperation agreement with Russia could not take effect under the AEA until this new period of continuous session was complete.[23] If, on the other hand, Congress were not to adjourn sine die on September 26, but were to remain in session without taking any further recess, the 90th day of continuous session could be reached on October 8, and the agreement with Russia could accordingly take effect on that date.

POTENTIAL EFFECT OF ALTERED RECESS SCHEDULES

The projections in the previous section could potentially be altered by departures from the schedule of recesses assumed there. Possibilities with some practical likelihood of occurring may include the following: (1) a later beginning for the August recess; (2) the reconvening of Congress for a "lame duck" session after the November elections; and (3) the use of periodic pro forma sessions rather than recesses of more than three days during scheduled state and district work periods. The following sections consider the possible effects of each of these possibilities.

Change in August Recess. The estimate presented in the previous section presumes that the House will be in recess during the first week of August, as projected in the schedule given on the website of the House Majority Leader. Schedules displayed on some other House websites, however, presume that the House will begin its August recess not on Saturday, August 2, but on the following Saturday, August 9.[24] As previously noted, the Senate is expected, in any case, to be in session during the week in question. As a result, if the House is also in session, the week will become one of continuous session rather than of recess. The additional seven days of continuous session could make the scheduled sine die adjournment day of September 26 the 85th day of continuous session, rather than the 78th day as estimated above. Under these circumstances, additional small changes in the congressional schedule might enable the 90-day period to be completed before the end of the 110th Congress.

"Lame Duck" Session. Rather than adjourning sine die on September 36, Congress might recess its session on or after that date and return for a "lame duck" session after election day (November 4). In this case, the occurrence of the 90th day of continuous session would depend on the dates of recess and reconvening. For example, Congress might recess on September 26 and reconvene on November 12 (the day after Veterans' Day). Under these conditions, if September 26 had been the 78th day of continuous session, the 90th day could occur on the 12th calendar day following the reconvening, which, in the case supposed, could be November 23 (the Sunday preceding Thanksgiving). If both houses were to remain in session during the first week of August, so that September 26 was the 85th day of continuous session, the 90th day could be reached a week earlier, on Sunday, November 17.

Similar considerations could apply if the 1 10th Congress were to adjourn sine die before the 90th day of continuous session was reached, but were called back by the President, pursuant to his constitutional authority,[25] before its expiration on January 3, 2009. Another possibility is provided by the authorization, included in most recent concurrent resolutions providing for sine die adjournments, for the bicameral leadership to call Congress back into session before the next session is slated to convene "if the public interest shall require it."[26] The leadership's exercise of this authority would presumably vitiate the sine die character of the previous adjournment, and if so, the previous count of days of continuous session would presumably resume from the point at which it had left off. By this means as well, the existing period of continuous session might reach 90 days before the end of the 1 10th Congress.

Pro Forma Sessions. The occurrence of pro forma sessions might also affect whether or not the continuous session of the 1 10th Congress may reach its 90th day before its adjournment sine die. Pro forma sessions are those held merely "for the sake of form," or as a formality. Typically, no legislative business is conducted; on some occasions, the chamber provides in advance (usually by unanimous consent) that no business may occur. These sessions count as days of session for purposes of determining whether an adjournment of more than three days is occurring.[27]

The resolution authorizing the non-legislative period for George Washington's Birthday in 2008, for example, did not provide for a recess in the constitutional sense.[28] Although the resolution covered essentially the period defined by the announced schedules, it did not provide for a recess of more than three days, but instead directed pro forma sessions of the House at least every fourth day, and authorized the Senate to arrange a similar schedule. Inasmuch as the Senate proceeded to exercise this authority, no "adjournment of more than three days," as contemplated by section 130.g.(2) and the Constitution, occurred in either house during this period.[29] Instead, every day of the non-legislative period counted as a day of continuous session.

At the July 12 hearing, Under Secretary Rood noted that days with pro forma sessions count as days of continuous session.[30] He did not note that this will be true only if the other house is not in recess. Nor, conversely, did he explicitly note that if both houses hold pro forma sessions at least every fourth day during a non- legislative period, no "adjournment of more than three days" occurs; as a result, not only the days of pro forma session themselves, but also the remaining days of the non-legislative period, will count not as days of recess, but as days of continuous session. If, accordingly, both houses were to hold periodic pro forma sessions during every non-legislative period in the remainder of the current session, every remaining calendar day before sine die adjournment would be a day of continuous session as defined by the AEA. Under these conditions, the "clock" defined by section 130.g. would run far more quickly, and the 90th day of continuous session could occur as early as August 11, 2008, instead of in early October.

Under these conditions, moreover, the 90th day of continuous session might fall within a non-legislative period. If one or both houses had provided that no legislative business occur in the pro forma sessions during this period, Congress could become unable to act on a joint resolution of disapproval during the period, and in the absence of that disapproval, the agreement with Russia would presumably take effect on the date specified. On the other hand, concurrent resolutions providing for recesses of the session, like resolutions for a sine die adjournment, often provide contingent authority for the bicameral leadership to call Congress back into session before the expiration of the recess. This authority might be used to give Congress an opportunity to consider a disapproval resolution rather than allow the agreement to enter into force by default.

The use of pro forma sessions might affect the occurrence of days of continuous session in another way as well. The announced schedule for the House includes at least one period not identified as a recess period, but in which "no votes" are scheduled for both a Friday and the following Monday (July 18-21).[31] If no session of the House occurs on any of these days, the period would constitute a break of more than three legislative days. It would be a recess of the House in the constitutional sense, for which a concurrent resolution would be required. In that case, these four days would not count as days of continuous session, and as a result, the projected sine die adjournment date of September 26 would presumably become the 74th rather than the 78th day of continuous session (or, under the alternate assumption discussed in the previous section, the 81st rather than the 85th).

It is possible that no pro forma sessions will be used in these ways to affect the length of continuous session of the current session of Congress. Unlike that for George Washington's Birthday, the resolution providing for the 2008 Memorial Day non-legislative period authorized only the Senate to schedule pro forma sessions, and provided for a recess of the House in the constitutional sense. Pursuant to section 130.g.(2) of the AEA, inasmuch as one house was in recess during this period, the days of this recess are excluded from the count of days of continuous session. If the two houses follow this practice for their remaining scheduled recesses, the date scheduled for sine die adjournment of the House will arrive, as already discussed, before the 90th day of continuous session after submission of the agreement has been reached.

Similarly, the schedules used to arrive at the initial estimates set forth above did not project a recess for any long weekend during the remainder of the 1 10th Congress. The estimates given were based, accordingly, on a presumption that on any such long weekend, at least one pro forma session would be held, in order to avoid the occurrence of a recess long enough to require a concurrent resolution. If, however, either house were to decide to obtain a concurrent resolution to cover a period of this kind, rather than holding pro forma sessions, the days of continuous session accomplished by September 26 could be diminished by the length of that recess.

Possible Need to Renew Action in the 111th Congress

If the 1 10th Congress adjourns sine die before the 90th day of continuous session after May 13, 2008, the period during which Congress could act to disapprove the agreement will not yet have elapsed, and the agreement with Russia will be unable to take effect under the AEA at that point. Instead, a new period of continuous session will begin with the convening of the 111th Congress in January 2009. Until this new period of continuous session reaches the requisite length, the entering into effect of the agreement will be postponed, and the opportunity for Congress to disapprove it pursuant to the AEA will remain available.

It is not clear from the statute, nor do any previous proceedings appear to establish, whether or not failure of the 1 10th Congress to complete the periods required under section 123. would necessitate starting from the beginning, in the 111th Congress, of the entire approval process or of only such parts of it as the 1 10th Congress did not complete.

At the June 12 hearing of the House Committee on Foreign Affairs, Under Secretary Rood took the position that, if the full period of 90 days of continuous session is not completed within the 1 10th Congress, the entire period must begin de novo in the 111th Congress.[32] In favor of this view, it could be argued that the newly constituted committees in the 111th Congress might not wish to be compelled to rely on the consultations and deliberations engaged in by their predecessors. In addition, of course, any resolution of disapproval submitted in the 110th Congress will die with a sine die adjournment, so that any such resolution could be considered in the 111th Congress only if it was introduced anew in that Congress. Finally, this interpretation might be held to imply, under these circumstances, the President would also have to retransmit the agreement itself to Congress, in the way provided in the AEA, in the new session. Absent this resubmittal, it could be argued, no date could be fixed at which the disapproval resolution would be automatically introduced.

A contrary argument might hold that, inasmuch as the AEA makes provision for the process it prescribes to continue after a break in the continuity of session, it intends that the submission of an agreement will trigger a single process of congressional action that may carry over into a subsequent Congress. On this view, the new period of continuous session required by the act would begin automatically with the convening of the 111th Congress. Rigorously applied, this view could hold that the 111th Congress would not have to repeat statutory requirements that had already been accomplished in the 1 10th Congress.

On this interpretation, for example, inasmuch as the President has already submitted the text of the agreement to the committees, made the required approval and determination, submitted the agreement itself to Congress, and submitted the NPAS and its classified annexes, he would not have to carry out these requirements anew in the 111th Congress. It could be argued, as well, that if at least 30 days of continuous session in the 1 10th Congress elapse between the May 13 submission of the text and the sine die adjournment, the 30-day consultation period required by section 123 .b. will not have to repeated in the 111th Congress. If all these conditions are fulfilled in the 1 10th Congress, on this view, the first day of the 111th Congress could be construed as the beginning of the 60-day period prescribed by section 123.d. for congressional action on the agreement and, accordingly, as the day on which new joint resolutions of disapproval should automatically be introduced. Further, by this interpretation, if no joint resolution of disapproval were to be enacted by the end of the 60th day of continuous session of the 111th Congress, the agreement would automatically go into effect.

STATUTORY PROCEDURE FOR DISAPPROVAL SUBMISSION OF THE AGREEMENT

Requirements for Submission. Several features of the language of section 123. indicate differences in purpose and intent between the 30-day period for consultation under section 123.b. and the 60-day period for congressional action under section 123.d. Under section 123.b., the President submits the text of the agreement to the committees having jurisdiction for consultation; under section 123.d. he submits the agreement itself to Congress for its action.

Section 123.b. then directs that the President consult with the committees receiving the submission for a period of "not less than 30 days of continuous session ... concerning the consistency of the terms of the proposed agreement with all the requirements of" the non-proliferation provisions of the AEA. He is also to approve the proposed agreement and make "a determination in writing that ... [it] will promote, and will not constitute an unreasonable risk to, the common defense and security." Under section 123.d., the 60-day period for congressional action begins when the President submits the agreement itself to the Congress, along with his "approval and determination," and then only when the NPAS, including any classified annexes, has also been submitted to Congress.

The reference of section 123.d. to the "approval and determination of the President," appears to address the same act of approval "determination in writing" required by section 123.b. Further, although section 123.b. does not explicitly require that the President must approve the agreement and make the required determination following the consultation with the committees, it can be read as implying that the consultation should precede this action. This reading of the statute appears to imply that the 60-day period required by section 123.d. will not run concurrently with the 30-day period prescribed by section 123.b., but will instead follow that 30-day period. On the other hand, the AEA does not appear to require that the submission to Congress of the agreement itself must immediately follow the 30-day period for consultation.

Submission of Agreement with Russia. Two features of the President's submission on May 13 do not appear to comport clearly with the statutory scheme. First, the President's letter of transmittal made explicit reference only to submitting the agreement to Congress for approval; it did not explicitly submit the text of the agreement to the committees of jurisdiction as well. Nevertheless, inasmuch as the submission did result in referral of the agreement to the committees, the President and Congress are apparently agreed in treating the submission of the agreement to Congress as also constituting submission of the text to the committees. It is this understanding, in effect, that enables the President by a single submission to fulfill the requirements of both sections 123.b. and 123.d.

Second, inasmuch as all requirements for both the periods required by the statute were met by the time of the submission on May 13, it might be questioned why the 30-day and the 60-day period should not both be considered as beginning at once. The chief reason against doing so appears to be the apparent presumption of the statute that the President's "agreement and determination," the submission of which is required for the beginning of the 60-day period for congressional action, is to follow and, in some sense, result from the consultation with committees that is supposed to occur during the period of at least 30 days.

Under this rationale, however, the President's declaration of his "approval and determination" at the outset of the 30-day period could be viewed as rendering moot the consultive purpose of that period. The President's letter of transmittal, nevertheless, also declares the readiness of the Administration to "begin immediately the consultations ... provided in section 123.b."

Resolutions of Disapproval

Requirements for Disapproval Resolution. Section 130.i. of the AEA regulates the form of the joint resolution to disapprove a proposed agreement for nuclear cooperation and proceedings thereon. Pursuant to section 130.i.(2), joint resolutions of disapproval are to be introduced automatically in each house "on the day on which a proposed agreement for cooperation is submitted" to Congress under section 123.d. The date specified would be the first day of the period of 60 days of continuous session for congressional consideration mandated by section 123.d. In order for the disapproval resolution to be eligible for expedited consideration under section 1 30.i., section 1 30.i.(1) prescribes that its text must simply state: "That the Congress does not favor the proposed agreement for cooperation transmitted to the Congress by the President on [the appropriate date]."

The automatically introduced measure is to be sponsored in the House by the chairman and ranking minority member of the Committee on Foreign Affairs, and in the Senate by the two party floor leaders, or (in each case) their designees.[33] The AEA, however, also appears to contemplate that other Members may also introduce similar resolutions. Pursuant to section 1 30.i.(3), a disapproval resolution is to be referred, in the Senate, to the Committee on Foreign Relations, and in the House to "the appropriate committee or committees," which presumably would be, or at least include, the Committee on Foreign Affairs.

Resolutions to Disapprove Agreement with Russia. Some elements of congressional proceedings in relation to the proposed agreement with Russia do not clearly reflect the distinctions between the period for consultation with committees and the period for action by Congress that the AEA appears to intend. For this agreement, as noted earlier, the first day of the 60-day period provided by section 123.d. must presumably occur on the 31st day of the full 90-day period contemplated in the President's submission letter. Inasmuch as the House maintained its scheduled Memorial Day recess, it appears that this point will be reached on or about June 24, 2008. A joint resolution to disapprove the proposed agreement (H.J.Res. 85), however, had already been introduced on May 14, the day after the President had submitted the agreement to Congress. This resolution has the text specified by section 130.i.(2), and was referred to the Committee on Foreign Affairs. It was introduced, however, at the beginning not of the 60-day period, but of the 30- day period, immediately after the President's initial transmission of the proposed agreement. Accordingly, it is not clear whether or not this measure is being regarded as meeting the requirements of section 130.i.(2) for the automatically introduced resolution.

In any case, however, the provisions of the statute do not seem to preclude any resolution having the required text from consideration pursuant to the expedited procedure of section 1 30.i. If H.J.Res. 85 were to be enacted before the end of the 60-day period, it would presumably suffice to prevent the agreement from going into effect, as contemplated by the statute.

Committee Action

Consultations With Committees. Section 123.b. of the AEA directs that after the President submits the text of the agreement to the pertinent committees, he is to consult with them thereon during the stated period of "at least 30 days of continuous session." This provision does not specify the form to be taken by these consultations. During the 60 days of continuous session after the agreement itself is submitted to Congress, on the other hand, section 123.d. specifies that the committees of referral are to "hold hearings on the proposed agreement ... and submit a report to their respective bodies recommending whether it should be approved or disapproved."[34] Presumably, if the committee decides to recommend disapproval, the report in question could be that which accompanies the resolution of disapproval itself. If the committee favors approval, the report might simply be explanatory, rather than accompanying any legislation.[35]

Committee Action on Agreement with Russia. The relation between these statutory requirements and initial congressional action on the proposed agreement with Russia also reflects possible ambiguities. This congressional action began with the hearing of the House Committee on Foreign Affairs on June 12 and the closed briefing with the Senate Committee on Foreign Relations on June 17. It is not clear whether either committee conceived its session as meeting the requirement of section 123.d. for hearings on the agreement. If they did, it is not clear whether hearings held after the agreement has been submitted and referred, but before the 60-day period during which section 123.d. calls for them, could appropriately be regarded as also satisfying that requirement. On the other hand, inasmuch as officials of the Department of State appeared at both sessions, they could no doubt be understood as means of implementing the consultations for which section 123.b. calls. There seems no reason to suppose that consultations pursuant to section123.b. might not take such a form.

DISCHARGE OF COMMITTEE

Timing of Discharge. Under section 130.i.(4) of the AEA, each committee of referral is automatically to be discharged from the further consideration of all disapproval resolutions referred to it at the end of 45 days from the date of submission of the agreement. This provision appears intended to guarantee that a disapproval resolution will become eligible for timely floor consideration in each chamber even if the committee takes no action. The statute, however, does not define this time period in terms of days of continuous session. Instead, it is the practice of Congress to construe references in its procedures to "days," if not otherwise specified, as legislative days. For each house, a legislative day ends each time the chamber adjourns, and another begins each time it convenes after an adjournment. Accordingly, "legislative days" in each chamber normally correspond to its days of session.[36] For this reason, although days of continuous session are measured in a way that maintains a single count for Congress as a whole, the number of legislative days in the two houses may differ.

As a result, if either chamber convenes Monday through Friday except during recess periods, five legislative days would probably occur per week there, although seven "days of continuous session" would elapse. If both houses held pro forma sessions during a recess period, days of continuous session would elapse even more quickly compared to legislative days in each chamber. (For example, if each house convenes two pro forma sessions during a "recess" period running from one Saturday through the second following Sunday, the recess would consume nine days of continuous session, and only two legislative days in each chamber.) Under these conditions, the 45th (legislative) day after referral of a disapproval resolution might not occur, in either or both chambers, until 60 days of continuous session from the submission of the agreement had already elapsed. In this case, the discharge of the committee(s) might not occur until after the agreement had already gone into effect and could no longer be disapproved under the statute.[37] It is not clear whether the possibility of such a result was intended by the statute or arises from an inadvertent oversight in drafting.

Possible Discharge of Agreement with Russia. In the present instance, if either house meets five days a week, except during recesses, during the period after the resolutions of disapproval are to be introduced on June 24, the required 45 legislative days in that house will not have elapsed by the time of the scheduled sine die adjournment on September 26. Under these conditions, that house will never reach the point at which discharge would occur by the time the 1 10th Congress ends.

Alternatively, if Congress continues meeting after September 26 on the same schedule, and without recesses, committees could be discharged pursuant to the statute on or about October 10, 2008. As estimated above, however,[38] the 90th day of continuous session will already have been reached on October 8, so that the discharge will come too late to prevent the agreement from going into effect. Similarly, if both houses hold two pro forma sessions per week during the scheduled Independence Day and August recesses, the additional legislative days represented by these pro forma sessions of discharge could advance the point of discharge in each house to about September 24. As also explained earlier, however, the pro forma sessions would also give rise to the days of the "recess" period being counted as days of continuous session. Under these conditions, as a result, the 90th day of continuous session would already have been reached on about August 11. In either case, if the committee in each chamber did not choose to report a joint resolution of disapproval for the agreement with Russia, the provision of section 1 30.i. for automatic discharge would not afford the 1 10th Congress an opportunity to act on the resolution.[39]

CHAMBER ACTION

Section 1 30.i. of the AEA provides that, once the committee in either chamber reports or is discharged from a joint resolution to disapprove a nuclear cooperation agreement, the measure is to be placed on the chamber's calendar of business.[40] The provision then directs that the disapproval resolution be considered under expedited (or "fast track") procedures, the purpose of which is to ensure that Congress will have an opportunity to consider and vote on the measure before the arrival of the time at which the agreement would otherwise automatically take effect. Section 130.i., however, does not itself specify procedures for floor consideration of a resolution of disapproval. Instead, for the Senate, it applies an expedited procedure contained in another statute, and for the House, it presumes that the procedures used will be established by a special rule.

For the Senate, section 130.i.(5) of the AEA provides that floor consideration shall occur pursuant to section 601 (b)(4) of the International Security Assistance and Arms Export Control Act of 1976 (ISAAECA).[41] This provision of law established an expedited procedure, for the Senate only, that has been made applicable to additional classes of measure by several subsequent laws. Pursuant to this expedited procedure, the joint resolution of disapproval is privileged, meaning that the Senate may take it up by approving a non-debatable motion to proceed to consider. ISAAECA also limits debate on the resolution itself to 10 hours (equally divided and controlled by the two floor leaders or their designees), and precludes any amendment (or motion to recommit). A non-debatable motion to limit debate further is allowed, various other potentially dilatory actions are prohibited, and limits are placed on the debate of questions arising during consideration. Provisions similar to these are standard components of statutory expedited procedures.

Section 1 30.i.(5) establishes no regulations for House floor consideration of the resolution of disapproval, nor does it even make the measure privileged for consideration (which, in the House, means that the measure could be called up with priority over the regular order of business). Instead, section 1 30.i.(5) authorizes the Committee on Rules to report a special rule providing for consideration of the measure under terms that "may be similar, if applicable" to those of ISAAECA. Any special rule for consideration of a disapproval resolution would surely place limits on debate, and would most likely prohibit amendments as well, inasmuch as any change in the text of the resolution would render it inconsistent with the requirements of section 1 30.i.(1), and therefore, presumably, ineligible for further consideration under the expedited procedure of section 1 30.i.

This provision of the AEA grants the Committee on Rules no power that it would not otherwise have. Nevertheless, unless the Committee on Rules reports a special rule for considering a disapproval resolution, or unless privilege for consideration is conferred on the measure by some other means (e.g., suspension of the rules or unanimous consent), section 130. would afford no means by which House floor consideration of the measure could be ensured.

FINAL CONGRESSIONAL ACTION

Section 1 30.i.(6) of the AEA makes provision to preclude the necessity to resolve differences between disapproval resolutions passed by the two chambers. If one chamber adopts its resolution and transmits it to the other, then the receiving chamber considers its own companion measure, but takes the final vote on the measure received from the first house (which, under the statute, must be substantively similar). This automatic "hookup" is evidently intended to ensure that final action in both houses will occur on the same measure in the same form, so that it can be cleared for presentation to the President without the necessity for a conference committee or other process of resolving differences between versions of the measure adopted by the two chambers.[42]

PRESIDENTIAL ACTION

Pursuant to section 123.d. of the AEA, the proposed nuclear cooperation agreement with the Russian Federation will take effect at the end of the total period of 90 days of continuous session unless a joint resolution of disapproval is enacted before that time. It is not sufficient for Congress to complete action on the disapproval resolution within the required time; the measure must actually become law before the end of the prescribed period. Enactment into law of the resolution requires either that (1) the President signs it or allows it to pass into law without his signature; or (2) the Congress overrides his veto. For Congress to prevent the agreement from taking effect, one of these actions would have to take place before the end of the 90-day period.

Under the Constitution, the President has 10 days (Sundays excepted) to act on a measure after it is presented to him. As a result, if the resolution were to be presented when fewer than 10 calendar days (excluding Sundays) remained in the total period of 90 days of continuous session, it appears that the President could render the measure moot by failing to act until the 90-day period expired and the agreement went into effect. Similarly, if the President were to return the resolution with a veto, the agreement would take effect unless Congress were to complete action to override the veto before the 90th day of continuous session after the initial submission of its text to the committees.

In practice, the President is likely to veto a resolution disapproving an agreement of which, under the statute, he has already certified his approval. For Congress to make effective use of its opportunity under the AEA to disapprove the agreement, accordingly, it would presumably have to present the resolution of disapproval to the President at a point when a minimum of 11 days of continuous session remain in the 90-day period before the agreement automatically becomes effective. (The minimum is 11 if Congress remains in session, such that every calendar day is a day of continuous session, inasmuch as any period of 10 calendar days will contain at least one Sunday that will count as a day of continuous session but not as a day of the period for presidential action.) A still longer period would afford Congress a more practicable opportunity to act to override the veto.

Specific implications of this circumstances for the agreement with Russia can be illustrated only through assumptions about the sine die adjournment of the 1 10th Congress. Assume, for example, that Congress maintains the announced schedule described above, in the section on "Days of Continuous Session in the 1 10th Congress," through September 26, 2008, but instead of adjourning sine die on that date, recesses its session until November 12. As shown earlier, September 26 would then presumably be the 78th day of continuous session, and November 12 would be the 79th . Under these circumstances, if Congress completes action on the resolution of disapproval and presents it to the President on September 26, just before recessing, the 10-day period allowed for presidential action would extend until October 8, and when Congress returned on November 12, it would have until the 90th day of continuous session (presumably Sunday, November 23) to prevent the agreement entering into effect by overriding the veto.

If, on the other hand, Congress does not complete action on the resolution of disapproval until it reconvenes on November 12, the 10 days allowed for presidential action would last until Monday, November 24. Assuming Congress remains in session, however, its 90th day of continuous session after submission of the agreement would still be November 23. Under these circumstances, it appears that the President could ensure that the agreement would go into effect by delaying his veto of the measure until November 24.

Finally, if Congress were to adjourn sine die shortly after adopting the disapproval resolution, the President could pocket veto it. If this sine die adjournment occurred after the 90th day of continuous session, the agreement would go into effect. On the other hand, if the adjournment occurred on or before the 90th day of continuous session, the agreement presumably could not go into effect until the appropriate period of continuous session had elapsed beginning with the convening of the 111th Congress, and then only if no congressional disapproval was accomplished during that period.[43]

Alternative Action

Although the AEA provides the expedited procedures described above for congressional action on a joint resolution of disapproval, it does not require Congress to use these procedures to act on the matter. If, during the period for action provided by the statute, Congress were to adopt a disapproval resolution meeting the requirements of section 1 30.i. under any of its regular procedures, enactment of the resolution would have the same effect of disapproving the agreement as would that of a similar measure under the expedited procedures of the statute.

Under its general legislative power, Congress could also determine the status of the agreement by acting on a measure other than the one prescribed by the statute. Such action occurred in the 99th Congress (1985-1986), when Congress enacted a measure (P.L. 99-183) providing that a nuclear cooperation agreement with China would become effective only when certain further conditions were met. Just as with the disapproval resolution specified by the statute, however, any such measure would have to be enacted before the end of period required by the AEA, because otherwise the agreement as submitted would automatically go into effect. On the other hand, inasmuch as any such alternative measure would not meet the requirements of section 130.i. for a joint resolution of disapproval, the measure would not be eligible for consideration under the expedited procedures of section 130.i. Instead, each house would have to consider it under its regular legislative procedures (unless it chose, in accordance with its own general procedures, to apply the expedited procedure to the alternative measure).

Any measure granting approval with conditions to the proposed agreement with Russia would presumably have to contain language specifying that its provisions apply "notwithstanding section 123. of the Atomic Energy Act of 1954, as amended." Section (a)(2) of P.L. 99-183, granting conditional approval to the agreement with China, contained a provision of this kind. In the absence of such a provision, the provision of section 123. for automatic unconditional approval at the end of the 90 days would presumably continue to apply, so that in spite of the conditional approval, and unless the joint resolution of disapproval specified by section 1 30.i. were enacted into law, the agreement might take effect without conditions at the end of the period.

The President might also be able to vitiate an attempt by Congress to place conditions on its approval of the agreement with Russia by vetoing the measure. Unless Congress could override the veto (or secure enactment into law of a joint resolution of disapproval), the agreement would then instead go into effect without conditions at the end of the period prescribed in accordance with section 123.

REFERENCES

[1] For information on policy issues associated with the proposed agreement with Russia, see CRS Report RS22892, U.S.-Russian Civilian Nuclear Cooperation Agreement: Issues for Congress, by Mary Beth Nikitin.

[2] Legislation governing atomic energy was originally enacted by the Atomic Energy Act of 1946 (Public Law 585, 79th Cong., 60 Stat. 755). The 1946 act was comprehensively amended by Atomic Energy Act of 1954 (Public Law 703, 83rd Cong., 68 Stat. 919), which added the initial version of the non-proliferation provisions, now codified chiefly at 42 U.S.C. 2151-2 160d (Subchapter X, "International Activities," of Chapter 23, "Development and Control of Atomic Energy," of Title 42, "Public Health and Welfare"). These provisions included pertinently sec. 123. (68 Stat. 940, 42 U.S.C. 2153), which defines requirements for nuclear cooperation agreements and for their approval. Sec. 308 of the Nuclear Nonproliferation Act of 1978 (P.L. 95-242, 92 Stat. 120 at 139) added the initial version of section 130. (42 U.S.C. 2159), which establishes expedited procedures for legislation to approve or disapprove nuclear cooperation agreements. Section 301(b)(2)(B) of P.L. 99-64 (99 Stat. 120 at 161) added subsection 130.i. (42 U.S.C. 2159(I)), which establishes the expedited procedure now applicable to the proposed agreement with the Russian Federation.

[3] This report follows the form of the enacting statutes in using periods in the designation of sections and subsections (for example, sections 123.d. and 130.i.). The codified versions of these provisions are designated with the more usual parentheses (for example, 42 U.S.C. 2 153(d) and 2 159(i)).

[4] The requirements of section 123.b. (42 U.S.C. 2 153(b)) apply to agreements not "arranged pursuant to subsection 9 1(c), 144(b), 144(c), or 144(d)" of the Atomic Energy Act (42 U.S.C. 2121(c), 2164(b), 2164(c), or 2164(d)), which cover military uses of atomic energy.

[5] The NPAS is described in section 123.a. (42 U.S.C. 2153(a)).

[6] The requirements of section 123.d. (42 U.S.C. 2 153(d)) apply to agreements "entailing implementation of [42 U.S.C.] 2073, 2074(a), 2133, or 2134 ... in relation to a reactor that may be capable of producing more than five thermal megawatts or special nuclear material for use in connection therewith." In practice, this category includes most reactors other than some that serve purposes of research alone.

[7] Section 130.i. does not specify that the 45 days allowed for committee action are days of continuous session; accordingly, they would presumably be treated instead as legislative days. The significance of this difference is addressed below in the section on "Discharge of Committee."

[8] U.S. Congress, House, Proposed Agreement Between the United States of America and the Russian Federation Concerning Peaceful Uses of Nuclear Energy, message from the President of the United States transmitting a proposed agreement between the Government of the United States of America and the Government of the Russian Federation for cooperation in the field of peaceful uses of nuclear energy, pursuant to 42 U.S.C. 2153(b), (d), H.Doc. 110-112, 1 10th Cong., 2nd sess. (Washington: GPO, 2008).

[9] Ibid., p. 3.

[10] Ibid., pp. 26-5 1.

[11] "Proposed Agreement With Russian Federation for Cooperation in the Field of Peaceful Uses of Nuclear Energy — Message from the President of the United States (H.Doc. No. 110-112," message inserted in House proceedings, Congressional Record [daily ed.], vol. 154, May 13, 2008, pg. H3701; "Text of a Proposed Agreement Between the Government of the United States of America and the Government of the Russian Federation for Cooperation in the field of Peaceful Uses of Nuclear Energy — PM 48," message inserted in Senate proceedings, ibid., pp. S4103-S4104.

[12] H.J.Res. 85 (Markey).

[13] Section 130.g.(2) (42 U.S.C. 2159(g)(2)).

[14] "Recesses of the session," in the sense used here, includes such periods as the "non-legislative periods," or "state [or "district"] work periods" scheduled, in 2008 as in most recent years, around Memorial Day and Independence Day, as well as during August.

[15] A concurrent resolution is used because this form of measure requires the agreement of both houses, but is not presented to the President for approval.

[16] Several other expedited procedure statutes also make use of this means of counting days.

[17] CQ Transcriptwire, "House Committee on Foreign Affairs Holds a Hearing on Russia, Iran, and Nuclear Weapons," June 13, 2008, available at [http://transcriptswire.cq.com /do/ transcriptView?id=259 144].

[18] The question of how long the period of continuous session in the new Congress would have to be is addressed below in the section on "Possible Need to Renew Action in the 11 1th Congress."

[19] CQ Transcriptwire, "House Committee on Foreign Affairs Holds a Hearing on Russia, Iran, and Nuclear Weapons," June 13, 2008.

[20] This recess occurred pursuant to H.Con.Res. 355, 1 10th Congress, adopted May 22, 2008.

[21] This calculation, like all the calculations and projections presented in this report, presumes that the first day of the 30-day period is the day following the submission of the text to the committees, and that the first day of the 60-day period is the day immediately following the 30th day of the 30-day period. These ways of counting conform to the usual congressional practice for day counts.

[22] The schedules used in making these calculations were those posted on the respective chamber websites at [http://www.senate.gov/pagelayout/legislative/two_column_table/2008_Schedule.htm] and [http ://www.maj orityleader. gov/docUploads/2008-CALENDAR.pdf].

[23] The required length of this new period of continuous session, and other considerations relevant to the extension into a new Congress of action on the proposed agreement with Russia, are pursued below in the section on "Possible Need to Renew Action in the 11 1th Congress."

[24] See, for example: [http://www.house.gov/house/House_Calendar.shtml] and [http://majoritywhip.house.gov/house_calendar/2008/go.pdf], both visited on June 13, 2008.

[25] Article II, section 3.

[26] For a recent example of an adjournment resolution providing this authority, see H.Con.Res. 531, 108th Cong., adopted December 9, 2004.

[27] It is, in fact, exactly this "formality" for the "sake" of which pro forma sessions are held.If a chamber holds a pro forma session at least every fourth day, it can avoid the need to obtain the permission of the other for the intervening days on which no sessions are held.

[28] H.Con.Res. 293, 1 10th Cong., agreed to February 14, 2008.

[29] The resolutions providing for these "recesses," accordingly, were technically not necessary to meet constitutional requirements. Media reports indicate that Senate leadership decided to hold regular pro forma sessions in that chamber during scheduled recess periods in an attempt to prevent the President from making certain "recess appointments." See Paul Singer, "Masters of a Pro Forma Senate," Roll Call, January 7, 2008. These reports do not ascribe any motivation for the House to meet in pro forma session during these periods.

[30] CQ Transcriptwire, "House Committee on Foreign Affairs Holds a Hearing on Russia, Iran, and Nuclear Weapons," June 13, 2008.

[31] "In figuring the length of an adjournment, Sundays are not counted, but "either the day of adjourning or the day of meeting ... must be taken into the count." W[illia]m Holmes Brown and Charles W. Johnson, House Practice: A Guide to the Rules, Precedents, and Procedures of the House (Washington: GPO, 2003), chapter 1, sec. 10.

[32] CQ Transcriptwire, "House Committee on Foreign Affairs Holds a Hearing on Russia, Iran, and Nuclear Weapons," June 13, 2008.

[33] The joint resolution is to be introduced "by request," signifying that the introducing Members do not necessarily advocate the measure.

[34] Section 123.d. (42 U.S.C. 2153(d)).

[35] The committee might also wish to advocate approval with conditions. In this case, the report might accompany a measure providing for that action, as described in the section on "Alternative Action," below.

[36] Exceptions today are not common, but in recent decades were more frequent in the Senate than in the House. Exceptions occur when a chamber does not adjourn, but takes a recess, overnight or longer, or, conversely, when it adjourns briefly and reconvenes in the course of a single calendar day. See "Day" in U.S. Congress, Senate, Riddick's Senate Procedure: Precedents and Practices, S.Doc. 101-28, 101st Cong., 2nd sess. by Floyd M. Riddick and Alan S. Frumin, rev. and ed. by Alan S. Frumin (Washington: GPO, 1992), pp. 712-715; U.S. Congress, House, Hinds' Precedents of the House of Representatives of the United States, by Asher C. Hinds (Washington: GPO, 1907), vol. IV, sec. 3192; and U.S. Congress, House, Cannon's Precedents of the House of Representatives of the United States, by Clarence Cannon (Washington: GPO, 1935), vol. VI, sec. 723.

[37] On the other hand, if one house held pro forma sessions during a period when the other was in recess, additional legislative days would occur while the count of days of continuous session would remain static. This circumstance would tend to allow the committee to be discharged earlier in the 60-day period when action to disapprove must occur.

[38] See "Days of Continuous Session in the 1 10th Congress," above.

[39] It is also possible, as suggested in footnote 21, that the Senate might hold two pro forma sessions per week while the House actually took its scheduled recesses for Independence Day and during August. In this case legislative days would accrue in the Senate during a period in which no days of continuous session were occurring. Under these conditions, discharge might occur in the Senate on about September 24, even though the period for disapproval might still potentially extend until October 8. Such an arrangement, nevertheless, could provide no corresponding help for the House.

[40] In the Senate, the resolution would be placed on the Calendar of General Orders, which carries most measures eligible for floor consideration. In the House, the measure would most likely be placed on the Union Calendar, which is for measures that may affect revenues or expenditures.

[41] P.L. 94-329, 90 Stat. 729 at 766.

[42] Similar provisions, again, appear in several other statutory expedited procedures.

[43] This period might encompass either 90 or 60 days, depending on interpretation, as explained above under "Possibility of Renewing Action in the 111th Congress."

INDEX

A

academic, 8
ACC, 144
access, x, 23, 45, 52, 55, 63, 69, 106, 121, 122, 137, 139
accidents, 22
accountability, 2, 74
accounting, 18, 105, 126, 130, 139
accuracy, 72
achievement, 29, 49, 75
acquisitions, 43, 110
acute, 49, 72
ad hoc, 78
adjustment, 142
administration, 53, 54, 60, 62, 63, 64, 109
administrative, 108
advocacy, 47
AEA, x, xi, 147, 148, 149, 150, 152, 154, 155, 156, 157, 158, 159, 160, 161, 162
Afghanistan, 9, 12, 14, 28, 31, 52, 69, 70
age, 103, 135
aggressiveness, 37
Agreement on Subsidies and Countervailing Measures, 130
agricultural, 105, 107, 108, 117, 124, 128, 131, 132, 136, 143
agriculture, x, 11, 100, 107, 108, 117, 121, 126, 129, 131, 132, 137, 141, 142
aid, viii, 2, 12, 22, 23, 32, 58
air, 31, 74, 139
Aircraft, 110, 134, 135, 137
Al Qaeda, 12, 14
alcoholism, 103
Aleksandr Lukashenko, 13
allies, viii, 19, 20, 25, 36, 43, 46, 58, 61, 63, 64, 65, 66, 75, 78, 117
alternative, xi, 14, 66, 73, 75, 148, 163
alternative energy, 75
alternatives, 55
aluminum, 116, 139, 142
ambassadors, 57
ambivalence, 46, 50
amendments, xi, 148, 149, 160
analysts, 12, 16, 27, 32, 36, 37, 38, 39, 42, 44, 55, 56, 58, 72, 74, 77, 87
anger, 15
antagonism, 12, 30, 34, 46
anti-American, 37, 38
anti-Americanism, 38
antidumping, 129, 139
ants, 27, 84, 85
anxiety, 70, 75
APEC, 136
application, ix, 19, 61, 108, 121, 122, 123, 124, 125, 138, 139, 148
appointees, 4, 6
appropriations, 23
appropriations bills, 23
Arabia, 4, 110
Arctic, 74
Argentina, 132
argument, 30, 39, 44, 51, 70, 71, 73, 155
armed conflict, 52
armed forces, viii, 2, 16, 17, 32, 41, 49, 52, 60, 69, 73, 74, 77
Armed Forces, 79, 81
Armenia, viii, 1, 13, 14, 24, 110, 115, 120
arms control, vii, viii, 4, 21, 25, 33, 44, 46, 48, 52, 53, 59, 61, 69, 73
Army, 24, 31, 80, 82, 84, 86, 94
arrest, 5, 37
Asia, 4, 14, 24, 31, 34, 35, 36, 37, 43, 55, 59, 64, 65, 66, 67, 71, 76, 78, 81, 82, 83, 90, 91, 92, 93, 95, 96

Asian, 14, 30, 58, 64, 71, 74, 75, 76, 78, 91, 92, 93, 95, 101, 118, 125
assault, 9
assertiveness, 30
assessment, 28, 31, 32, 33, 38, 39, 40, 43, 44, 48, 49, 60, 62, 63
assets, 3, 5, 19, 74, 99, 100, 104, 109, 110, 117, 127
assumptions, 152, 162
Atlantic, viii, 2, 17, 65, 70
Atlas, 119
atmosphere, 12, 42
Atomic Energy Act (AEA), x, 147,148, 150, 163, 164
attacks, 9, 10, 14, 15, 18, 22, 34, 45, 49, 50, 58, 59, 64, 70, 73
attitudes, 33
attractiveness, 53, 69
Australia, 132
Austria, 21
authoritarianism, 6, 55, 57
authority, 4, 19, 61, 66, 105, 140, 153, 154, 165
autonomy, 3, 9, 15, 124
avian influenza, 133
aviation, 40, 110, 142
avoidance, 107
AWACS, 71
Azerbaijan, viii, 1, 17, 21, 24, 32, 63, 115

B

background information, 144
bad behavior, 61
Balkans, 65
ballistic missile, 20, 30, 32, 40, 47, 49
ballistic missiles, 30, 40, 47
Baltic states, 35, 39, 46, 50, 51, 68,74, 77
banking, 108, 127, 133, 134, 137, 142
banking industry, 109
bankruptcy, 101
banks, 100, 109, 134, 145
bargaining, 76
barriers, x, 47, 52, 121, 122, 123, 125, 143
beef, 132, 136
behavior, vii, viii, 25, 33, 60, 61, 64, 65, 66, 73
Beijing, 36, 47, 64, 66, 67, 75, 86
Belarus, viii, 1, 13, 17, 18, 39, 55, 56, 57, 58, 63
beliefs, 53, 60, 69
benchmark, 129
benefits, 32, 53, 57, 69, 72, 73, 75, 104
benign, 43
Beslan, 6, 9
beverages, 129, 135
bilateral relations, 26, 30, 34, 37, 41
bilateral trade, 4, 117, 139, 140
binding, 40, 45, 67, 141
biological weapons, 22, 38
bipolar, 36
birth, 10, 77
birth rate, 10
Black Sea, 15, 34, 80
blame, 42
bloodshed, 9
Boeing, 117, 139
bomb, 9
bonds, 67, 101
Boris Yeltsin, 4, 40, 99
borrowers, 133
Boston, 86
bounds, 51
bovine, 136
bovine spongiform encephalopathy (BSE), 136
Brazil, 98
breeding, 48
Bretton Woods, 125
Bretton Woods conference, 125
broadcast media, 5
Brussels, 21, 90
budget cuts, viii, 2, 16
budget deficit, 100, 101, 106
budget surplus, vii, 1, 106
buildings, 9
Bulgaria, 31, 44, 51
bullying, 35
Bureau of the Census, 116, 139
bureaucracy, 127, 128, 142
Bush administration, vii, x, 12, 14, 18, 19, 20, 22,26, 53, 54, 59, 63, 66, 91, 122
Bush Doctrine, 90, 93
business environment, 107, 115
by-products, 136

C

campaigns, 31
Canada, 74, 82, 132
candidates, 7, 8
capacity, 43, 49, 66, 75, 114, 116, 135
capital flight, vii, 1, 100
capital flows, 104
Capitol Hill, 91
carbon, 73
carbon dioxide, 73
carrier, 32
cartel, 26
cash payments, 106
Caspian, 14, 36, 69, 74, 118

cast, 19, 33
catastrophes, 10
cattle, 136
Caucasus, 9, 14, 23, 31, 41, 65, 72, 73, 77, 89, 94, 96
cement, 49
Census, 116, 139
Central Asia, 14, 24, 30, 31, 36, 37, 43, 55, 64, 65, 71, 74, 78, 82, 83, 90, 91, 92, 118
Central Bank, 104, 109,118, 128, 134
Central Europe, 52, 81
Central Intelligence Agency, 36
central planning, 103, 107, 125, 127, 128
centralized, 44, 107
CEO, 5
certificate, 133
certification, 133, 136
certifications, 136
Chad, 95
chain of command, 17
chaos, 99, 105, 106, 117
Chechen rebels, 10, 14
Chechnya, 3, 4, 9, 10, 14, 23, 30, 37, 39, 58, 72, 73, 74, 90
chemical weapons, 52, 69
chemicals, 116, 126
chicken, 117, 133, 139
Chief of Staff, 5, 27
children, 9
China, 2, 10, 12, 14, 19, 30, 34, 35, 36, 37, 38, 39, 45, 47, 48, 57, 65, 67, 71, 74, 75, 76, 82, 92, 95, 98, 99, 105, 114, 140, 143, 162, 163
CIA, 36
citizens, 2, 99, 134, 139
civil society, 38
civil war, 14
civilian, 9, 17, 18, 22, 32, 74, 127
classes, 160
classical, 34
Clinton Administration, 35
CNS, 93
Co, v, 4, 7, 9, 14, 24, 29, 84, 90, 92, 95, 119, 147, 148, 150, 158, 163, 164
coal, 15, 75, 110, 112, 126
coalitions, 67
cognitive, 42, 59
coherence, 65
cold war, 26
Cold War, 12, 15, 22, 26, 27, 31, 32, 33, 34, 40, 43, 44, 45, 46, 47, 50, 51, 53, 61, 63, 68, 77, 82, 86, 89, 94, 116, 138, 139, 140
collateral, 100
collectivism, 107
colleges, 78
commerce, 124
commodity, 112, 128
Commonwealth of Independent States, viii, 1, 28
communication, 36, 114
Communism, 93
communist countries, 125, 139
Communist Party, 7
community, vii, viii, x, 25, 47, 61, 72, 122, 138, 141, 142, 143
comparative advantage, 130
competition, 36, 55, 107, 108, 115, 133, 135, 141, 142
competitive advantage, 130
competitiveness, 10, 117, 134
complexity, 77
compliance, 21, 22, 26, 27, 130, 139, 140
components, 160
composition, 4, 47
computation, 150
computer software, 131
concentration, 70
concrete, 70
confidence, 2, 3, 21, 114, 127, 134
conflict, ix, 9, 10, 14, 17, 36, 46, 48, 50, 52, 56, 73, 77, 98, 107
conformity, 42, 72
confrontation, 12, 36, 40, 49, 50, 98
confusion, 128, 135
Congress, iv, ix, x, xi, 6, 18, 19, 22, 23, 31, 35, 37, 81, 87, 90, 91, 98, 121, 122, 131, 136, 140, 145, 147, 148, 149, 150, 151, 152, 153, 154, 155, 156, 157, 158, 159, 160, 161, 162, 163, 164, 165, 166
Congressional Record, 164
congruence, 37, 65
consensus, 13, 62, 64, 76, 125, 143
consent, 151, 153, 161
consolidation, 26, 35, 36
Constitution, 3, 151, 154, 161
constraints, 28, 31, 70, 73
construction, 18, 19, 40, 58, 109, 117
consumer price index, 103
consumers, 74, 75, 117, 127, 131
consumption, 39, 75, 102, 114, 117
contingency, 68
continuity, x, 8, 147, 150, 151, 152, 155
contracts, 75, 136
control, vii, viii, ix, 4, 5, 6, 7, 11, 14, 17, 18, 25, 32, 33, 39, 40, 44, 47, 52, 53, 54, 69, 70, 73, 74, 77, 97, 100, 106, 109, 110, 118, 127, 128, 134
convergence, 65
conviction, 35, 56
copyrights, 131
corporate governance, 107, 128

correlation, 41
corruption, vii, 1, 5, 6, 10, 11, 54, 107, 109, 115
costs, 60, 74
counterfeit, 131
counterintelligence, 73
countermeasures, 130
counterterrorism, 30
courts, 4, 109
coverage, 8, 44, 123, 140, 143
craving, 26, 42
credibility, 105
credit, 10, 139
crime, vii, 1, 10, 23, 72, 109
crisis management, 61
critical points, 78
criticism, 9, 15, 18, 20, 21, 54, 55, 61
CRS, viii, 1, 2, 23, 24, 90, 97, 99, 102, 111, 114, 116, 118, 119, 120, 121, 139, 147, 163
crude oil, 110, 112, 126
cruise missiles, 31
CT, 80
Cuba, 12, 125
culture, 60
currency, 75, 99, 101, 115, 120
current account, 105, 126
current account balance, 105
current account surplus, 126
customers, 64, 76, 130, 135
Customs Service, 119
Cyprus, 117, 139
Czech Republic, 2, 3, 12, 20, 21, 26, 31, 40, 45, 114

D

danger, vii, viii, 14, 18, 25, 30, 43, 48, 49, 55
database, 120
dating, 40, 54
de novo, 155
death, 15, 50, 68
deaths, 9
debt, 10, 100, 101
debts, 5, 100, 106
decisions, 11, 17, 28, 43, 62
decoding, 32
decoupling, 66
defects, 60
defense, viii, 2, 3, 12, 16, 17, 18, 19, 20, 21, 22, 25, 26, 29, 30, 31, 32, 34, 37, 39, 41, 42, 43, 44, 46, 47, 48, 53, 58, 69, 70, 77, 100, 110, 134, 149, 156
defenses, 20, 40, 41, 45
deficit, 106, 112
deficits, 70, 100, 101, 106, 138
definition, x, 105, 147, 148, 151
degradation, 10, 18
delivery, 19, 134, 135, 137
demand, 27, 41, 45, 47, 56, 66, 70, 71, 74, 75, 105, 107, 111, 115, 117, 127, 133, 134
democracy, viii, 2, 6, 28, 30, 33, 34, 35, 43, 52, 55, 56, 60, 61, 62, 70, 71, 72, 74, 77, 140
Democratic Party, 7, 8
democratization, 22, 35, 36, 37, 39, 53, 60, 62, 63, 65, 69, 70, 71, 72, 73, 77
democrats, 12
Department of Agriculture, 136
Department of Commerce, 116, 139
Department of Defense, 30, 92
Department of Energy, 22, 111, 119, 120
Department of State, 88, 91, 92, 149, 158
deposits, 106, 109, 134
depreciation, 105, 107, 126, 128
depressed, 16, 44
depression, 126
desertion, 16
desire, vii, viii, 25, 32, 39, 43, 47, 50, 53, 69
destruction, 38, 42
deterrence, 41, 42, 43, 44, 47, 53, 64
devaluation, 10
developed countries, 103, 108, 132
developing countries, 124, 144
dichotomy, 62
dictatorship, 64
direct cost, 74
direct costs, 74
direct investment, 100, 108, 117, 127, 137, 139
Director of National Intelligence, 30, 80
discipline, viii, 2
discourse, 26, 70
discretionary, 137
discriminatory, 123
disinformation, 32
dislocation, 10
displacement, 135
disposable income, 99, 102, 103
disposition, vii, viii, 25
disputes, 4, 12, 52, 66, 124, 141, 143
disseminate, 75
distribution, 103, 104, 126, 137
distribution of income, 103
diversification, 115
division, 125
divorce, 13
doctors, 29
Doha, 132
domestic demand, 64
domestic economy, 125
domestic industry, 143

domestic investment, vii, 1
domestic policy, 39, 46, 66, 74
dominance, vii, 1, 13, 15, 19
draft, 16
dream, 41
dual exchange rate, 128
Duma, vii, 1, 3, 6, 7, 8, 23, 108, 131, 142, 145
dumping, 139
duties, 137, 139, 141

E

early warning, 18, 21
earnings, 101
East Asia, 36
Eastern Europe, viii, 1, 12, 16, 21, 28, 34, 41, 46, 63, 135
ecological, 10, 45
economic activity, 107
economic crisis, 101
economic development, 123
economic growth, x, 10, 98, 102, 103, 104, 105, 111, 113, 114, 115, 116, 121, 122, 126, 127, 128, 133, 142, 144
economic institutions, 142
economic integration, 13, 108
economic performance, ix, 98
economic policy, 101, 107, 125, 128, 138
economic problem, 100, 126, 127
economic reform, ix, 10, 11, 97, 100, 101, 105, 106, 108, 115, 122, 123, 126, 127, 128, 140
economic reforms, ix, 10, 97, 105, 106, 115, 122, 123, 126, 140
economic stability, ix, 97, 98, 101, 106, 109, 117
economic theory, 142
economic transformation, 36
effective exchange rate, 118
election, vii, 1, 3, 7, 8, 13, 15, 23, 30, 57, 101, 153
election law, 8
electricity, x, 74, 121, 129, 130
elephant, 54
embargo, 14
emerging economies, 114
emerging markets, 122
emigration, 139, 140
emotional, 56
employers, 108
encephalopathy, 136
encouragement, 15
encryption, 137
energy, vii, ix, x, 1, 5, 11, 16, 30, 31, 33, 35, 36, 37, 38, 55, 58, 61, 63, 64, 65, 74, 75, 76, 97, 98, 104, 105, 106, 112, 114, 115, 117, 118, 121, 126, 127, 128, 129, 130, 137, 141, 142, 149, 163, 164
energy consumption, 75
Energy Information Administration, 111, 119, 120
engagement, ix, 25, 66, 67
enlargement, viii, 1, 12, 29, 32, 39, 46, 47, 49, 52
enterprise, 110, 127, 130
enthusiasm, 117
environment, ix, 4, 37, 59, 67, 74, 77, 98, 117, 123
environmental degradation, 10
equality, vii, viii, 25, 27
equity, 110
equity market, 110
erosion, 132, 135
espionage, 14
Estonia, 12, 15, 24, 26, 28, 52
estrangement, 37, 54
EU, vii, x, 1, 11, 12, 13, 14, 15, 16, 18, 27, 51, 55, 57, 58, 59, 62, 63, 65, 68, 75, 77, 81, 90, 91, 105, 121, 122, 129, 130, 131, 132, 133, 134, 135, 141
Eurasia, 3, 33, 35, 36, 42, 44, 51, 52, 56, 60, 62, 68, 72, 73, 77, 78, 82, 89, 90, 94, 95
Euro, 58, 70
Europe, ix, 4, 7, 9, 15, 16, 20, 21, 24, 26, 27, 29, 30, 31, 34, 35, 37, 39, 41, 42, 45, 46, 47, 51, 52, 53, 55, 57, 58, 59, 64, 65, 68, 69, 71, 72, 73, 74, 77, 78, 79, 82, 83, 85, 87, 89, 90, 91, 93, 94, 95, 96, 97, 98, 107, 117
European Union, x, 27, 58, 62, 90, 92, 105, 121, 122, 129
evil, 53
evolution, 43
exchange rate, 128
exchange rates, 128
excise tax, 135
excuse, 21
exercise, 56, 75, 78, 153, 154
expansions, 72
expenditures, 17, 106, 112, 134, 166
expert, iv, 32, 49, 114
expertise, 133
explosives, 9
export subsidies, 132
exporter, 4, 110, 117
Export-Import Bank, 138, 139
exports, vii, ix, 1, 10, 11, 98, 104, 105, 106, 108, 111, 112, 115, 116, 117, 120, 126, 128, 129, 130, 133, 137, 138, 139, 140
external environment, 66, 76
extortion, 58
extraction, 4, 6
extremism, 7, 14

F

failure, ix, 13, 28, 33, 42, 44, 46, 47, 50, 61, 68, 71, 97, 99, 101, 149, 155
Far East, 65, 95
farms, 132
FBIS, 78, 79, 80, 81, 82, 83, 84, 85, 86, 87, 89, 90, 91, 92, 94
FDI, 105, 127
fear, 38
fears, 51, 68, 74
February, 6, 9, 13, 19, 22, 23, 24, 26, 30, 70, 78, 79, 80, 81, 82, 84, 85, 86, 89, 90, 91, 94, 95, 106, 118, 119, 145, 165
federal government, 106, 107, 112, 132
females, 99
fertilizer, 130
fertilizers, x, 121
fighters, 9
films, 131
finance, 21, 100, 101, 106, 110
financial crisis, 100, 101, 105, 106, 107, 109, 115, 118, 128
financial markets, 117
financial sector, 128
financial support, 129
financing, 109
Finland, 26, 119
fire, 10, 37, 75
firms, 14, 55, 100, 114, 134, 138
fiscal policy, 106
fishing, 52
flank, 14
flexibility, 36, 66
flight, 118
float, 128
flooding, 37
flow, 108, 118
flow of capital, 108
focusing, 123
food, 4, 105, 115, 132
foreign aid, viii, 2, 22, 23
Foreign Broadcast Information Service, 78
foreign direct investment, 75, 105, 108, 117, 127, 137, 139
foreign experts, 126
foreign intelligence, 4
foreign investment, vii, x, 1, 26, 76, 105, 108, 121, 122, 124, 128, 133, 135, 137, 142
foreign policy, vii, viii, 1, 12, 25, 32, 35, 38, 43, 45, 48, 49, 54, 55, 56, 57, 58, 59, 60, 61, 62, 63, 64, 70, 71, 73, 78, 138
foreign producer, 131, 135
foreigner, 144
foreigners, 61
Fox, 85
France, 2, 8, 19, 21
fraud, 5, 15, 38, 109
freedom, 30, 73, 139, 140
Freedom Support Act (FSA), viii, 2, 22
freezing, 136
friction, 36
Friday, 151, 154, 159
friendship, 53
FSA, 22, 23
fuel, 19, 22, 76, 115, 126
fulfillment, 53, 63, 69, 137
funding, 21, 52, 69
funds, 17, 21, 52, 69, 106, 108, 109, 118
furniture, 142

G

gas, vii, ix, x, 1, 4, 5, 6, 10, 11, 14, 16, 17, 26, 35, 74, 75, 76, 97, 98, 104, 105, 110, 112, 117, 120, 121, 126, 129, 130
gas exploration, 110
GATS, 123, 134, 144
GATT, ix, 108, 121, 122, 123, 125, 134, 138, 144
Gazprom, 5, 6, 91, 110, 129
GDP, vii, 1, 10, 99, 100, 101, 102, 103, 104, 105, 106, 108, 110, 111, 113, 114, 115, 116, 120, 126, 131
General Agreement on Tariffs and Trade, ix, 108, 121, 122, 123
General Agreement on Trade in Services, 123, 134, 144
Generalized System of Preferences, 128, 135
generation, 110
Geneva, 144
Georgia, viii, 1, 2, 12, 13, 14, 16, 17, 24, 26, 28, 39, 46, 51, 57, 58, 68, 70, 71, 72, 73, 77, 89, 94, 110, 115, 120, 140
Germany, 8, 19, 21, 31, 77, 105
Global Insight, 113, 120
global leaders, 27, 29, 34
global markets, 76
global warming, 73
Globalization, 95
goals, 20, 32, 34, 46, 48, 52, 53, 59, 61, 62, 69, 142
gold, 101
goods and services, 101, 123, 124, 126, 127
Gore, 63
governance, 70, 72, 73
government, viii, ix, 2, 3, 4, 5, 6, 9, 10, 11, 13, 14, 15, 16, 22, 23, 28, 29, 32, 34, 35, 39, 43, 46, 47,

49, 57, 60, 61, 63, 70, 71, 73, 75, 76, 77, 97, 99, 100, 101, 103, 105, 106, 107, 108, 109, 110, 112, 115, 118, 123, 124, 127, 128, 129, 130, 131, 132, 133, 134, 135, 136, 137, 138, 139, 140, 141, 142
government budget, 112
government expenditure, 115
government procurement, 124
government revenues, 106
government-to-government, 14
governors, 5, 6
GPO, 164, 165, 166
grants, 160
graph, 111
gravitation, 38
gravity, 31
Great Britain, 26, 64, 74
Great Depression, 10, 99
gross domestic product, 99
ground-based, 20
grouping, 56
groups, 3, 67, 106, 126
growth, ix, x, 10, 71, 97, 98, 102, 103, 104, 105, 111, 112, 113, 114, 115, 116, 117, 121, 122, 126, 127, 128, 133, 142, 144
growth rate, 10
GSP, 128, 138, 144
Guam, 26, 74
Guantanamo, 70
guidance, 48
guilty, 5

H

Hamas, 26
hands, 5, 6, 29, 48, 54, 127
harassment, 2
hard currency, 10, 112, 129
harm, 18, 30
harmony, 18
Harvard, 81
health, 10, 37, 101, 103, 106, 109, 111, 126, 134
health care, 106, 109
health insurance, 134
hearing, 150, 152, 154, 155, 158
heart, 27, 74
heat, 45, 129
heating, 7, 130
hedging, 55
hegemon, 28
hegemony, 12
Hezbollah, 64
high-level, 6, 27
high-tech, 28, 46
hip, ix, 27, 29, 34, 121, 122, 141, 142
horse, 57
host, 31, 37, 49
hostage, 6, 9, 47, 55
House, x, xi, 22, 92, 118, 147, 148, 149, 150, 151, 152, 153, 154, 155, 157, 158, 160, 161, 164, 165, 166
household, 102, 109, 114
housing, 109, 127, 132
human, ix, 2, 9, 25, 35, 65, 71, 74
human rights, ix, 2, 25, 35, 36, 65, 71, 74
humanitarian, viii, 2, 9, 22, 23
humanitarian aid, viii, 2, 22
Hungary, 44, 77, 144
hysteria, 57

I

ice, 30
identity, 37, 67, 93
ideology, vii, viii, 16, 25, 34
IEA, 75
IFRS, 109
imagination, 59
IMF, viii, 2, 11, 12, 106, 111, 113, 117, 120, 125
immediate gratification, 60
immunity, 5
imperialism, 33, 55, 72, 73
implementation, 13, 14, 32, 62, 63, 71, 108, 109, 128, 129, 135, 148, 164
import prices, 107
import restrictions, 136
imports, 10, 105, 108, 112, 115, 116, 117, 123, 124, 125, 126, 127, 128, 131, 132, 133, 136, 137, 138, 139, 140, 143, 144, 145
in situ, 73
in transition, 143
inattention, 78
incentive, 37, 55
incentives, 107
inclusion, 35, 150
income, 11, 99, 102, 103, 104, 105, 107, 111, 126
income distribution, 103, 104, 126
income tax, 11, 107
increased competition, 143
independence, 3, 10, 12, 14, 15, 29, 57, 58, 59, 64
India, 12, 35, 36, 57, 75, 98
indicators, 10, 54, 131
indices, 110
indirect effect, 117
industrial, 3, 12, 37, 47, 106, 114, 115, 117, 130, 137
industrial democracies, 12
industrial sectors, 37, 47

industrialized countries, 98, 125, 144
industry, 11, 76, 100, 108, 110, 126, 129, 130, 131, 133, 135, 142, 143
infant industries, 133
inflation, vii, 1, 10, 11, 99, 100, 101, 102, 103, 104, 106, 115, 118
influenza, 133
Information System, 120, 145
Information Technology, 137
infrastructure, 19, 76
inherited, 3, 49, 53, 114
injections, 58
injunction, 54
injuries, 9
injury, iv, 130, 143
inorganic, 116
insecurity, 45, 70, 72
insight, 55, 72, 77
inspection, 18, 19, 133, 136
inspections, 21, 67, 107, 133
instability, 14, 38, 71, 72, 106, 115
institutions, viii, 2, 30, 54, 65
instruments, 20, 53, 61, 69, 76
insurance, 109, 133, 134, 137, 142, 145
insurance companies, 133, 137
integration, viii, 1, 12, 13, 16, 24, 37, 58, 61, 72, 75, 108
integrity, 35, 54, 57
intellectual property, x, 108, 121, 123, 124, 129, 130, 131, 137, 139, 141, 142
intellectual property rights, x, 108, 121, 123, 124, 129, 130, 131, 137, 139, 141, 142
intelligence, 17, 30, 31, 37, 61, 70
intensity, 74, 75
intentions, 31, 43
interactions, 30, 105
interdependence, 61, 125
interest groups, 67, 126
interest rates, 100, 101
interference, 9, 29
intermediaries, 133
international division of labor, 125
International Energy Agency, 75
International Financial Reporting Standard, 109
international law, 33, 39, 48, 71, 72
International Monetary Fund, 111, 117, 125, 142
international relations, 29, 39, 42, 46, 50
international standards, 139
international terrorism, 6, 49, 71
International Trade, 99, 130, 141, 144, 145
internationalism, 56
Internet, 78, 79, 80, 82, 86
interpretation, 32, 151, 155, 156, 166
interval, 8
intervention, 30, 38, 51, 57, 59, 68, 77, 94, 117
interviews, 56
intimidation, 7, 58
investment, vii, x, 1, 4, 11, 26, 75, 76, 101, 105, 108, 111, 114, 116, 117, 121, 122, 123, 124, 127, 128, 133, 135, 137, 138, 139, 140, 141, 142, 143
investment capital, 4
investors, 101, 107, 117, 138, 139, 140, 142
Iran, viii, ix, 2, 18, 20, 22, 23, 24, 26, 29, 30, 32, 35, 36, 38, 42, 43, 44, 45, 47, 48, 53, 54, 61, 63, 64, 65, 66, 67, 69, 71, 76, 79, 85, 86, 92, 97, 98, 150, 164, 165
Iraq, 19, 21, 22, 28, 30, 31, 35, 43, 54, 59, 64, 65, 66, 78
iron, 35
irritation, 30
IS, 28
Islam, 50, 70
Islamic, 9, 14, 70
isolation, 28
Israel, 64, 69
ITA, 137

J

January, x, 11, 13, 16, 19, 20, 23, 80, 83, 85, 86, 87, 88, 89, 90, 93, 95, 99, 106, 117, 121, 123, 125, 128, 132, 139, 140, 145, 147, 151, 153, 155, 165
Japan, 10, 36, 57, 65, 66, 75, 76, 82, 95, 141
Japanese, 135, 142
jobs, 142
joint-stock companies, 129
Jordan, 91
judges, 4, 109
judgment, 60
judiciary, 109
jurisdiction, 150, 156, 157
jury, 4
justification, 21, 53, 59, 66, 69, 71

K

Kazakhstan, 13, 14, 18, 115, 120
Kentucky, 96
Korea, 26, 36, 37, 61, 64, 67, 91, 93
Korean, viii, 1, 20, 36, 43, 52, 62, 65, 67, 69, 92, 135
Kosovo, viii, 1, 12, 23, 49, 70, 89, 94
Kyoto Protocol, 11
Kyrgyzstan, 13, 14, 39, 57, 71, 72

L

labor, 4
labor force, 4
lack of confidence, 118
land, 11, 107, 108, 127, 128
language, 58, 151, 156, 163
large-scale, 9, 17, 39, 43
Latvia, 12, 120
laundering, 7
law, 2, 3, 6, 7, 17, 23, 33, 39, 48, 53, 62, 65, 71, 72, 74, 105, 106, 108, 131, 143, 149, 160, 161, 163
law enforcement, 2
laws, 8, 11, 54, 73, 101, 108, 123, 127, 128, 129, 130, 131, 134, 139, 141, 160
lead, 17, 35, 41, 48, 52, 71, 75, 142
leadership, ix, 11, 12, 17, 19, 32, 34, 35, 38, 55, 76, 97, 98, 105, 108, 152, 153, 154, 165
leaks, 64
Lebanon, 64, 66, 92
legal protection, 131, 139
legality, 4
legislation, 4, 22, 126, 128, 158, 163
legislative, 20, 124, 148, 153, 154, 159, 162, 164, 165, 166
LexisNexis, 82
liberal, 7, 8, 11, 53, 55, 124
liberalization, 142
liberty, 73
licenses, 5, 107, 135
licensing, 107, 110, 135
life expectancy, 10, 99, 103
lifetime, 4
likelihood, 30, 37, 53, 69, 153
limitations, 17, 27, 51
Lincoln, 78, 80
links, ix, 29, 33, 36, 98
Lithuania, 12, 35, 120
livestock, 131
living standard, vii, 1, 102, 142
living standards, 102
loans, 100, 107, 109
local government, 132
location, 49
London, 88, 90, 95
long distance, 134
long period, 126
longevity, 132
long-term, ix, 25, 34, 50, 58, 60, 71, 75, 78, 105, 126, 142
Los Angeles, 79, 90
losses, 9, 10
love, 61
low-intensity, 74
Luxembourg, 117, 139

M

machinery, 105, 112, 116, 117, 127, 139
macroeconomic, 10, 100
mad cow disease, 136
magnetic, iv
Maine, 21
mainstream, 142
maintenance, 112
major cities, 126
males, 99, 103
malicious, 20
management, 61
manipulation, 4, 13
manufacturer, 6, 22
manufacturing, 6, 114, 115, 120
marginalization, 59
market, viii, ix, 2, 5, 11, 13, 22, 55, 64, 75, 76, 98, 99, 100, 101, 105, 106, 109, 110, 117, 125, 126, 127, 131, 133, 134, 137, 138, 139, 140, 141
market access, 137
market economy, 99, 100, 106, 127, 131, 133, 138, 140
market prices, 100, 101, 126, 131
market value, 5, 100, 109
market-based economy, 125
marketing, 137
markets, x, 14, 100, 121, 122, 125, 141, 142
marriage, 30
mass media, 4
measures, ix, 2, 6, 21, 22, 97, 98, 99, 100, 105, 106, 124, 127, 129, 136, 142, 166
meat, 116, 117, 131, 132, 136, 139
media, 2, 4, 5, 7, 9, 37, 49, 61, 84, 100
Mediterranean, viii, 2, 17, 26
membership, x, 12, 14, 15, 51, 58, 68, 108, 117, 122, 123, 124, 132, 137, 143, 144
men, 6, 16, 32, 41, 42
mentor, 8
merchandise, 105
metals, 105, 129, 135
metaphor, 88
metric, 21
metropolitan area, 114
Mexico, 141
Middle East, 4, 21, 30, 34, 54, 56, 59, 61, 64, 65, 75, 92, 95
migration, 10
militarism, 21

military, viii, 2, 3, 4, 9, 12, 13, 14, 15, 16, 17, 19, 20, 26, 27, 28, 29, 30, 31, 32, 33, 34, 35, 36, 37, 38, 39, 40, 41, 42, 43, 45, 46, 47, 49, 50, 51, 52, 54, 57, 59, 64, 65, 68, 71, 73, 74, 76, 98, 127, 130, 149, 164
military aid, 12
minorities, 3, 23
minority, 3, 107, 128, 134, 149, 157
misleading, 26
missile defense, viii, 1, 2, 3, 12, 19, 20, 21, 22, 26, 28, 29, 30, 31, 32, 40, 41, 45, 47
missile launches, 18
missiles, 20, 21, 30, 31, 32, 39, 40, 42, 45, 47, 48, 49, 64, 68, 69
missions, 31, 73
misunderstanding, 40
MIT, 82
MOD, 46
models, 72
modernization, 30, 35, 40, 41, 42, 50, 55, 135
Moldova, viii, 1, 13, 14, 17, 28, 30, 39, 46, 51, 55, 65, 68, 70, 71, 73, 77, 87, 89, 93, 94, 110
momentum, 27, 65
money, 6, 31, 46, 56
monograph, viii, 25
monopoly, 3, 5, 6, 15, 29, 109, 110, 118, 128, 133, 134
morale, viii, 2, 16
moratorium, 21, 27, 100
mortality, 103
mortality rate, 103
Moscow, viii, ix, 1, 2, 5, 8, 9, 10, 11, 12, 13, 14, 15, 16, 18, 19, 20, 21, 22, 26, 27, 28, 30, 31, 32, 33, 34, 35, 36, 37, 40, 41, 43, 44, 45, 46, 48, 50, 51, 52, 53, 55, 60, 61, 62, 63, 64, 65, 66, 67, 68, 69, 70, 71, 72, 73, 77, 78, 79, 80, 81, 82, 83, 84, 85, 86, 87, 88, 89, 90, 91, 92, 93, 94, 96, 114, 119, 126, 142, 145
motion, xi, 148, 149, 160
motivation, 125, 165
motives, 14, 20, 61
mountains, 9, 114
movement, 9, 124
multidimensional, 76
multi-ethnic, 3
multilateral, 108, 122, 125, 131, 141, 142
multilateralism, 66
multiplier, 111
multiplier effect, 111
murder, 30
music, 131
Myanmar, 38
myopic, 74

N

nation, 5, 23, 123, 130, 134, 138
national, viii, ix, 2, 3, 4, 6, 12, 17, 26, 27, 33, 38, 42, 50, 57, 59, 60, 73, 74, 75, 97, 98, 106, 109, 117, 124, 127, 130, 134
National Intelligence Estimate, 19
national interests, ix, 98
national security, ix, 4, 12, 26, 27, 42, 74, 97, 98, 117
National Security Council, 91, 92
National Security Strategy, 95
National Trade Estimate Report, 144
nationality, 3
nationalization, 6
NATO, viii, 1, 2, 4, 12, 14, 15, 16, 17, 20, 21, 26, 29, 31, 32, 33, 35, 39, 41, 42, 43, 45, 46, 47, 48, 49, 50, 51, 52, 54, 57, 58, 59, 65, 68, 72, 73, 74, 77, 80, 81, 83, 86, 87, 92, 93
natural, ix, x, 3, 4, 6, 11, 14, 16, 34, 50, 68, 97, 98, 104, 105, 110, 112, 117, 120, 121, 126, 129, 130
natural gas, ix, x, 4, 6, 11, 16, 97, 98, 104, 105, 110, 112, 117, 120, 121, 126, 129, 130
natural resources, ix, 3, 4, 14, 97, 110, 112, 117, 126
Navy, 15, 30
Nazi Germany, 26
negative consequences, 32
neglect, 62
negotiating, 50, 53, 64, 66, 67, 132
negotiation, 53, 65, 71
net exports, 112
Netherlands, 90, 105
network, 5
New World, 96
New York, iii, iv, 24, 79, 88, 89, 91, 92, 93, 94, 144
New York Times, 24, 79, 91, 92, 93, 94
New Zealand, 132
newspapers, 62
NGO, 6
NGOs, 2, 6, 23, 29, 34
nightmares, 45
nongovernmental, 71
nongovernmental organization, 71
non-nuclear, 18, 49
nonproliferation, 4, 22, 33, 37, 38, 48, 59, 62, 65, 66, 67
nontariff barriers, 123
normal, ix, x, 7, 22, 98, 122, 138, 140
norms, 71, 72, 73
North Atlantic, 26, 81
North Atlantic Treaty Organization, 26, 81

North Korea, viii, ix, 1, 20, 36, 43, 44, 45, 52, 53, 54, 62, 64, 65, 66, 67, 69, 75, 76, 81, 82, 91, 92, 97, 98
Northeast, 34, 36, 64, 66, 67, 75, 76, 81, 92, 95, 96
Northeast Asia, 34, 36, 64, 66, 67, 75, 76, 81, 92, 95, 96
Norway, 26, 74
NPR, 43
NSC, 19
nuclear, viii, ix, x, 1, 2, 4, 17, 18, 19, 20, 21, 22, 23, 25, 26, 28, 29, 30, 31, 33, 34, 38, 39, 40, 41, 42, 43, 44, 45, 46, 47, 48, 49, 50, 51, 52, 53, 59, 64, 66, 67, 68, 69, 73, 74, 75, 76, 97, 98, 147, 148, 149, 150, 152, 157, 160, 161, 162, 163, 164
nuclear arms race, 20
nuclear charge, 49
nuclear energy, 64, 149, 164
nuclear material, 164
nuclear matter, 53
nuclear power, 18, 49, 74, 76
nuclear program, 40, 64, 66, 67, 75, 76
nuclear reactor, 18, 22, 23, 38
nuclear technology, 30
nuclear threat, 64
nuclear weapons, 18, 19, 21, 22, 28, 39, 40, 42, 43, 44, 46, 47, 48, 49, 50, 51, 52, 53, 64, 68, 69, 76

O

obligate, 63
obligation, 51, 68
obligations, 100, 135, 141
observations, 55, 59, 65, 72
obsolete, 114
obstruction, 58
OECD, 110, 114, 115, 118, 119, 120, 144
offenders, 144
Office of the U.S. Trade Representative, 144, 145
Office of the United States Trade Representative, 145
offshore, 33
oil, vii, ix, x, 1, 3, 4, 5, 10, 11, 13, 14, 15, 16, 17, 52, 74, 75, 76, 97, 98, 100, 101, 104, 105, 106, 109, 110, 111, 112, 115, 116, 117, 121, 126, 129, 130, 138, 139
oil production, 5, 52, 106, 111, 116
oil revenues, 106, 111
open economy, 125, 127
openness, 124, 143
opposition, viii, 1, 7, 13, 16, 19, 21, 23, 29, 36, 46, 49, 71, 109, 132, 140, 142
optical, 137
optimism, 2, 21
orbit, 32
organization, ix, 29, 49, 74, 75, 108, 121, 122
Organization for Economic Cooperation and Development, 119
organizations, viii, 2, 6, 29, 38, 65, 70, 71, 75, 117, 122, 125
organized crime, 10
orientation, 17
OSCE, 7, 8, 9, 14, 29, 34, 42, 51, 70
Overseas Private Investment Corporation, 138
oversight, 159
ownership, 5, 109, 110, 127, 129, 134
oxide, 22
oxygen, 78

P

Pacific, 3, 43, 44, 75, 85, 93
Pakistan, 70
Paper, 27, 4449, 82, 83, 84, 88, 89, 91, 145, 146
paralysis, 61
paranoia, 30, 35, 70
parents, 9
Paris, 46, 50, 68, 83, 90, 92, 106
Paris Club, 106
partnership, 18, 21, 26, 33, 36, 37, 42, 48, 54, 55, 56
passports, 2
patents, 131
patriotism, 38
pay off, 106
peacekeeping, 14, 28, 70
pedal, 62
pegged exchange rate, 128
penalties, 109
pension, 106, 108
pensions, 108
Pentagon, 47, 51, 63
per capita, 75
perception, 32, 33, 44, 46, 49, 54, 56, 57, 67, 72
perceptions, 33, 39, 43, 45, 47, 54, 55
performance, ix, 97, 98, 112
periodic, 31, 153, 154
permit, 132, 136
Persian Gulf, 95
personal, 11, 18, 60, 63, 101, 103, 107, 133
personal relations, 18, 60, 63
personal relationship, 60, 63
petroleum, 105
pharmaceutical, 137
pharmaceutical companies, 137
pharmaceuticals, 129, 135
philosophy, 42
pipelines, 14, 16, 76, 109, 118

piracy, 131
pirated, 131, 137
planning, 17, 47, 49, 52, 68, 103, 107, 125, 127, 128
plants, 133, 137
platforms, 7
play, 4, 13, 59, 76, 101, 107
plutonium, 21, 22
PM, 164
Poland, 2, 12, 20, 21, 26, 28, 31, 40, 45, 46, 48, 78, 80, 139, 144
police, 5, 38, 83
policy choice, 72
policymakers, 43, 54, 57, 64, 75, 107, 139
political crisis, 15
political instability, 115
political leaders, ix, 18, 31, 41, 121, 122, 140, 141, 142
political parties, 5, 109
political power, 7
political stability, 9
politicians, 14, 15, 31, 58
politics, vii, viii, 5, 25, 27, 28, 29, 33, 36, 37, 38, 41, 44, 49, 54, 56, 60, 61, 70, 77
poor, 100, 101, 103, 126, 139, 142
poor health, 126
popular vote, 7
population, vii, ix, 1, 3, 10, 15, 32, 56, 97, 98, 99, 100, 102, 103, 104, 126
pork, 132, 136
ports, 135
post-Cold War, 51, 68, 116, 138, 139
post-Soviet states, 38, 51, 74
posture, 38, 42, 44, 46, 47, 51, 53, 54
poultry, ix, 98, 117, 131, 132, 133, 136
poverty, vii, 1, 10, 37, 102, 108, 126
poverty line, vii, 1, 102
poverty rate, 126
power, ix, 2, 4, 5, 6, 7, 8, 13, 17, 18, 27, 28, 29, 31, 32, 33, 35, 36, 37, 38, 39, 41, 42, 47, 52, 53, 54, 55, 56, 57, 58, 59, 60, 61, 65, 66, 71, 72, 73, 74, 76, 77, 97, 98, 99, 110, 115, 122, 127, 160, 162
powers, 29, 34, 59, 88, 141
PPP, 99
pragmatism, 55
predictability, x, 121, 122, 124, 130
presidency, 3, 7, 14
president, 3, 4, 5, 6, 7, 8, 10, 12, 18, 87, 98, 100, 101, 109
President Bush, x, 6, 16, 21, 22, 39, 59, 147, 148, 150, 152
President Clinton, 63
President Vladimir Putin, ix, 26, 121, 122
pressure, viii, 2, 5, 14, 15, 36, 51, 53, 63, 66, 68, 69, 70, 71, 74, 77, 101, 115, 117, 132
preventive, 42, 59
prices, ix, x, 11, 17, 64, 75, 97, 100, 101, 104, 106, 109, 111, 112, 115, 116, 117, 121, 126, 129, 130, 131, 138, 142
pricing policies, x, 121, 130
primacy, 44, 70
priorities, 4, 17, 55, 62
private, 53, 69, 107, 109, 110, 127, 134
private banks, 134
private ownership, 107, 110
private sector, 109, 110, 127
privatization, 5, 11, 100, 110, 127, 129, 132
probability, 32
producers, ix, x, 36, 74, 98, 100, 115, 121, 126, 127, 130, 131, 132, 135, 139, 142, 143
production, ix, 11, 17, 39, 47, 58, 75, 97, 100, 105, 107, 110, 111, 112, 114, 117, 127, 130, 131, 132, 134, 139, 142
productive capacity, 75
profits, vii, 1, 11
program, 11, 12, 18, 19, 21, 22, 26, 28, 35, 40, 45, 52, 64, 69, 76, 100, 106, 109, 128, 134, 135, 138, 144
proliferation, ix, 18, 28, 34, 44, 45, 48, 49, 50, 64, 66, 67, 69, 71, 73, 76, 97, 98, 148, 156, 163
promote, ix, 38, 97, 99, 124, 133, 140, 143
propaganda, 16, 37, 38, 57
property, iv, x, 11, 55, 101, 108, 121, 123, 124, 129, 130, 131, 137, 139, 141, 142
property rights, 101, 129, 130, 131, 137
proposition, 28, 61
prosperity, 73
protection, x, 58, 107, 108, 121, 124, 127, 128, 130, 131, 133, 135, 137, 139, 142, 145
provocation, 66
pseudo, 23
public, vii, 1, 8, 9, 10, 38, 44, 57, 70, 71, 133, 153
public health, 133
public interest, 153
public opinion, vii, 1
public support, 9
pumping, 16
purchasing power, 17
purchasing power parity, 17
Putin, vii, viii, ix, 1, 2, 3, 4, 5, 6, 7, 8, 9, 10, 11, 12, 13, 14, 15, 16, 17, 18, 19, 20, 21, 24, 27, 28, 30, 31, 32, 35, 37, 38, 39, 40, 41, 46, 48, 50, 52, 54, 59, 60, 61, 63, 69, 70, 73, 76, 80, 82, 83, 87, 89, 90, 91, 92, 94, 95, 97, 98, 101, 102, 105, 106, 107, 108, 109, 118, 122, 125, 127, 128, 141, 142, 145

Pyongyang, 64, 66, 67, 91

Q

quality of life, 99
question mark, vii, viii, 25
Quinones, 91, 92
quotas, 124, 132, 136, 141

R

race, 21, 26, 28, 32, 33, 39, 41, 44, 45, 49, 52, 53, 69
radar, 3, 20, 21, 32, 44
radical, 62, 100, 101
radio, 5
radio station, 5
range, 17, 20, 30, 32, 40, 42, 43, 47, 48, 63, 74, 115, 117, 128, 129, 133, 136, 139
rat, 106
raw material, ix, 6, 55, 98, 105, 115, 116, 126, 138, 142
raw materials, ix, 55, 98, 105, 115, 116, 126, 138
reading, 156
real estate, 99, 114
real terms, 10, 99, 115
real wage, 102, 103
realism, 73
reality, 32, 33, 54, 67
rebel, 9, 10
recess appointment, 165
recession, 126
recognition, 26, 43, 56
reconcile, 45
recovery, 10, 35, 65
recreation, 63
recurrence, 54
redistribution, 55
reduction, viii, 2, 16, 21
reelection, 100
reforms, 6, 11, 51, 68, 74, 76, 106, 107, 109, 115, 126, 128
refugees, 9
regenerate, 48
regeneration, 52, 69, 76
regional, 4, 6, 7, 23, 33, 34, 35, 36, 44, 59, 65, 71, 107, 108, 128, 132, 142
regression, 26, 35, 38, 41, 43, 60, 67
regular, 43, 160, 162, 163, 165
regulation, 110
regulations, 8, 107, 123, 124, 129, 130, 134, 135, 141, 142, 149, 160
reinforcement, 57
relationship, viii, 2, 8, 16, 18, 22, 27, 29, 30, 33, 34, 35, 36, 37, 39, 41, 42, 43, 46, 53, 54, 62, 63, 70, 78, 98, 116, 123, 138
relationships, 60, 63, 64
relative prices, 120
reliability, 37
Renaissance, 94
rent, 74, 115
reporters, 27, 31
repression, 15
reprocessing, 18, 19
reproduction, 131
Republican, 7
Republican Party, 7
reputation, 7
research, 44, 67, 130, 164
resentment, 20, 27, 42
reserves, 4, 10, 36, 63, 75, 98, 101, 110
residential, 6, 130
resistance, 9, 10, 19, 36
resolution, x, xi, 10, 13, 19, 129, 133, 140, 143, 147, 148, 149, 150, 151, 154, 155, 156, 157, 158, 159, 160, 161, 162, 163, 164, 165, 166
resources, ix, 3, 4, 14, 16, 17, 29, 39, 61, 63, 66, 97, 110, 112, 117, 126, 131, 132
responsibilities, 78, 128
restaurants, 133
restructuring, 51, 58, 100, 107, 115, 126, 128, 132
retail, 136
retaliation, 22, 44
retirees, 108
retirement, 108
reunification, 57
revenue, 11, 13
Reynolds, 90
RF, 88, 89, 93
rhetoric, vii, viii, 25, 27, 32, 35, 37, 38, 41, 54, 64, 67, 70
rice, 129
risk, 38, 41, 50, 68, 69, 72, 77, 107, 149, 156
risks, 98
roadblocks, ix, 97
Robert Gates, 30, 80
Romania, 2, 28, 31, 51, 77, 110, 144
Rome, 12, 50, 68
rule of law, 53, 62, 65
rural, 132
rural communities, 132
Russia, v, vii, viii, ix, x, 1, 2, 3, 4, 5, 6, 7, 8, 9, 10, 11, 12, 13, 14, 15, 16, 17, 18, 19, 20, 21, 22, 23, 24, 25, 26, 27, 28, 29, 30, 31, 32, 33, 34, 35, 36, 37, 38, 39, 40, 41, 42, 43, 44, 45, 46, 47, 48, 49, 50, 51, 52, 53, 54, 55, 56, 57, 58, 59, 60, 61, 62,

63, 64, 65, 66, 67, 68, 69, 70, 71, 72, 73, 74, 75, 76, 77, 78, 79, 80, 81, 82, 83, 84, 85, 86, 87, 88, 89, 90, 91, 92, 93, 94, 95, 96, 97, 98, 99, 100, 101, 102, 103, 104, 105, 106, 107, 108, 110, 111, 112, 114, 115, 116, 117, 118, 119, 120, 121, 122, 123, 125, 126, 127, 128, 129, 130, 131, 132, 133, 134, 135, 136, 137, 138, 139, 140, 141, 142, 143, 144, 145, 147, 148, 149, 150, 152, 154, 155, 157, 158, 159, 160, 162, 163, 164, 165
Russian, i, iii, v, vii, viii, ix, x, 1, 2, 3, 4, 5, 6, 7, 9, 10, 11, 12, 13, 14, 15, 16, 17, 18, 19, 20, 21, 22, 23, 24, 25, 26, 27, 28, 29, 30, 31, 32, 33, 34, 35, 36, 37, 38, 39, 40, 41, 42, 43, 44, 45, 46, 47, 49, 50, 51, 52, 53, 54, 55, 56, 57, 58, 59, 60, 61, 62, 63, 64, 65, 67, 68, 69, 70, 71, 72, 73, 74, 76, 77, 78, 79, 80, 81, 82, 83, 84, 85, 86, 87, 88, 89, 90, 91, 92, 93, 94, 95, 97, 98, 99, 100, 101, 102, 103, 104, 105, 106, 107, 108, 109, 110, 111, 112, 113, 114, 115, 116, 117, 118, 119, 120, 121, 122, 123, 125, 126, 127, 128, 129, 130, 131, 132, 133, 134, 135, 136, 138, 139, 140, 141, 142, 143, 144, 145, 147, 148, 150, 161, 163, 164

S

sacrifice, 62
safeguard, 143
safeguards, x, 67, 121, 122, 129
safety, 56, 123, 133
salaries, 109
sales, 22, 26, 30, 36, 37, 71, 76
sanctions, viii, 2, 14, 19, 22, 64, 71
satellite, 44, 77
Saturday, 152, 153, 159
Saudi Arabia, 4, 110
savings, 99, 109, 115, 134
scandal, 68
scarcity, 15
school, 6, 9
scientists, 19
search, 32
searches, 5
Seattle, 95
secret, 39, 107
Secretary of Defense, 35, 80, 85
Secretary of State, 6, 54, 62, 77, 78, 85, 92, 150
Secretary-General, 26
securities, 101, 133
security, ix, 2, 4, 5, 8, 9, 12, 14, 17, 21, 22, 24, 26, 27, 28, 29, 31, 32, 33, 34, 35, 36, 37, 41, 42, 44, 45, 46, 48, 50, 51, 52, 53, 55, 58, 59, 62, 64, 65, 66, 67, 68, 69, 71, 72, 73, 74, 75, 76, 77, 78, 85, 97, 98, 117, 132, 149, 156
Security Council, 2, 17, 19, 64, 91, 92
seizure, 37, 115
seizures, 5
self-interest, 60
senate, 80, 165
Senate, x, xi, 30, 80, 81, 147, 148, 149, 150, 151, 152, 153, 154, 155, 157, 158, 160, 164, 165, 166
September 11, 12, 14, 18, 19, 22, 24, 78
Serbia, 12, 56
series, 9, 26, 50, 65, 68, 74, 129
services, iv, x, 5, 8, 30, 31, 70, 71, 100, 101, 105, 121, 123, 124, 126, 127, 129, 132, 133, 134, 137, 141, 142, 143
Shanghai, 14
Shanghai Cooperation Organization, 14
shape, 28, 41
shaping, 46, 141
shareholders, 107
shares, 100, 109, 110, 117, 126, 139
Shell, 110
shock, 36, 100
shock therapy, 100
shocks, 101
shoot, 10
short run, 142
shortage, 74
short-term, 101
Siberia, 5, 76, 82
sign, 11, 32, 44, 47, 59, 63, 71, 102, 109, 114, 118, 135, 142
signs, vii, viii, 25, 74, 108, 116, 128, 161
sine, x, 147, 150, 151, 152, 153, 154, 155, 156, 159, 162
Singapore, 115
sites, 21
Slovakia, 77
Slovenia, 20
small and medium sized enterprises, 107
small banks, 109
social development, 72
social influence, 72
sociocultural, 32
solar, 59
solar system, 59
solutions, 28
South Korea, 36, 66, 67, 75, 76, 114
sovereignty, 15, 30, 35, 57, 58, 71, 74
Soviet Union, viii, 2, 3, 4, 10, 13, 16, 24, 30, 41, 45, 56, 65, 91, 100, 102, 104, 110, 111, 112, 115, 123, 124, 125, 126, 127, 129, 131, 133, 135, 140, 144
Spain, 8
specter, 33, 39

spectrum, viii, 25, 73
speculation, ix, 7, 26, 97
speech, 24, 26, 27, 28, 48, 50, 82, 93, 141
speed, 108
spheres, 58
spin, 29
sponsor, 38
sporadic, 10
St. Petersburg, 5, 8, 37, 84, 114, 122, 126, 142
stability, ix, x, 9, 37, 39, 41, 46, 49, 97, 98, 101, 106, 109, 117, 121, 122, 134, 143
stabilization, 10, 69, 105, 106
stabilize, 126
stages, 129
standard of living, ix, 97, 98, 102, 104
standards, 56, 70, 71, 115, 122, 124, 133, 139
stars, 33
starvation, 17
state control, 110, 115, 128
State Council, 86
State Department, xi, 2, 22, 63, 148
statehood, 58
state-owned, 4, 5, 6, 74, 100, 108, 109, 110, 115
state-owned banks, 108
statutes, 163, 164
statutory, x, 144, 147, 148, 149, 151, 156, 157, 158, 160, 166
steel, x, 116, 121, 139, 143
stock, 5, 101, 108, 132
storage, 20, 133
strain, 18, 19, 116
strategic, vii, viii, 2, 6, 11, 12, 17, 18, 19, 20, 25, 26, 29, 31, 32, 33, 34, 35, 36, 37, 39, 40, 41, 42, 43, 44, 45, 46, 47, 48, 49, 50, 51, 52, 53, 55, 57, 58, 62, 65, 68, 71, 73, 77, 78, 110, 115
strategies, 99
strength, 3, 16, 39, 48, 51
stress, 48
stretching, 3
strikes, 40, 73
structural changes, 124
submarines, 40
subsidies, x, 52, 69, 100, 106, 107, 108, 121, 124, 129, 130, 131, 132, 143
subsidy, x, 121, 130
substitutes, 60
suburban, 15
suffering, 73, 74
sugar, 128, 135
suicide, 9
summer, 5, 152
Sunday, 85, 152, 153, 159, 161, 162
superiority, 60
superpower, vii, 1, 4, 28, 43, 58, 59
supervision, 67, 109
suppliers, 13
supply, 31, 75, 127, 132
Supreme Court, 4, 7, 15
surging, 74
surplus, vii, 1, 105, 106, 112, 126
surprise, 4, 6, 21, 27
surveillance, 47
survivability, 44, 47
survival, 56, 57
sustainable economic growth, 142
Sweden, 95
syndrome, 33
Syria, viii, 2, 26, 30, 64, 66
systems, 3, 17, 40, 47, 56, 72, 74

T

tactics, 45, 58, 64, 70
Taiwan, 36, 37
Tajikistan, 13, 14, 110
Taliban, 12
tangible, 27, 35, 57
tangible benefits, 57
tanks, 77
targets, 9, 20, 31, 32, 130
tariff, 123, 128, 132, 135, 136, 138, 140, 144, 145
tariff rates, 128, 136
tariffs, x, 13, 121, 123, 124, 129, 132, 135, 136, 137, 138, 142
tax collection, 107
tax evasion, 5, 109
tax reform, 101, 128
taxation, 111, 118, 139
taxes, 11, 99, 102, 107
teachers, 9
technical assistance, 138
technicians, 19
technology, viii, ix, 2, 4, 18, 23, 30, 31, 49, 75, 98, 117, 137
technology transfer, 18, 30
Tehran, 18, 26, 32, 47, 64, 66, 78, 92
telecommunication, 134
telecommunications, 134, 137, 142
telephone, 134
television, 5
temporary protection, 135
tension, viii, 1, 14, 15, 18, 22, 30
term plans, 46
territorial, 52, 77
territory, 3, 9, 17, 18, 20, 38, 55, 70, 71, 124

terrorism, 4, 6, 9, 18, 23, 34, 35, 39, 46, 47, 49, 52, 59, 66, 69, 70, 71, 73
terrorist, 9, 10, 38, 48, 49, 73
terrorist attack, 9, 73
terrorists, 9, 14, 22, 48, 72, 73
testimony, 30, 31, 59, 70, 151
theory, 29
thinking, 29, 39, 47, 53
Third World, 16
threat, vii, viii, 2, 4, 14, 20, 25, 27, 28, 29, 30, 31, 32, 33, 35, 36, 37, 38, 39, 40, 41, 42, 43, 44, 45, 47, 48, 49, 50, 51, 52, 56, 57, 58, 63, 64, 65, 66, 67, 68, 72, 73, 75, 76, 77, 85, 99
threat of force, 66, 76
threatened, 6, 14, 19, 21, 22, 33, 46, 47, 57, 63, 68
threatening, 21, 29, 44, 47, 50, 54, 60
threats, vii, viii, 9, 18, 25, 26, 28, 29, 31, 32, 33, 34, 36, 39, 40, 41, 42, 44, 45, 46, 48, 49, 50, 51, 52, 53, 54, 64, 66, 68, 69, 73
threshold, 3, 7, 44, 49, 106
thresholds, 143
time, vii, x, 1, 3, 6, 8, 9, 11, 13, 17, 18, 26, 33, 34, 35, 41, 44, 45, 47, 49, 53, 58, 60, 65, 66, 70, 71, 73, 74, 76, 77, 78, 101, 102, 105, 106, 107, 111, 116, 121, 122, 123, 124, 125, 126, 128, 130, 132, 139, 141, 142, 143, 148, 149, 150, 151, 157, 159, 160, 161
time periods, 150
timetable, 20
tin, 78
titanium, 110
Tonga, 123
totalitarian, 32
trade, ix, x, 4, 14, 19, 22, 29, 37, 64, 98, 99, 101, 104, 108, 112, 115, 116, 117, 120, 121, 122, 123, 124, 125, 126, 128, 129, 130, 131, 132, 134, 135, 137, 138, 139, 140, 141, 142, 143
Trade Act, 139, 143, 144
trade agreement, 22, 108, 140
trade deficit, 138
trade liberalization, 142
trade policies, 124
trade policy, 139
trade preference, 138
Trade Representative, 124, 131, 145
trademarks, 131
Trade-Related Aspects of Intellectual Property Rights, 144
Trade-Related Aspects of Intellectual Property Rights (TRIPS), 144
trading, x, 4, 59, 105, 121, 122, 142, 143
trading partners, x, 121, 122, 142, 143
tradition, 63, 70
traditionalism, 55
training, viii, 2, 8, 22, 31, 71
trajectory, 44, 54
trans, 82
transactions, 101, 109
transfer, 15, 18, 30
transformation, 62
transition, 28, 99, 100, 101, 103, 107, 110, 127, 131, 133
transition period, 107, 127
transitions, 142
transmission, xi, 148, 158
transmits, 161
transparency, 45, 52, 75, 109, 115, 143
transparent, 5, 47, 60
transport, 109
transportation, 4, 106, 114, 127
traps, 66
Treasury, 101
Treasury bills, 101
treaties, 45, 46, 47, 50, 51, 52, 53, 55, 56, 60, 61, 66, 67, 68, 69, 71, 73, 74, 77
trend, 3, 26, 44, 53, 55, 65, 69, 103, 115, 143
trial, 4, 5
triggers, 35
TRIPS, 123, 130
trust, 41
tuberculosis, 103
Turkey, 21
Turkmenistan, 94, 110
turnout, 7, 23
turnover, 107

U

U.N. Security Council, 19
U.S. Department of Agriculture, 136
U.S. Export-Import Bank, 138
U.S. military, 14, 19, 20, 27, 30, 46
ubiquitous, 32, 101
Ukraine, viii, 1, 2, 12, 13, 15, 16, 17, 18, 24, 28, 29, 35, 39, 57, 58, 63, 64, 65, 71, 72, 74, 77, 80, 89, 110, 117
uncertainty, 8, 38, 117, 118
unclassified, 149, 150
unemployment, vii, 1, 102, 132, 142
unemployment insurance, 142
unemployment rate, 102
unhappiness, 27
unilateralism, 19, 21, 27, 28, 33, 41, 42, 53, 58, 66, 67
unions, 57, 59
United Kingdom, 8, 78, 92, 95

United Nations, 28
United States, v, viii, ix, x, 2, 3, 4, 8, 10, 12, 13, 14, 16, 18, 19, 20, 21, 22, 23, 24, 25, 26, 27, 29, 34, 36, 37, 38, 39, 41, 42, 43, 44, 45, 51, 52, 58, 59, 61, 62, 63, 64, 65, 66, 68, 70, 71, 73, 75, 81, 82, 88, 91, 94, 95, 97, 98, 99, 107, 116, 117, 121, 122, 123, 124, 125, 129, 130, 131, 132, 133, 135, 136, 137, 138, 139, 140, 141, 142, 143, 144, 145, 164, 166
unpredictability, 50, 55
Urals, 106
uranium, 2, 18
uranium enrichment, 2
Uruguay, 123, 124, 125, 132, 134
Uruguay Round, 123, 124, 125, 132, 134
Uzbekistan, 14, 70, 72, 94, 120

V

validity, 30, 35, 53, 61, 69
values, 34, 53, 62, 69, 73
variance, 70
vehicles, 116, 117, 135, 139
velvet, 71
Venezuela, 30, 56
veterinarians, 133
Vice President, 85
Vietnam, 123, 136
violence, 37, 38, 72, 78
violent, 9, 73, 77
visas, 7
visible, 27, 35, 37, 39, 52, 69
vision, 32, 55
voice, 67, 141
volatility, 55, 112
voter turnout, 7, 23
vulnerability, 36

W

wages, 34, 102
walking, 74
Wall Street Journal, 86, 87, 91
war, 4, 5, 6, 14, 15, 19, 23, 26, 28, 33, 34, 35, 37, 39, 42, 47, 58, 59, 64, 66, 72, 73, 94
war on terror, 4, 23, 35, 59
warfare, 9, 63
Warsaw, 20, 45, 82, 84
Warsaw Pact, 20, 45
Washington Post, 23, 24, 83, 87, 88, 91, 93
weakness, 30, 55, 109
wealth, 74, 100, 126
weapons, viii, 2, 4, 17, 18, 20, 21, 22, 28, 32, 39, 40, 41, 42, 43, 44, 46, 48, 49, 50, 52, 53, 59, 64, 68, 69
weapons of mass destruction, 4, 28, 38, 48, 50, 59
weapons of mass destruction (WMD), 28, 81
web, 80
websites, 15, 131, 137, 153, 165
well-being, 141
Western Europe, 16
White House, 18, 62, 95
winning, vii, 1
wisdom, 64, 65, 66, 67
withdrawal, 9, 13, 14, 20, 27, 40, 46, 47, 48, 52
WMD, viii, 2, 28, 33
workers, 11, 115
workforce, 11
World Bank, 115, 117, 125, 142, 144
World Trade Organization, ix, 98, 108, 117, 121, 122, 144
World War, 125
World War I, 125
World War II, 125
worldview, 29
WP, 124, 128, 129, 130, 133, 135, 136
writing, 156
WTO, v, ix, x, 11, 22, 23, 98, 99, 108, 117, 121, 122, 123, 124, 125, 128, 129, 130, 131, 132, 133, 134, 135, 136, 137, 138, 139, 140, 141, 142, 143, 144, 145, 146

Y

Yabloko, 7
yield, 19, 44, 77
Yugoslavia, 139